Working the Night Shift

Working the Night Shift

Women in India's Call Center Industry

Reena Patel

Stanford University Press
Stanford, California

Stanford University Press
Stanford, California

Reena Patel, Ph.D., works as a Foreign Service Officer at the Department of State. The opinions expressed in this book are those of Patel only and do not necessarily reflect those of the Department of State or the U. S. Government.

Printed in the United States of America on acid-free, archival-quality paper

Library of Congress Cataloging-in-Publication Data

Patel, Reena, 1970–
    Working the night shift : women in India's call center industry / Reena Patel.
        p.   cm.
    Includes bibliographical references and index.
    ISBN 978-0-8047-6913-6 (cloth : alk. paper)
    ISBN 978-0-8047-6914-3 (pbk. : alk. paper)
    1. Women employees—India—Social conditions.   2. Call centers—India—
Employees.   3. Night work—India.   4. Women—Employment—India.   5. Women—
India—Social conditions.   I. Title.
    HD6189.P375   2010
    331.4'813811420954—dc22
                                                                                          2009038919

*To my grandparents—Jayaben C. Patel,
Chaturbhai B. Patel, Manibhai S. Patel, and
Savitaben M. Patel—for having the courage and
integrity to build a better life for their family.*

*And of course to Mom and Uncle Charlie, who taught
me the true meaning of unconditional love.*

Contents

Acknowledgments

During a leadership conference at The University of Texas at Austin, a panelist pointed out the importance of remembering that "it's not all about me." Drawing from this, there are a number of people for whom I am grateful. I wish to thank my co-advisors and committee members for their guidance and encouragement throughout the writing process. Dr. Emily Skop flew all the way to India not only for her own research interests but more so to see how I, her befuddled student, was faring. Armed with gifts of beef jerky and a willingness to understand the challenges of international fieldwork, she kept an eye on me and brought me back to reality when I started to get a little crazy. And yes, fieldwork in India made me a bit crazy at times. When I returned, she provided the space necessary to allow this book to expand in directions I had not anticipated.

When hit with writer's block, Dr. Paul Adams could always be counted on to help me. Our discussions allowed me to look at my work from a perspective I often had not considered before. When I started to get lost in what I perceived to be the enormity of this project, he reminded me to look at my book as capturing a moment in time that would someday be history. His guidance allowed me to remain focused on the writing at hand. His willingness to challenge my assumptions as well as his encouraging me to speak my opinion—detractors be damned—made for a stronger learning experience.

In addition, I want to thank three professors who at varying stages of this project provided much needed encouragement. Dr. Cecilia Menjivar served as a member of my thesis committee at Arizona State University and for years after provided invaluable advice, particularly when it came time to publish this book. Dr. Winifred Poster and Dr. Margaret Abraham, both sociologists conducting their own research on the call center industry, happily shared their resources with me and on more than one occasion took time from their hectic schedules to provide commentary and guidance on the direction of this study.

My mother once told me, "Do you know how happy it would have made my parents to know that their grandchild used what they left behind to pursue a Ph.D.?" Thanks to my grandparents, Jayaben C. Patel and Chaturbhai B. Patel, for passing on a flat in Mumbai that served as my home base during the course of this project.

Whether through coincidence or connection, individuals unwittingly came into my life at just the right time during my fieldwork. I wish to thank Kavita and "Indiana Jones" for being a listening ear and for, on more than one occasion, helping me during frantic phone calls when I was lost somewhere in Mumbai. When it came to laughter and adventure, I always knew I could count on Jasbir Sachdev Singh (Jassi_taxi@hotmail.com), who is by far the best taxicab driver in Mumbai but, more important, also my now-adopted brother. When I needed refuge from gritty city life, my aunties in Ahmedabad, Ranjan Foi and Sumi Foi, could always be counted on to take care of me and fatten me up when I got too thin. And when it came to cheap flights, my cousin Cookie, a savvy travel agent, saved the day on more than one occasion.

Thanks to Raven (her call center name) for helping me get into what was by far the coolest of all call centers. When it came to expanding the scope of this project to Ahmedabad and Bangalore, Sukumar Parikh, Shailaja Parikh, and Dipa Patel were key in providing contacts that I would not have been able to secure on my own. Thanks also to Ralph Jude for sharing his home with me in Bangalore during the course of fieldwork. There are many more people I would like to thank for contributing directly to this book, but due to issues of confidentially I am unable to name them.

When I returned from fieldwork, it was suggested that in order to write a book I needed to hunker down and stay in one place. A writing desk to return to regularly and a set environment are supposedly key to creating and maintaining the writing process. This confined work ethic did not work for me and thankfully I had the support of grants and of friends and family around the country whom I could visit while writing chapters in some of my favorite places. The bulk of this book was written among my dear friends Leona and John in upcountry Maui. To awake every morning to a view of the Pacific

Ocean and West Maui Mountains on one side and Haleakala on the other was more than I had ever imagined. To end a day of writing with two friends who shared laugher, merriment, good food, and wine with me was a gift. Add to that their eighty-five-pound lab, Kula, who made sure that my daily walk stayed daily, and I was living a writer's dream. The foundation of this book was laid in Maui, and to Leona and John I am grateful.

Cleaning up this book—and the arduous task of revising—were done in Manhattan in a corporate apartment two blocks from Times Square. I have my cousin Amish to thank for this. Sent to New York on a one-year consulting assignment, he opened up his place to me, rent free, and happily shared his couch, laundry service, maid, gym, and doorman. When he would leave early in the morning to begin his fourteen-hour workday I would tell him, "Don't get fired! I like this job." Amish, I will never forget the magical "yellow bag": clothes went in dirty, clothes came back out washed and folded. Every writer should have one. And when I needed respite from the city, my brother, Meehir, was just over the bridge to take me in. My father made it a point to tell me, "Between your brother and cousin you have over $8,000 a month worth of free housing!" Thank you for providing me with a lifestyle that few beginning writers have the luxury to enjoy. I love you both.

Although the bulk of this book was written in Maui and Manhattan, sections were also completed in Kauai, Phoenix, Chicago, St. Louis, Austin, Boston, Santa Barbara, and Hollywood. Many thanks go to friends and family who took me in, along with the fifty-pound bags of books and articles I insisted on dragging along.

This book would not have come to fruition without support from the following organizations: the American Association of University Women, the National Security Education Program's David L. Boren Fellowship, the National Science Foundation (NSF-Grant No. 0703463),[1] and numerous grants and scholarships from The University of Texas at Austin: the Huston Endowment President's Excellence Scholarship, the International Education Fee Scholarship, the David Bruton Jr. Graduate Fellowship, the Ward Fellowship, and travel grants from the Department of Geography and the Environment, the Department of Women's and Gender Studies, and the South Asia Institute.

Special thanks also go to Vivé Griffith in Austin, the finest editor a writer could ask for. Her eye for detail was invaluable.

This is my first time publishing a book. Kudos to the staff at Stanford University Press for literally holding my hand throughout the process. Thanks to Stacy Wagner, acquisitions editor, for believing in this manuscript; to Tim Roberts, production editor, for patiently guiding me through the production process; and to Alice Rowan for fine-tuning the book.

Finally, I wish to thank my parents, Lavang Patel and Shirish Patel, for their unwavering support. My pursuing a doctorate at an age when parents expect their daughter to be "settled" (that is, married with children) certainly went against the path they had envisioned. Yet never once during the process did they burden me with judgment about what I should be doing with my life. Thank you both for providing me with the space to pursue my dreams.

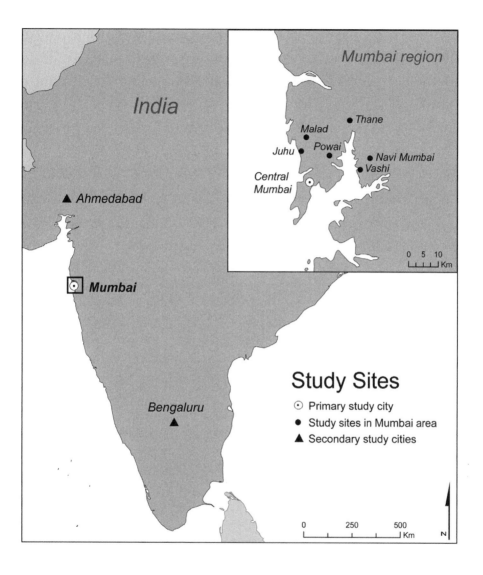

Study Sites

⊙ Primary study city
● Study sites in Mumbai area
▲ Secondary study cities

1 Introduction

For many young people, especially women, call-center work means money, independence, and an informal environment where they can wear and say what they like. Along with training in American accents and geography, India's legions of call-center employees are absorbing new ideas about family, material possessions and romance.

—*Wall Street Journal*, 2004[1]

"Housekeepers to the World"—this headline gracing the cover of a 2002 issue of *India Today* was accompanied by an image of a woman wearing a headset.[2] Other reports that emerged at the same time suggested that these twenty-something "housekeepers" were trading in *salwar kameez*'s and arranged marriage for hip-hugger jeans, dating, and living "the good life."[3] The call center industry, with its relatively high wages and high-tech work environment, was heralded as a source of liberation for women.[4]

A closer look reveals a different aspect of the story. On December 13, 2005, Pratibha Srikanth Murthy, a twenty-four-year-old employee of Hewlett Packard, was raped and murdered en route to her night shift call center position in Bangalore. Reported by the *India Times* to the BBC and CNN, the Bangalore rape case attracted worldwide attention. Just two years prior, in December 2003, a speaker at the 2003 Women in IT Conference in Chidambaram, India, had reported that one of her employees in Chennai called her company's New York office in a complete panic because the shuttle van used to transport employees during the night had been pulled over by the police. Despite having identity cards, the women were accused of prostitution. Global night shift labor was intersecting with the lives of women in ironic and unsettling ways.

In the late 1990s, Fortune 500 companies in the United States began moving customer service jobs to India because of the availability of an English-speaking population and lower wages than those paid to U.S. workers. Call centers fall under the umbrella of the business process outsourcing (BPO) industry in India. Estimates suggest that approximately 470,000 people work in the industry, and it is currently the fastest growing sector in the nation.[5]

Due to the time difference between India and the United States, one of the primary requirements for employment in a transnational call center—besides fluency in English—is working the night shift.[6] Typical night shift hours range from 10 P.M. to 6 A.M. or 8 P.M. to 4 A.M. Mobility is vitally important to those who seek to work in this industry. In other words, *physical* mobility (getting to and from work) and *temporal* mobility (going out when one is expected to stay in) are job requirements. Because leaving home at night is generally considered inappropriate for and off-limits to Indian women, companies offer transportation as part of their recruitment strategy.

In this book I examine how women employed in the industry experience this rapidly expanding "second shift" in the global economy. During the course of research for this book it became evident that call center employment affects the lives of women workers in ways that run counter to standard expectations, such as the belief that when women are educated and earn a relatively high income, their status in a given society will be transformed for the better; and that as part of this transformation women will experience increased levels of independence and empowerment, such as substantive changes in the household (for example, men contributing equally to household labor) and the ability to come and go as they please. This has not necessarily been the case.

Instead, I argue, employment in this industry, particularly working at night, brings with it both new challenges and new opportunities for women workers. The notion of a woman's "place" in the urban nightscape, which until now, for most women, has been characterized as "being safe at home," is transforming as a result of the night shift requirement in the BPO industry. My research for this book was shaped by three broad, interconnected questions related to this transformation: (1) How does the demand for night shift workers recodify women's physical and temporal mobility? (2) How does call center employment translate into social and economic mobility? and (3) What spatial and temporal barriers do women face, both in the household and in urban public space, as a result of BPO employment? In-depth qualitative analysis revealed that the answers to these questions are by no means unified and singular, because of a variety of factors such as age, economic status, and living situation (that is, whether married, single, living alone, living with parents or within a joint family).

For the most part, educated, middle-class women working in call centers are earning an income that far exceeds what they could previously earn. Proponents of the industry believe this serves as a catalyst for empowering women. Yet no one has considered whether increased income and education mean that women experience expanded physical and temporal mobility (that is, are now able to go out, day or night, as freely as their male counterparts). Thus, underlying *Working the Night Shift* is concern about whether women continue to face strict regimes of surveillance and control of their physical and temporal mobility, despite increased income and education, and what this tells us about power and dominance in a given society.

Spatializing the Night

Social science tends either to ignore space completely, to view it as merely a container of difference, or to conceptualize it as "dead," absolute, or neutral.[7] According to Fincher and Jacobs, this framework is problematic because class and gender differences are "experienced in and through place."[8] Thus geographers are on the forefront of illustrating that space matters, particularly in terms of the social construction of identities.[9]

For instance, Dalits, also called untouchables or the backward caste, were barred from entering Hindu temples because of the low status assigned to them by society.[10] Likewise, in many Hindu temples, the body of a menstruating woman is considered dirty.[11] Menstruating women are forbidden to enter because it is believed they will contaminate the perceived sanctity and purity of this sacred space. In this context, a temple is far from a neutral space. It marks people as pure or impure, as compatible with the sacred or essentially profane. Who belongs in a temple is determined by multiple categories such as age, gender, religion, and class.

Similarly, the nightscape is not a static geographic or temporal landscape. It is a dynamic space with a spatiality that is different from the day. Who belongs out at night and who does not is similarly determined by multiple categories such as gender, class, age, and religion. Areas perceived as safe during the day transform into spaces of danger at night, and stories about the dangers of going out at night are used to control women's mobility. As a result, women who break the rules about their place are viewed as "asking for it" if they meet with violence, even rape, when they go out at night.

The conception of space as interrelational is illustrated in the view of women as both a site and a source of contamination. As global customer service workers, women must now traverse the nightscape. As a result of this relocation, perceptions about women's place in society also have the potential to be transformed. As the research in this book illustrates, however, generally speaking "women of the night" continue to be viewed as loose, bold, and mysterious. In some instances a woman is assumed to be a prostitute, transformed symbolically by time and space into "a dirty girl." Just as women supposedly bring contamination to sacred sites because they are, at certain times of the month, out of *place*, they are also, at certain *times* of the day, out of place simply by leaving the home.[12] The profane space of the street, particularly at night, contaminates women's bodies just as the sacred space of the temple is contaminated by women's blood. This reflects how flows of the body (that is, moving about) and flows from the body (that is, menstruation) are spatialized in a variety of ways.

When women leave their homes or migrate from their villages, the act of "stepping out" can place them in positions of experiencing disdain, and possible violence, even when the act of stepping out is done for the good of their families and society. In Dhaka, Bangladesh, for instance, migrant women working at night in export-oriented garment factories experience hostility and abuse both inside the factory and when they travel to and from work.[13]

The violence these workers face when they are out at night includes verbal harassment from male supervisors, such as "Daughter of a whore, why don't you work? You can die for all I care, but you have to finish your work"; rape, both inside and outside the factory; and the very real threat of assault and kidnapping.[14] The independence of earning their own money and living away from the family unit is viewed as a threat to the urban, male order. As Siddiqi aptly points out, "Symbols of inverted moral order, women workers signify through their bodies male inadequacies and national failure."[15] In addition, society relegates female garment workers to a low-class status, and the factories they work in are sometimes referred to as whorehouses and baby-producing centers.[16] This low-class status combined with working at night renders garment workers extremely vulnerable. They are perceived to be indecent women because they are out of place. At the same time, the local government provides little intervention or protection to garment workers. This is especially ironic given that their labor serves as the primary contributor to foreign exchange income and is a key benefit to the government in the form of economic development.

Barring women from sacred spaces because their bodily functions are viewed as dirty and attacking women workers who labor at night are just two examples of the restrictions and challenges women face when they venture outside the home. As some women gain increased access to night spaces outside the household, their experiences are further complicated as their bodies become imbued with stereotypes of sexual impropriety, questionable moral values, and "bad character."

Why Do Physical and Temporal Mobility Matter?

The ability and freedom to drive a car, traverse the urban nightscape, and explore neighborhoods beyond the confines of one's community speak volumes in terms of gender equality. Massey's seminal work on space, place, and gender finds that "the mobility and control of some groups can actively weaken other people."[17] Hägerstand also points out that "one individual's use of his freedom influences what other individuals are able to do with theirs."[18] Although they are often overlooked, physical and temporal mobility, or the lack of them, provide an important perspective in terms of understanding which groups or individuals hold domain over certain spaces and which groups do not.

Studies on women's mobility are conducted in a variety of settings as scholars seek to understand how mobility shapes their lives.[19] From Worcester, Massachusetts, to Porto Novo, Benin, West Africa, a lack of mobility impacts women's access to education and job opportunities.[20] Sujata, a fifty-eight-year-old woman I interviewed one sunny afternoon in San Antonio, Texas, described growing up in her small town in the state of Gujarat, India. She was not allowed to leave home after 6 P.M. As a child, she wanted to participate in sports that were offered to girls but was forbidden because she would not be home by the curfew imposed on her. She recalled that restrictions on her mobility undermined her ability to compete with her fellow students as she grew older. She remarked that "the bitterness still remains" as she looks back on her childhood. Sujata made it a point to tell me that she would ensure that her daughters not experience the same confinement in their lives.

Mobility reflects more, however, than the physical act of walking or driving from point A to point B. Paromita Vohra's 2006 documentary, *Q2P*, provides an important perspective on how physical and temporal mobility, toilets, and health are intertwined.[21] By examining women's access to toilets in Mumbai, she revealed how the lack of public toilets combined with societal rules about where women are expected to relieve themselves hinders women's mobility. Vohra also linked the lack of access to toilets to ongoing health problems that women face, such as urinary tract infections.

Going to the bathroom is a fundamental issue for women in Mumbai because many lack toilets in their homes but are still expected to relieve themselves incognito. Under these conditions, women will hold off going to the bathroom until nightfall so as not to be seen. They also walk far distances to access a place to urinate away from the view of men, or they try to stay near areas that provide them access to a toilet. Poor women, especially, bear the brunt of this situation.[22] Even women who have toilets in their homes are aware of how long they can be gone from home before the need to go to the bathroom arises, and how this need can be satisfied. Often it's a choice between relieving oneself in a tucked-away public space or enduring physical pain.

In comparison, men have the privilege of urinating in public spaces, such as in street gutters and on the road. Women walking by are expected to turn away and pretend not to see. It is out of the question for women to behave in a similar manner. "It would be chaos!" is how one man in Vohra's film responded to the idea. This dynamic illustrates how men hold dominion over public space. It also shows one graphic way in which male behavior in public space is used to define gendered perceptions of mobility and spatial access. As a result, women modify their actions in order to respect a man's need for privacy in public spaces. Women are treated as an *intrusion* in the male domain of public spaces and they hide themselves as a means to justify their existence outside the household.

During a discussion I had with Madhusree Dutta, filmmaker of *7 Islands and a Metro*, she concurred with Vohra's film, adding, "If you want to increase women's social mobility, make more public toilets available."[23] As a means of addressing concerns about women's safety, Dutta also pointed to the current trajectory of increasing the presence of female police stations. These stations are generally staffed by female officers and serve as a place for women to lodge criminal complaints. She believes, however, that public toilets would be more effective in addressing safety concerns because women would no longer have to go into dark, faraway spaces to relieve themselves. Providing public toilets would not only increase women's mobility but also help to integrate them into mainstream spaces.

Shilpa Ranade's work on gender and space in Mumbai provides an additional perspective.[24] By mapping women's mobility in four public spaces of Mumbai, she illustrates not only how gender segregation is spatialized, but also how a woman's access to public space intersects with maintaining a particular reputation. The areas she mapped were (1) Central Avenue, Chembur, a suburban middle-class neighborhood; (2) Zaveri Bazaar and Mumbadevi, dense, commercial areas in old southern Mumbai; (3) Nariman Point, a commercial district of South Mumbai; and (4) Kalachowki, a working class neighborhood. By mapping women's mobility in these diverse settings, Ranade found that men have almost free access to public space whereas women self-regulate their physical and temporal mobility in order to (re)produce respectability:

> Women cross the road between one to four times to avoid situations in which they might find themselves uncomfortable/unsafe. This is sometimes done indirectly by producing respectability such as when a woman crosses the road to avoid a wine shop. At other times, it is direct such as when she crosses to the other side to avoid groups of men hanging out at the *paan* shop, or when she chooses not to walk between trucks and a dead wall. (The working class drivers [of these trucks] in this case are regularly perceived as threatening.)[25]

If women dodge streets and avoid dead walls during the day, what happens at night?[26] In the course of the study from which this book grew, it became apparent that one of the ways in which women produced respectability in the nightscape was to be in the presence of a man and to adhere to a strict work-to-home journey. This does not mean, however, that there were not instances in which women would "bunk off" (take a day off from work) to hang out. Yet it was made clear during interviews and participant observation, and through my own experience, that women, compared to men, are held to far stricter rules of mobility in terms of where they can move in the urban nightscape.

Theoretical Overview

The research for this book is informed by feminist literature on the public versus private sphere. I draw from this literature because it provides a foundation for looking at how women experience inequality in a variety of settings, ranging from gender relations in the household to their participation in the paid labor force. Notions of public and private are generally viewed through the lens of the home as the private sphere and spaces outside the home as the public sphere, or the lens of business as a private sphere and government as a public sphere. These structural conceptions, problematic as they may be, are in turn embedded in the body. To articulate how the distinction between public and private spheres is embodied and subsequently used to socially construct women as inherently different from men, I also draw from literature on body politics.

Public Versus Private

The distinction between the public and private spheres gained popularity in the 1970s as a means to explain a woman's place, or lack thereof, in society.[27] As illustrated in Table 1, women were relegated to private sphere traits and men were relegated to public sphere traits.

According to feminist scholar Spike Peterson, in the 1980s feminist political theorists in the West began to move away from this distinction because the notion of the public sphere shifted and was used to describe the state government while the private sphere moved into the realm of business.[28] Scholars from a range of disciplines have gone on to critique the use of this distinction. Its binary nature (that is, one is either dependent or independent on the basis of the sphere to which one is relegated), for example, fails to consider difference and overlap at the individual level.[29] Although it is important to understand how the perception of a woman's place (that is, in the home) reflects her overall status in society, the public-private framework mirrors the belief that women and men actually belong in distinct categories.[30] Indeed, as demonstrated by the popularity of books that perpetuate sexist beliefs about masculinity and femininity, such as *Men Are from Mars, Women Are from Venus*, the illusion of separate spheres certainly remains real and relevant in the lives of men and women, despite the fact that there is difference and overlap at the individual level.[31]

When a man says, "My wife will stay at home because we can afford to have her at home," certain assumptions related to the public versus private distinction are revealed. Although gender is in fact fluid and interrelational— some men have traits that are deemed feminine and some women have traits that are deemed masculine—public versus private traits are constructed as real. The relegation of women to private spaces appears to be a privilege of the upper class and a prerogative of men.

Table 1. Associated differences of the public and private sphere

Public Sphere	Private Sphere
Masculine	Feminine
Production of goods and services	Reproduction—childbearing
Paid labor	Unpaid labor
Leaders	Followers
Visible	Invisible

Sources: Derived from Andersen, *Thinking About Women;* Peterson and Runyan, *Global Gender Issues.*

The dichotomy perpetuated in notions of a private sphere versus a public sphere contribute to a form of gender hierarchy in which society deems the adoption of supposed masculine traits as positive and the adoption of feminine traits as negative. For example, being aggressive is considered better than being nurturing. Being told "you throw like a girl" or "don't be such a pussy" is an insult for men.

The distinction between public and private spheres also reflects the supposition that once women step out of the domestic hearth and into a masculine, public domain they will be allowed equal access to other aspects of the public sphere. From this perspective, getting out of the house and pursuing a career is viewed as a means of achieving liberation.[32]

This is not necessarily the case, however, because traits categorized according to the distinction between public and private spheres are replicated in the paid labor force. Research on female engineers in India illustrates that gender roles as defined by the public-private distinction are embedded in the information technology (IT) industry and have a negative impact on women's participation in that industry.[33] An employer who participated in Parikh and Sukhatme's 2002 study on the challenges that female engineers face stated:

> I do not have specific bias for women engineers. I do agree that they are more competent, intelligent, possess more integrity, and are more efficient than men engineers, but they are helpless. In spite of their full willingness to perform their duty perfectly they are not able to meet with the requirement of the organization in which they are employed due to family responsibilities like their responsibilities towards their children, in-laws, parents, and other social obliga-

tions towards family, illness, etc. In Indian culture men expect everything from women.[34]

In general, both academia and industry fail to consider women as equal, contributing participants in the realm of technological development.[35] This occurs because more women, compared to men, continue to be viewed as "out of place" in the workforce and as such they are discriminated against.[36] The persistence of traditional gender roles deems some women's participation in the paid labor force as secondary to their reproductive role in the household, and thus hinders women. The dichotomy embedded in the public-private distinction—despite how inaccurate it may be from a theoretical stance or unjustified in an ethical sense—is a real social force in the lives of women.

Another critique of the framework is that it is couched within Western ideals of what constitutes public traits and private traits and therefore these kinds of definitions cannot be generalized across cultures. It would appear evident, however, that traits deemed masculine in a given society will often be linked to higher status and thus the framework does have validity across cultures.[37] For instance, the traits listed in Table 1 held throughout my study. From stereotypes that helping children with their homework is a woman's job to men having a visible presence in the urban night while women are relatively out of sight, beliefs about public traits and private traits are pervasive and, in turn, spatialized in a variety of settings.

The public-private sphere distinction is now almost three decades old and is less often used in scholarly pursuit than it used to be. Nevertheless, Melissa Wright demonstrates that "the myth of public and private spaces" remains.[38] Myths in this case are essentialized ideas of difference—such as women's "natural" capacity for nurturing—that take on the status of biological destiny, thus erasing the history of their complex social construction. In the world of global capitalism, for example, this myth justifies the assignment of a disposable value to female factory workers in Mexico and China. Wright shows how this disposability narrative is used to justify inequality both inside and outside the factory setting. Her work illustrates that the conception of public and private space, however mythical it may be, continues to affect the lives of women in ways that are far beyond the imaginary.

In this book I reposition the public-private sphere distinction in ways that allow for an understanding of how night shift employment, gendered norms of mobility, and the global economy interact with one another. In-

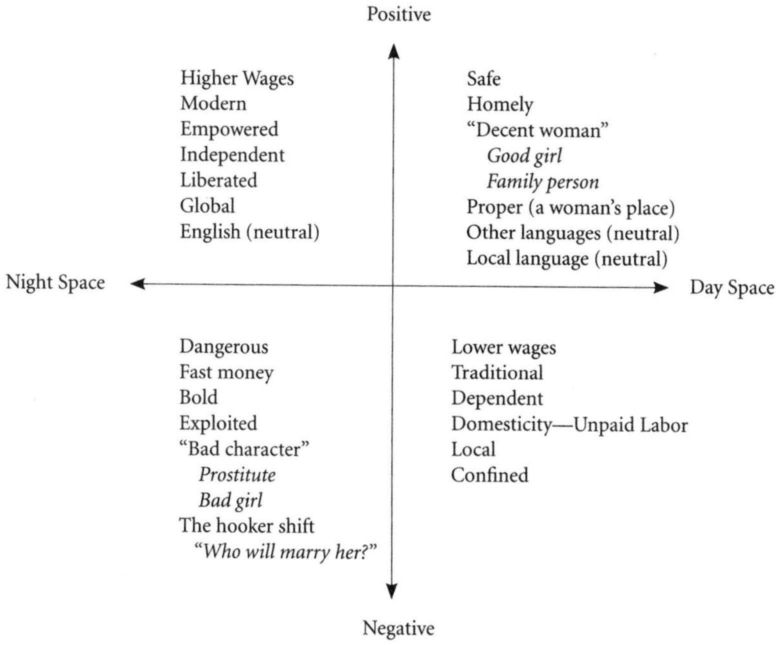

Positive

Higher Wages	Safe
Modern	Homely
Empowered	"Decent woman"
Independent	*Good girl*
Liberated	*Family person*
Global	Proper (a woman's place)
English (neutral)	Other languages (neutral)
	Local language (neutral)

Night Space ← ——————————————————— → Day Space

Dangerous	Lower wages
Fast money	Traditional
Bold	Dependent
Exploited	Domesticity—Unpaid Labor
"Bad character"	Local
Prostitute	Confined
Bad girl	
The hooker shift	
"Who will marry her?"	

Negative

Figure 1. Spaces embodied and experienced by female call center employees. *Note:* Quotes indicate terms used by the individuals I interviewed; italics denote common sayings or remarks that emerged during fieldwork and fall under the broader theme presented here.

stead of denying binary oppositions, such as that women are homemakers and men are breadwinners, I acknowledge the existence of such beliefs and seek to expose how women experience them. Instead of examining the public-private distinction from an either/or perspective (such as dependent versus independent), I conceptualize categories such as "homely" (that is, domestic) and "bold" as *spaces* that individuals embody and experience, often in overlapping and conflicting ways. As illustrated in Figure 1, the variety of spaces that women traverse do not always follow a linear path (for example, work = money = mobility) that can be mapped out and set as the standard.

There are several conclusions to be drawn from this matrix. For some women, call center employment, by providing them the opportunity to go out at night and earn a higher wage, represents a space of *empowerment*. Simultaneously, however, the global circuitry from which their employment draws is deemed an *exploitative* space because of stressful work conditions and wages that are lower than those paid to a U.S. employee in the same job.

At the same time, participation in this industry gives some women new forms of *independence* because they are able to access *night spaces* in ways that were previously deemed off-limits. Yet they are hampered by the assumption that women should embody a space of *dependency* and vulnerability. Therefore, a male escort is required for physical safety and the protection of the woman's reputation so that she will not be viewed as too *bold*, a term used to describe a defiant woman, or as a "bad girl" who lacks family values. The term *homely*, in contrast, is commonly used to describe women who prefer to stay at home and is included in matrimonial ads to refer to women who are family oriented. Although the IT infrastructure and the *global* nature of call center employment is associated with *modernization*, it also intersects with a woman's worth in ways that conflict with and degrade their bodily value in spaces deemed *traditional*, such as arranged marriage. Obviously, global night shift labor intersects with the lives of women in ironic and unsettling ways.

Body Politics

The literature on body politics provides an additional conceptual understanding of how individuals both embody and experience stereotypes of gender in a variety of spaces. Feminists are on the forefront of critiquing the social and biological construction of women's bodies, from being marked as a site of reproduction to being considered a source of provocation.[39] Donna Haraway, for instance, points out that when sex is conceptualized under the guise of biological determinism, the space of emerging work in critical social theory is limited.[40] The body, as scale of analysis, provides a powerful understanding of how space and place are conceived on the basis of gender.[41] Furthermore, it is a key site for understanding how gender differences are maintained and spatialized.[42] Women's bodies, when read as a text, are also saturated with gendered symbols and meaning.[43]

Regarding the status of women in spaces deemed sacred, for instance, Susan Wadley points out that Hindu mythology assigns lower ritual status to women, and within this hierarchy it is believed that "the woman's menses are polluting, but not as polluting as childbirth."[44] Shan Ranjit's description of why women remain barred from Ayyappa Temple in Kerala illustrates that gendered symbols become spatialized in ways that degrade women:

> The curse on the women starts on the very first day she menstruates, a period in which the girl's body is considered to be very hot and polluting. It is also

believed that the release of blood from a body orifice (opening)—in this case from the vagina—attracts spirits and demons that can devastate a family's happiness and its power of vitality. Women during this period are considered to be impure, unclean, polluted and contaminated.[45]

Judith Butler theorizes that gender is an act of performance.[46] When women and men "perform" gender, notions of womanhood and manhood are inscribed on their bodies, thus marking them as a biological site of difference. It is generally believed, for example, that women are the nurturing force in the family unit and that in this capacity they are better equipped than men to take care of children and elders. Such beliefs are spatialized in ways that mark the home as women's territory, and generation after generation of women are socialized to aspire to such, even if they pursue a career outside the home.

Subsequently, from a young age, women are taught how to perform this nurturing role. Be it cooking and cleaning or behavioral expectations such as obedience and being deferential in the presence of men, such training does not only operate in a vacuum of home space. It is reiterated and reproduced in a variety of settings and mediums ranging from the education received in school to media images such as movies and television advertising. This social construction of what constitutes feminine behavior in turn becomes marked as a biological difference. This leads to the assumption that women are *naturally* adept in behavior that society demarcates as feminine.[47] Those who fail to perform gender in ways that adhere to this societal expectation are seen as out of place.

Utilizing Butler's framework for examining how women perform gendered norms of mobility, Anna Secor examines how gender is presented through "regimes of veiling" in Istanbul.[48] She finds that veiling allows women to deter the male gaze when they travel, but it also reinforces the belief that women's bodies are a source of provocation that must be controlled and concealed. Shilpa Phadke too found that wearing a *burkha* or *hejab* in Mumbai increased women's access to urban space, as a means to gain permission from one's family to leave the confines of the household, but she also found that the practice of veiling did not reduce sexual harassment.[49] This dynamic illustrates that performing gender—in ways that conform to patriarchal norms of honor— does not always protect women. Nonetheless, it does demonstrate how women perform gendered norms of mobility through their bodies.

Conceptualizing the body as a site that produces and performs gender in a variety of settings gives us a greater understanding of women's mobility. The body also provides an understanding of how globalization and gender interact with one another.[50] Instead of contributing to universalizing discourses that present women who work at night as either victims of exploitation or exemplars of empowerment, I draw from the literature on body politics to critically examine how notions of a woman's place are recodified to meet the growing demand for twenty-four-hour workers.

Sites of Study

The research for this book took place primarily in Mumbai, India. Labeled the "City of Dreams" among residents and in popular literature, it was the ideal setting for exploring the juxtaposition of day and night, traditional and modern, female and male. As the financial center of the Indian economy, Mumbai provides the largest income tax base for the country. As of 2001, an estimated 11,976,439 individuals live in this city, and at 64,263 people per square mile, it is one of the densest cities in the world.[51]

Due to the exorbitant real estate prices in Mumbai's central business district, call centers set up shop in suburban areas such as Thane, Malad, Powai, and Navi Mumbai. Employees who participated in this study worked primarily in Navi Mumbai and Malad. Located more than thirty miles from downtown Mumbai, Navi Mumbai measures 212.3 square miles and is India's largest urban planning project to date.[52] Development of Navi Mumbai began in 1971 with the goal of creating fourteen suburbs that would hold a population of approximately two million people.[53] It was conceived as a satellite township to slow the expansion of downtown Mumbai by serving as a countermagnet to draw incoming migrants and to re-settle some of its current population.[54]

Malad is home to Mindspace, the largest high-tech commercial business park in Mumbai (see Figure 2). At approximately 125 acres, this commercial minicity is home to multinational corporations such as Deutsche Bank and J.P. Morgan. Mindspace has transformed this backroad area, formerly a municipal dumping ground for solid waste, into a premier destination for corporations.[55] For instance, to service the demands of its workforce, the surrounding areas include large-scale malls and retail stores such as Inorbit Mall and HyperCITY, movies theaters, and restaurants. At the same time, the office park itself is home to sleek designs of steel and glass that reflect the industry's desire to showcase itself as the place to work in India.

Figure 2. Aerial shot of the Mindspace area in Malad. *Source:* Sahu, "Present Scenario of Municipal Solid Waste (MSW) Dumping Grounds in India," 330.

Despite development in both Navi Mumbai and Malad, evidence of poverty and class inequality endures. Dust, pollution, dirt roads, and dilapidated housing remain in view of the sleek office buildings and upscale malls in Malad. Winifred Poster comments on this dichotomy in her research on the call center industry in Gurgaon, a suburb of Delhi:

> Adjacent to Convergys (one of Gurgaon's premier call centers), and literally lined up on its side, is a migrant worker ghetto camp composed of tent cities of blue plastic tarps held up by bamboo poles and tree branches. These workers, without homes, electricity, running water, or sanitation facilities, are the sweepers, dishwashers, and construction workers for the ICT [information and communications technology] industry, fundamental to its physical creation and daily maintenance in the night time city, but excluded from its global and virtual operations.[56]

Call center operations have emerged throughout India. Given the variety of available settings in which to conduct this study, the question arose, "Why Mumbai?" especially given that Bangalore is considered the Silicon Valley of India. According to Linda, an American call center executive in Mumbai, even though Bangalore is the IT hub of India, it is not necessarily the call center hub. The presence of an educated, English-speaking population and of space in the outlying areas of Mumbai in which to build call centers are the key magnets drawing companies to this area. Mumbai is also viewed as more cosmopolitan and professional compared to other Indian cities, and it is ahead of cities such as Delhi in terms of fiber-optic connectivity and electricity infrastructure.[57]

Seven years after this industry began in Mumbai, there is an abundance of call center advertisements, recruitment brochures, and training centers. Job fairs, such as the one I visited in Mumbai, are also held (see Figure 3).

Mumbai is also the setting of films on the call center industry such as *Bombay Calling*, a documentary that chronicles the lives of call center workers, and *John and Jane Toll-Free*, a film that examines the impact of globalization on six call center employees. And in 2009 *Slumdog Millionaire*—a rags-to-riches film about a young man who serves tea in a Mumbai call center—took the big screen by storm as it won eight Oscars at the Academy Awards. Yet it is not only filmmakers who have set their sights on the call center industry, whether as the central focus or as a backdrop to a larger storyline. Journalists and scholars are also exploring the ramifications of this industry in a variety of ways.

What is missing thus far, however, is an in-depth exploration of how gender roles and beliefs about a woman's place fare when low-wage, day shift call center jobs—generally deemed "women's work" in the United States—move offshore and transform into a high-wage, night shift position.

Mumbai, for the most part, is generally depicted as one of the more women-friendly cities in India. Time and again I was told that Mumbai is a great place for Indian women to live because fewer limitations are placed on them, particularly related to going out. Yet depicting an entire city as "women-friendly" is problematic because it obscures the ways in which city spaces continue to be gendered, thus taking away from future struggles to secure for women their rights to the city. Also, women-friendly is inaccurate because this statement tends to be based on the lives of professional upper-middle-class women who in reality constitute a very small percentage of the population.[58]

After six months of research in Mumbai, I expanded the scope of my study to include Bangalore (also known as Bengaluru) and Ahmedabad.[59] I decided to include Bangalore and Ahmedabad when it became clear that I needed a greater understanding of the context of women's mobility in Mumbai. Put another way, I wanted a comparative understanding of how women in other

Figure 3. BPO job fair held at Bhavan's College in Mumbai. Source: Photo by author.

major cities in India experience gendered norms of mobility and spatial access. Prior to expanding the scope of the study, I was stuck in comparing women's mobility in Mumbai to that of women in major U.S. cities. From a rational standpoint, I knew that such a comparison was inappropriate for the project at hand. I was also aware that it could be subject to the criticism that researchers from the United States are unwilling or unable to see beyond the lens of Western feminism. To address this problem, I sought to understand how BPO employees in other Indian cities experience working the night shift. The two other cities are included because Bangalore is generally viewed as more conservative, and Ahmedabad is considered the most conservative, particularly in terms of gender relations. Although Mumbai was the primary site of study, my findings from Bangalore and Ahmedabad are included when they provide an appropriate context or comparative understanding.

In this research, I discovered that unlike Bangalore and Ahmedabad, Mumbai is viewed as a city of ill-repute, danger, and sin. Thus, focusing on all three cities provided a complementary understanding of how a city's reputation intersects with the demand for night shift workers. Mumbai, in particular, provided an understanding of how IT intersected with a city that was already labeled fast, progressive, and cosmopolitan. Bangalore, in contrast, was a small, quiet city that transformed into the Silicon Valley of India in a period of less than twenty years, while Ahmedabad is in the midst of ramping up its IT industry to compete with neighboring cities. These three cities, distinct in many ways, provided the opportunity to see how the demand for night shift workers plays out in a variety of settings.

Sources of Information

In 2006 I conducted interviews with seventy-two employees over a ten-month period. To understand how women from varying backgrounds experience night shift employment, I sought to interview a range of women: single, married, separated, living with their families, or living on their own. Women who had left the industry also participated in this study because their retrospection provided insight into how call center employment shaped the lives of some employees. Interviews were conducted in cafes, restaurants, and in three cases, family homes. I also sat on the stoop of call centers in Mindspace to interview employees who were on a break or waiting for a shuttle to transport them home. Upon my return to the United States, some employees kept in touch with me via e-mail, text messaging, and occasional phone calls. Their willingness to maintain contact served as a forum for asking follow-up questions that emerged during the course of writing this book.

Of the seventy-two interviewees, nine were men. Taking into account that men constitute 50 to 70 percent of the employment pool, critics may argue that this study is incomplete because they were underrepresented. The sample was purposely skewed because it is the presence of women that disrupts gendered notions of place during the night. I also interviewed managers and executives, family members of employees, industry consultants, and film directors who have made documentaries on the call center industry. In total, ninety-six people were interviewed. This sample provided an understanding of how the various players inform and impact the experiences of female night shift workers.

I also conducted four focus groups, two mixed-sex and two women-only, during the course of this study. The focus groups were particularly useful because the spontaneous interaction between the participants allowed for the emergence of important issues that were relevant to this study but were not made evident during interviews. [60] Some of the findings from the focus groups, such as workers getting into car accidents due to reckless drivers, were certainly not generalizable to the experiences of all center employees. Nevertheless, interviewing in a group setting provided an understanding of the varying issues and concerns that workers deal with and of the relative importance they placed on these matters. Additionally, the focus groups allowed for unique and interesting perspectives to emerge because the camaraderie within the group in some cases led to more candid responses than in the interviews.

I also visited various locales, such as malls, cafes, and bars frequented by call center employees. In relation to mainstream media reports about call center employees spending their money on branded clothes at the latest mall, sipping coffee while hanging out in cafes, and partying all night at bars, spending time at these places provided an understanding of the lifestyle changes with which call center employment is associated. Certainly hanging out at a suburban bar in the middle of the night may strike some as a questionable research method. Specific to the goals of this study, however, it provided a firsthand glimpse of how gendered conceptions of space informed where it was acceptable for women to hang out and where it was not.

Participant observation was also conducted inside two call centers in Mumbai. Both call centers are located in Navi Mumbai and are referenced as TYJ Corporation and Company A throughout this book. These are fictitious names used to protect the identity of the companies. Entry into TYJ Corporation took place during preliminary fieldwork in 2005 and entry into Company A occurred during research conducted in 2006. Both companies are 100 percent Indian owned, service U.S. and U.K. businesses, and are listed as top ten call centers by the National Association of Software and Service Companies (NASSCOM), the industry association for India's IT sector. [61] They are considered a "third party process," which means that overseas firms outsource their customer service requirements to them. As such, they provide customer service to credit card companies, telephone providers, major electronics stores, and airlines.

During my interactions with these companies I was allowed to interview employees and conduct participant observation, under the supervision of a company executive at TYJ Corporation and an operations manager at Company A. Employees of both companies were primarily in their early twenties, reflecting the demographics of the industry. Participant observation in this study refers to watching employees work and, in some instances, listening in on phone calls. I was not allowed to answer calls or engage an employee in discussion when they were working.

TYJ Corporation is a ninety thousand square foot facility (equivalent in size to a Wal-Mart Supercenter) with a little more than two thousand employees. On any given shift, the company had up to a thousand employees working the phone lines. The starting salary as of January 2005 for a full-time, entry-level employee was Rs 10,000 per month (US$225).[62] I was allowed to conduct participant observation only in a department that serviced U.K. clients because TYJ Corporation was under strict contractual agreements with its U.S. clients not to allow outsiders access to their processes. Even employees who work at TYJ Corporation are restricted in their access to the departments that service U.S. clients.

Company A employs approximately a thousand people and was one of the first call center operations to open in Mumbai. As of October 2007, the starting salary for a full-time call center employee ranged between Rs 10,000 to Rs 14,000 (US$222 to US$310) depending on her level of experience.[63] I was given limited, closely supervised access to observe the employees taking phone calls. Unlike TYJ Corporation, where my interviews with women were conducted in the cafeteria in the presence of an executive, at Company A I was allowed to conduct interviews on a private, one-on-one basis.

Popular fiction, documentaries, and newspaper accounts on the call center industry were also collected in order to evaluate how the call center industry was portrayed popularly and to understand reaction to this relatively new industry. Popular fiction, such as *One Night @ the Call Center*, often provided a talking point when conducting interviews.[64] In addition, documentaries such as *Q2P* and *Do You Know How We Feel? Aaaaaaargh!* provided a visual understanding of how women's mobility and spatial access remain hindered despite the economic and IT development taking place.[65] Meanwhile, media reports served as excellent data sources for interpreting how women who work in the call center industry are represented and perceived.

Interviews were taped when permission was granted by the participants; otherwise, I recorded their responses by hand. Subsequently I transcribed both tapes and handwritten notes. I then performed a narrative analysis based on coding and categorizing interviewee responses using NVivo 7, a qualitative data analysis software program.[66] I also integrated into this narrative analysis research notes taken during participant observation, as well as newspaper accounts, journal articles, and popular fiction relating to women's participation in the call center industry. This level of coding allowed me to analyze the data across a broad spectrum of issues as well as sources (from interviews to newspaper reports). By centralizing all the data sources into NVivo 7 I was also able to uncover themes and patterns that I had failed to consider at the beginning stages of the project.

Pseudonyms are used throughout the book to protect the identity of the participants and the companies where they work.[67] Identity was a key source of concern for a number of participants, and on more than one occasion employees risked their jobs to contribute to this study. During a focus group interview at a mall in Malad, for example, one of the participants asked me to remove my interview notes from the table and stop the discussion because he saw the client for the account they service standing near the area where we were sitting. To be caught in an interview would jeopardize his and his coworkers' jobs because they had signed contractual agreements with their employer stating that they would not disclose information about their work.

Reflexivity and Positionality

Throughout this study, Haraway's concept of situated knowledge provided an innovative approach to thinking about my direction and goals as a researcher.[68] Rejecting notions of detached neutrality and the quest for universal findings, Haraway encourages scholars to aim for a partial perspective that is context-specific. This approach is based on the premise that detached neutrality is an attempt by modern science to perform a "god-trick" by viewing itself as a disembodied Other that can produce objective findings.[69] This veil of neutrality is unrealistic because it conceals the complexities of research. In regard to gender discrimination, Haraway uses the concept of vision to explain that subjects deemed feminine are not given sight.[70] They are instead viewed primarily through a lens of being observed, described, or conquered. Essentially, they become outsiders explained away by a so-called objective, detached, scientific gaze.

To address this problem, feminist scholars contend that it is important to think about how one's own position, in relation to the study topic at hand, can shape the findings of a study.[71] Engaging in this exercise—termed reflexivity and positionality—is viewed as a way to address the gap between the researcher and the researched. Although much of the literature on this topic focuses on anthropological research methods such as ethnography, feminist geographers also debate the merits and concerns related to reflexivity and positionality.[72] Inspired by this ongoing discourse, I provide here an overview of my background as a means for readers to be aware of the factors that may have influenced the direction and findings of this study.

Born and raised in the United States and being of Indian descent, for example, places me in the position of an "in-between entity" in terms of being identified as American and Indian at the same time. This dual identity brings forth multiple positionalities and associations. On the one hand, as a U.S. citizen I am positioned as hailing from a country that benefits from India's low-wage labor pool, and at the individual level I represent the customer that call center employees interact with on a daily basis. On the other hand, when in India, I am labeled a nonresident Indian (NRI) and associated with the term *American-Born Confused Desi* (ABCD). The acronym ABCD is used by Indians to characterize Indians born in the United States and reflects the notion that they are inherently "confused." This notion stems from an underlying belief that Indians raised outside of India have a disconnected or incoherent sense of identity and belonging.[73]

During fieldwork I resided in Juhu Vile Parle, a suburb of Mumbai. My inability to speak fluent Hindi as well as lack of ability to speak Gujarati prompted one neighborhood friend to say, "Do you have any idea how much you confuse people around here? You are the brown face that doesn't speak back!" Add to this that I didn't live with a husband, parents, or uncle, and some neighbors were befuddled by the arrival of a single, child-free, "young" woman (I was thirty-six years old) to the building.

Despite the fact that I am of Indian origin, specifically Gujarati, and was also living in a Gujarati neighborhood while in Mumbai, categorical aspects of my identity rendered me different from that community. For example, when I informed neighbors that I would be leaving to spend a weekend in Dubai, on a ticket purchased only two days prior, they were perplexed and told me that this would not be possible because there was not enough time to get my visa in order. I responded, "What visa? I'm American!" This spoke not only to my sense of identity and privilege, but also was a reminder of how citizenship played a direct role in mobilizing my lifestyle.

During the course of fieldwork I came to realize that the questions I initially focused on during the interview process were more about patriarchal concerns about a woman's place and less about what women actually thought of their call center experiences. At the beginning stages of fieldwork I would inadvertently hone in on the question, "What did your family think of you working at night?" As I conducted more interviews I realized that the question itself reflected the "What will people think?" narrative that women were already subjected to in many facets of their lives. By placing it foremost in the interviews, I was at some level taking on the belief that what other people think matters and is worthy of concern. When I moved these questions to the background and instead focused on what women themselves thought about working the night shift and on their opinions of how call center employment shaped their lives, I ended up with richer qualitative data that spoke to how women experience life beyond "family values" and marriage.

In writing this section it was difficult to ignore the irony of reflexivity and positionality discourse in relation to feminist concerns. My basic premise is that women have struggled for years to get jobs in academia and be taken seriously. As part of gaining entry they are compelled to work harder than men in order to prove themselves and justify their right to be scholars. After they gain entry some feminist scholars turn around and say, "Okay, now we have to justify our position"—that is, apologize for themselves, and their status, race, and gender—in the context of our research project and also relative to those on whom we are conducting research. In my opinion, it is as if we are so used to having to explain ourselves that we are compelled to do so even when it is not asked of us.

This is not to suggest that I disagree with reflexivity and positionality but instead to state that I am mindful of the irony that comes from engaging in this exercise. Researchers have to maintain a fine line between not showing off or partaking in what concerned skeptics see as an act of self-absorbed navel gazing. At the same time, they deal with notions of "propriety" that prefer women researchers to present themselves as "unassuming" and "down to earth" regardless of their accomplishments. I wrestled with these thoughts throughout the study.

The Scope of the Book and General Findings

During this study I have remained cognizant of how large structural forces such as national policy and economic liberalization fuel the development of the transnational call center industry and, subsequently, inform women's participation in this industry. Although these matters are certainly important, this book focuses on how individual women and their families experience being part of a global night shift labor pool. Rather than connect their stories to theories of how economic policy or unequal global relations shape the day-to-day lives of workers, I have instead sought to show how the body, as a scale of analysis, provides a rich, textual understanding of how globalization and gender inequality operate "on the ground." The willingness of participants and their family members to share intimate details of their lives allowed me to gain such an understanding.

To be clear, the purpose of this book is not to generalize mobility and spatial access to the entire population of call center employees. In fact, it became evident during the course of fieldwork that subgroups of women—such as divorced women and married women—merit further attention. Instead, I uncover how mobility is recodified in a variety of settings—from the household to the urban nightscape—for the women I encountered during my time in India.

Some women are certainly able to use the emergence of this globalized, night shift labor force to expand their mobility and gain access to social spaces that were previously off-limits. At the same time, call center workers are also more intensely protected than other female laborers; this draws from class conceptions about what types of women are *worthy* of protection and what types of women are not. This protection works against increases in mobility, as keeping women safe is used as an excuse to confine them in ways from which their male counterparts are relatively immune, such as relegating women to home space or controlling when they are allowed to go out. This protective attitude also plays into how some women's bodies are used as a site for promoting nationalistic attitudes. Body and nation converge around the motif of potential violation and the consequent need for boundary policing.

Furthermore, there is no linear path to how call center employment affects all workers, because the diversity in women's experiences exists on a spectrum from entrapment to liberation. In contrast to presenting night shift employment as a revolutionary turn that thoroughly reshapes women's lives, my fieldwork revealed that women use technology and societal expectations of their "place" to *recodify* their mobility in ways that allow them to go out at night while dealing with societal pressures. Some women, for example, used the mobile phone both to assert their autonomy and to placate family members concerned about them being out at night. Although the mobile phone was certainly key to getting some women out of the house, they continued to experience disdain and social stigma for working the night shift.

This dynamic draws on how women have come to embody gendered conceptions of space. Some such conceptions are protective, some are exploitative, and some are exclusionary. For example, women are seen as both contaminating (when temporally out of place in temples because it's the wrong time of the month) and contaminated (when temporally out of place in the street because it's dark). Their bodies, in turn, become sites on which family honor, religious piety, and national identity are performed. Key to this study is that women are held to higher levels of scrutiny, relative to their male counterparts, for when and where they go out. A woman out at night is seen as both *at risk* (in need of protection) and *risky* (in need of discipline and control). These dual anxieties are reflected in family, community, and media responses to the growing phenomenon of women working the night shift in call centers.

Yi Fu Tuan contends that "cultural geography remains almost wholly daylight geography" and that more attention needs to be given to the "after hours."[74] By moving into the geographies of the night, this book directly confronts how women experience spatial and temporal mobility beyond the daytime. The relatively high wages combined with the night shift requirement of this industry provide a unique platform for thinking about how gendered norms of mobility are recodified when the lure of high wages, an upscale office environment, and the opportunity to work in a global setting are brought together.

The Organization of the Book

To begin this exploration, Chapter Two presents a brief synopsis of the call center industry. I outline the growth of this industry in relation to gender, class, and education issues that affect who is able to gain access to these jobs and who is not. Chapter Three introduces the concept of mobility-morality narratives, a term I created to describe how the pressure placed on women to maintain their safety and reputation (for example, not to be a "bad girl") affects their physical mobility and spatial access. Chapters Four and Five provide detailed accounts of how call center employment affects women's temporal mobility and economic mobility. Each chapter explores how working the night shift reshapes women's lives in a myriad of ways, from being able to get out of the house at night and having the means to purchase a home to being able to be the sole support of a family unit. Chapter Six shifts the focus to the household and looks at how gender relations fare when women work at night and, in some instances, earn more money than their husbands or parents. Chapter Seven uncovers how perceptions about call center employment as well as its relatively high wages affect the social mobility of workers. The last chapter summarizes the findings of the study and articulates the varying ways in which call center employment has the potential to transform the lives of women workers while at the same time keeping them tethered to gendered notions of a woman's place.

2 Off-Shoring Customer Service

A New Global Order

One afternoon in the fall of 2004, while giving a guest lecture, I asked a roomful of students at The University of Texas at Austin how many of them had called an 800 number for customer support or technical assistance and found that the support person was in India. More than 80 percent raised their hands. I then asked these same students, "How many of you would like to use your college degree to work from midnight to 8 A.M., use an Indian accent, change your name from Sam to Shirish, and provide customer service for a product that you most likely have never owned yourself?" No hands went up. Even though call center employment is viewed by industry proponents as a vehicle to prosperity and career growth for young people in India, it was not seen the same way by this college population in the United States.

Since the U.S. call center industry workforce has gone global, it operates on a twenty-four-hour timeframe that shifts the work space and work time of customer service employees worldwide.[1] Twenty five years ago it would have been hard to imagine that a Texan would dial an 800 number at 2:30 P.M. and at 2 A.M. India time reach the suburb of a major Indian city where an employee named Jyothi would alter her accent and answer, "Good Afternoon, Delta Airlines, this is Julie speaking."[2] This transformation of time into a global resource is based on reorganizing employees identities, neutralizing their accents, and temporally adjusting the conventional nine-to-five work schedule.

The emergence of this transnational labor force represents a new level of social and spatial interaction between industrialized and developing nations. Unlike silicon chip production in Taiwan, maquiladoras in Mexico,[3] or McDonald's in France, transnational call center employment represents a shift from exporting the *production* of material goods or culture to a full-scale *reproduction* of identity and culture. For example, McDonald's sells French fries in Paris but does not require an American accent from its French employees. In contrast, call center operations are based on the availability of workers trained to embody an American identity and recognize cultural cues. This new local-global nexus of identity formation represents a dramatic shift in how the United States uses foreign labor to fuel its economy.[4]

In this chapter I provide a brief overview of the developments that led to the creation of transnational call centers, as well as some of the characteristics of transnational call centers in India. I also examine how the relatively high wages and the night shift requirement of this industry have implications for what is often termed the feminization of labor. I then discuss how employment in the industry is shifting from college to high school graduates (and even some high school dropouts) and how this new recruitment strategy intersects with gender and education. Finally, I outline what happens when call center employment, traditionally viewed as "pink-collar" employment, takes on the nightscape in India. When women begin to traverse the nightscape, wide-ranging opinions and concerns related to call center employment emerge. Here I incorporate comments and insights that emerged from interviews and participant observation during the course of fieldwork. Throughout the chapter I argue that the emergence of the industry is not only about economic development, but also about how gender, class, and education are linked to the English-speaking requirement that is imperative to getting a job in this industry.

Background on the Industry

Call center operations moved to India because the country provided a cheap, English-speaking labor force.[5] Indeed, the global demand for twenty-four-hour workers also emerged as transnational corporations took advantage of different time zones to access more and more laborers. Barbara Adam refers to this process as the *colonization of time,* a term that describes how the Western clock is commoditized, set as the standard, and exported throughout the world.[6] *Temporal imperialism* and *temporal entrapment* have also been used to define the shifting relationship between the timescapes of the global north and global south.[7]

At the same time, the global processes that fueled the emergence of the BPO industry in the late 1990s were a direct result of national policies of both

India and the United States. The restructuring of U.S. immigration policy, which reduced the number of H1-B work visas, along with the economic downturn of the U.S. IT sector starting in 2000 led companies to off-shore both high-wage engineering positions and low-wage call center jobs. Essentially, because the Indian worker could not migrate to the United States, the work migrated to India. The protectionist policy of limiting immigration in order to bring economic security to the American worker created the opposite effect, as more and more jobs were transferred overseas.[8]

The emergence of transnational call centers in India also came about because of a national policy that welcomed the presence of multinational corporations. Historically this was not the case. After independence, India went from being dubbed the "British Raj" to being called the "Permit Raj."[9] India was considered an impenetrable market because of its unending bureaucracy, notorious corruption, and protectionist policies that sought to shield India from the outside economy. This situation shifted dramatically in 1991 when the government, under Prime Minister Rao, removed import licensing requirements and sought to undo more than four decades' worth of bureaucracy under the Permit Raj.

In 2002, a decade after the pivotal 1991 reforms, NASSCOM estimated that 336 call centers had emerged throughout India. By 2006, approximately 470,000 women and men worked in this industry.[10] Amish, an industry consultant, expressed doubts about the accuracy of these numbers. When asked his opinion on approximately how many call centers there are in Mumbai, he stated that he was unable to provide an accurate estimate because numerous "mom and pop" call centers intermittently emerge and are shut down. Still, it is clear that the BPO industry is a significant employer of hundreds of thousands of Indian workers.[11]

Although this book focuses primarily on transnational call center employment, the BPO industry in India is far more expansive in scope. From payroll processing and legal and medical transcription to tax preparation services for individuals and financial analysis for Wall Street firms, this rapidly expanding industry encompasses a variety of processes that are key to both U.S. industries and individuals. American Express, Microsoft, General Electric, Delta Airlines, and even the State of Arizona Unemployment Division are just some of the firms that have transferred a portion of their operations to India. In essence, a variety of jobs that can be done "over the wire" (that is, by Internet or telecom connection) are up for grabs as India seeks to leverage its low-wage, English-speaking workforce in a competitive, global labor market.

Feminization of Labor

It turns out that a significant percentage of workers now employed by the BPO industry are female, but the social construction of women's role in society (such as nurturing, passive, unpaid household labor) conflicts with their participation in the paid labor force. Indeed, gendered narratives about what constitutes "a man's job" versus "ladies work" are becoming more and more common as more women become employed in these transnational call centers.

From Dublin, Ireland, to the rural American West and New Zealand, call center employment especially is defined as women's work and reflects what scholars term *the feminization of labor* or, more recently, *the feminization of service*.[12] Because it is associated with a part-time, flexible work schedule that allows women to manage the household and still bring home an income, call center employment is considered a "pink-collar" field.[13] Although research on women's employment in the industry has to date focused primarily on Western countries, the demand for a qualified low-wage labor pool to do this work is expanding the geography of the industry.

Literature on the feminization of labor focuses on women's participation in the paid labor force and uncovers how the status and value accorded to an industry is transformed when women gain a foothold. Anne Bonds, for instance, found that when women joined the call industry in the rural American West, the white-collar status associated with this job was devalued into that of a deskilled, feminized work space.[14] Her research refutes the idea that working in spaces that were traditionally male gives women higher status. Instead, the infusion of women transformed perceptions of call center work from professional to entry-level. Underlying this transformation is the belief that women must aspire to masculine forms of labor (such as work outside the household) if they want to achieve equality. At the same time, there is less emphasis on holding men accountable for contributing to what Arlie Hochschild and Anne Machung term "the second shift," namely, the unpaid labor of cooking, cleaning, and child care.[15]

When the transnational call center industry initially moved into Ireland, Proinnsias Breathnach stated:

Ireland has been on the forefront in acting as a host for internationally-mobile routine office work, initially involving mainly data processing and, more recently, teleservices. As elsewhere, teleservices employment in Ireland is characterized by a combination of female predominance, low pay, difficult working conditions and high turnover rates.[16]

As this characterization illustrates, even when labor processes are exported throughout the world, gendered notions of a woman's worth in the workforce remain in place. Unpaid labor in the household transforms into low pay when women step out. *Nurturing* becomes a code word for the belief that it is more acceptable for women than for their male counterparts to tolerate difficult working conditions with less reward. This idea applies not only to service jobs but to manufacturing as well. From describing women as workers with nimble fingers to defining them as disposable and replaceable in the realm of global manufacturing, women are marked as a secondary necessity in the paid labor force and are subsequently made the target of exploitation.[17]

With this comes, in some instances, the devaluation of labor processes from white-collar to "pink-collar." This devaluation not only intersects with gender and class, but also bumps up against the limited "professional" job opportunities available in developing countries. Carla Freeman's rich ethnographic account of the off-shoring of data processing for one of the largest insurance companies in the United States to Barbados in the 1990s is revealing:

> Locally, in Barbados, the pink-collar informatics operator represents a new category of feminine worker, symbolically empowered by her professional appearance and the computer technology with which she works. Her air-conditioned office appears to be a far cry from the cane fields and kitchens in which her mother and grandmother toiled. . . . [18]

The call center industry in India, with its upscale office environment and night shift requirement, is also a far cry from finishing one's education, having an arranged marriage with a dowry to seal the deal, and settling down to have children and be homebound.[19]

Freeman's study goes on to uncover the exploitative side of working in a transnational process, such as the low wages relative to the actual output demanded of workers. In fact, what makes her research unique is that the employees in her study would have earned more money if they had worked in sugar cane factories. Instead, what drew women to the industry was the sense of modernity and professionalism they associated with the office environment. Women used "dressing up" to go to work (that is, professional appearance) to create a new identity for themselves that challenged the Barbadian expectation that one's clothes must be in line with one's class status. While navigating between empowerment and exploitation narratives, Freeman brings to light the sense of independence that women gained from being part of the transnational data processing industry, and the gendered narratives about work that made women, instead of men, the choice labor pool for this industry.

A gendered narrative about work was also apparent in the call center industry and the demand for women draws from beliefs about what constitutes "ladies work." Previous research indicates that call centers in India prefer hiring young, educated women.[20] According to J. P. Pradhan and V. Abraham, call centers often prefer to hire women because they are seen as more hardworking, patient, attentive, and loyal; as less aggressive; and as having better interpersonal skills than men.[21]

Under the rubric that call center employment requires what Hochschild terms "emotional labor"—for example, empathizing with customers and soothing tempers—women are stereotyped as best suited for customer service.[22] In contrast, labor defined as aggressive and combative is considered a man's job and, in many cases, comes with a higher salary. These stereotypes are reflected in the occupational segregation interviewees described within the industry. Interviewees stated that call center work that involved credit collections had predominantly male workers because it required aggressive employees to harass late-payers. Processes such as airline reservations had more women workers. It was also reported that a collections job came with a much higher salary potential because many companies paid a commission on the collections an employee made. This was not the case for processes such as booking airline reservations.

In closing, the integration of women into the paid labor force is at times seen as a symbol of liberation. Women leaving the confines of the home to earn an income is viewed as an indicator of society moving along the path of "modernization" and thus emancipating women from traditional gender roles. Yet in most cases the demand for women workers is less about ensuring their equal participation in the paid labor force and more about meeting the demand for a steady supply of workers who can be purchased on the cheap. Disparity in wages between women and men is certainly nothing new. Narratives related to women being loyal, compliant, deferential, nimble fingered, nurturing, and not needing to earn as much money (because they are expected to have husbands who support them) are just some of the descriptions used to explain, and in many cases rationalize, the structural inequality that women continue to face in the paid labor force.

From College to High School

Research on the feminization of labor in relation to the global distribution of labor tends to focus on manufacturing. Examining the call center industry in India provides a context for comparing and contrasting how service workers relative to factory workers experience the feminization of labor. This is important because perceptions about the type of job one has overlap with both the content of the work and the class distinctions embedded in the labor. In contrast to factory work, which is perceived as drawing from the poor or working-class strata of society, call center employment in India is thought of as a job that recruits from the middle class.[23] Thus, the discussion about the feminization of labor becomes more complicated, and more enriched, when class dynamics are incorporated.

It is important to note that although transnational call centers in India originally sought recent college graduates, they have recently discovered that recent college graduates don't necessarily have the skill set they seek. As a result, some of them have begun to recruit high school graduates and high school dropouts. This shift in recruitment strategy has also lowered the age range for entry-level call center employees to include more eighteen- to twenty-one-year-olds. Indeed, one interviewee, Anan, explained that depending on the process (such as customer service for credit cards or airline reservations) some companies prefer high school graduates or dropouts because they are less likely to quit, can be hired at a lower cost, and are able to communicate on a par with college graduates.

The recruitment of high school students and dropouts is a source of concern to many people, both inside and outside the industry. Some suggest that the lure of fast money is causing some students to drop their education. Because call center employment is believed to be a stop-gap job instead of a viable long-term career option, foregoing school to work in this industry is considered shortsighted. Under the current educational system, students are expected to attend high school, college, and graduate school in order and, more important, with no interruptions. When a student opts out at the college level, it is generally very difficult to reenter the system.

To provide a context for "big money" as seen through the eyes of a high school graduate, consider that interviewees reported that the average entry-level salary in other fields is Rs 2,000 to Rs 3,000 (US$44 to US$67) a month. In contrast, call centers have starting salaries in excess of Rs 10,000 (US$222) per month. Swati, twenty-six years old and a three-year veteran of the industry, contended that regardless of what one studied in college, call center employment offers the highest starting salary. Offer this income level to an individual with a high school education or to a high school dropout and the lure is even stronger. This dynamic would be the equivalent of foreign corporations setting up shop in New York City and offering local high school graduates a salary of $40,000 to $60,000 per year, provided they work the night shift and mask their identity.

Interestingly, it turns out that men are more likely to drop out of school to pursue call center employment, whereas women are more likely to stay with their education. The two companies where I conducted interviews did not disclose the education and income levels of their employees, but my participant observation and in-depth interviews indicated that the majority of women were college graduates. During discussions about why men are more likely to drop out of school to work in a call center, Anan stated, "Women are more disciplined and less rebellious."

Conversely, I argue that gender-based discipline is related to the more stringent controls placed on women's lives rather than to an inherent quality based on sex. In this instance, the pressure on women to complete their education is less about providing them with the opportunity to pursue their career goals and more about increasing their worth on the arranged marriage market. Even the perceived value of what one studies runs along gender lines. Anjali, a twenty-seven-year-old former employee, for instance, has an arts degree and spoke in frustration about receiving comments such as "B.A. in arts? Oh, you're a girl. Arts, it's okay."

Thus it is important to note that gendered conceptions about education and working outside the home also inform the extent to which women participate in the paid labor force. Examining how the feminization of labor fares in work constructed as middle class, for example, is insightful from the perspective of *sanskritisation*, a process by which those of the lower class mimic the restrictive social norms of the upper class.[24] This dynamic draws from the assertion that women from the upper echelons of society experience more stringent regimes of control over their lives because their families can afford to keep them at home as a marker of class status. Staying out all night, therefore, is in direct conflict with this regime. Although the income from call center employment is certainly a marker of upward economic mobility and, subsequently, class mobility in some families, this mobility is bought at the price of sending women out at night to work. This practice disrupts the tradition of according higher status to families that keep women at home.

The "Pink Collar" Traverses the Nightscape

As a time to work, the night shift is generally looked down on, especially for women. In many instances, a night shift job is considered a last resort, the least favorable time to work. Because it is perceived as a space containing those who couldn't get a "better" job (code word for *daytime*) or for those who are paying their dues in order to move to the day shift, call center employment is viewed as a job that young people take while looking for other options to move up the economic ladder.

Although disparaging views toward women who work at night were pervasive during the course of this study, the growth of the call center industry in India brought with it a dramatic shift in some women's access to night shift jobs. Previously, night shift opportunities for women in the urban domain were primarily in the following fields: prostitution, bar dancing, medicine (nurses and OB-GYN doctors), and the hotel industry. To combat resistance, some employers, including hotels and dance bars, have assumed the responsibility of transporting women to and from work during the night. According to Annie, a former manager of five-star hotel properties in Mumbai:

> Okay, yes, hotels typically provide night shift drops to their women employees past 10 P.M., because it's a law in India that women should not work past that hour. The legalities I am not sure of, but I know that there used to be a drop on the hour every hour till 3 to 4 A.M. for women door-to-door and any woman could avail [herself] of the drop, no grade distinction. It's just that most higher management women had their own cars so didn't take the drop, but no one would stop them if they wanted to.

Following their lead, call centers transport employees to and from the office. This is offered not only as an incentive for joining the industry, but also because companies need to ensure the safety of women workers traveling during the night in order to recruit them effectively.[25]

As call center operations traverse the globe and the day turns to night, not only does the home-to-work journey become more complicated, but also the pink-collar framework associated with the industry is destabilized. Night shift employment now intersects with gendered notions of "skill" and mobility narratives in conflicting and often contradictory ways. According to Winifred Poster, the flexibility associated with call center employment in the West disappears and is replaced with a rigidification of time:

> While these engineers may experience cyclical time that has breaks and down time between heavy periods of overtime, there is no hiatus or respite for Indian call center workers. Reversed work time is continuous for the full duration of the year, and industry representatives are pushing for additional work days on national and international holidays. Call center work is also hyper-managed and monitored from numerous vantage points: from the quality control department at end of the production line, to the president/CEO of the Indian call center, to the client firm in the U.S. Needless to say, self-management is far from the picture here.[26]

The change in work time also creates a dynamic that runs counter to the gender and technology discourse. In terms of the interplay between technological development and the feminization of labor, for instance, B. A. Weinberg argues that computerization benefits women because it deemphasizes physical skills and thus women become an important part of a labor force that demands people skills and knowledge work.[27] From this perspective, it would be expected that the gendered aspects of the call center industry would remain the same as it traverses the globe. After all, the gendered narratives used to explain why women are well suited for this job—combined with the fact that technological development allows the United States to off-shore its demand for "emotional labor"—would arguably make Indian women the preferred labor pool for this position. In fact, it might even be expected that they would be on the forefront of the call center industry and, as illustrated by Figures 4 and 5, this appears to be the case.

In 2002, workers were depicted as "housekeepers to the world" (Figure 4) ready to do the dirty work. Four years later, *Time* magazine (Figure 5) depicted the Indian call center employee, wearing a *bindi* and *wedding* jewels, as a sparkly, *traditional* woman ready to enter the workplace and *serve* the global economy. The underlying themes of these images are marriage, tradition, and servitude. Women are constructed as the bodily site of a marriage (code word for *merger*) between the East and the West. They are presented as the recipients of Western development—jobs, money, and technology—who at the same time keep to tradition and culture. Put another way, these women don't forget where they *belong*; they keep to their place.

During fieldwork, however, I learned that this was not necessarily the case. Although Indian women are depicted as the face of the industry, in contrast to their U.S. counterparts they are, in some respects, losing ground in terms of industry participation. As customer service moves from the United States to India, the twelve-hour time difference that comes with it intersects directly with notions of a woman's place, namely at home. What was considered a flexible day shift job in the United States is rigid night work in India. As labor processes move from day to night and from low wage to high wage, ideas about what constitutes "ladies work" get complicated.

Unlike garment production, which was predominantly female in the United States and remained the same upon transfer to countries such as Mexico and Bangladesh, call center employment in India, at the time of this study, *appeared* to be moving toward gender integration in the labor pool. I italicize *appeared* to point out that what lies beneath the surface is more complex. The influx of men into positions that in the United States would be marked as "pink-collar" operates from multiple stances. Although this industry provides a flexible schedule that appeals to women in the United States who are expected to put family first, the temporal landscape of this industry shifted drastically once it was exported. Flexible work hours transformed into a night shift requirement that disrupts the traditional day and early evening schedule of this workforce.[28]

In fact, previous research suggests that a shift in the gender aspects of the industry is occurring. Poster's and Kiran Mirchandani's studies of call centers in Gurgaon and Noida, near New Delhi, found that 50 to 70 percent of the employees were men.[29] This finding coincides with the two call centers I visited in Mumbai; TYJ Corporation was approximately 60 percent men, and Company A was approximately 50 percent men. Employees I spoke to in Bangalore also cited rates that were in line with Mumbai. In addition, Shailesh, the training manager for a top-five call center in Mumbai, estimated that during the on-the-job (OTJ) training phase he has 40 percent women and 60 percent

Figure 4. *India Today*, November 18, 2002

Figure 5. *Time*, June 20, 2006

men. These findings contradict the media representation of call center employees in India as primarily female.[30]

Where I noticed an even further difference was at WebCorp and MedCorp in Ahmedabad.[31] Daksha, a human resources executive assistant at WebCorp, stated that approximately 80 percent of their employees are men and that few women there work at night because Ahmedabad is more conservative compared to other Indian cities. At MedCorp, *no* women were working the night shift. This was also the only company in the study that did not provide transportation to its employees. Although the company does have women working during the day shift, Parag, the company's owner, explained that in order to integrate women into his night shift, he would have to provide transportation.

The presence of men at the entry level of this industry certainly represents a shift in the gendered aspects of the industry. Drawing from interviews with employees, managers, family members, and industry experts, two reasons emerged as to why men move into "pink-collar" employment. First, the salary earned from working in this industry is well above average. In fact, some employees are paid more money to offset the night shift requirement.[32] Second, the night shift requirement of this industry is less of a hurdle for men to address. Although women may be the preferred gender for call center employment, it is men who are able to navigate the night more freely. This is not to suggest that families give men carte blanche to go out all night, but the physical and temporal mobility of men is a less contentious issue in comparison to the physical and temporal mobility of women.

In the upper echelons of this industry, men have always dominated. As one goes up the call center hierarchy from team leader to manager and director, women's participation dwindles. Women often plateau at mid-level positions while men progress further.[33] This disparity is linked to men's lack of responsibility to provide household labor and child care.

The cover story in Figure 4, "Housekeepers to the World," provides a glimpse of this occupational segregation.[34] In the story itself, photographs of customer service workers are mostly of young women whereas photos depicting high-level positions, such as chairman or president, show older men. The article presents only men as leaders of the industry and as experts in terms of discussing future growth and challenges. In contrast, the women interviewed are primarily entry-level workers. The one exception is a female vice president. She, however, works for a company that trains women to be effective customer service representatives. She is not in a direct position of power in terms of owning a call center or influencing policy surrounding the development of the industry. Interpreting this article, there is a sense that women are to be seen and *heard*, but not to serve as active participants in corporate decision making.

In closing, women experience temporal and spatial segregation in ways that generally limit their access to paid labor to the day shift. Although some critics present the BPO industry as subjecting workers to toiling the night away in IT sweatshops, a similar outcry did not emerge about women not participating in the industry because they are unable to go out at night as freely as their male counterparts.[35] Advocating against exploitative labor practices was certainly a focus of attention, but advocating for a woman's right to work was not. This is significant given the relatively high wages that come with BPO employment and its rapid expansion.

Opinions and Concerns Related to Call Center Employment

As I learned from my fieldwork, call centers in India are viewed and represented in a myriad of ways. Some accounts present them as a revolutionizing force that is reshaping the lives of India's youth.[36] Here the argument is that call centers provide jobs and a level of income that ten years ago were beyond the reach of eighteen- to twenty-five-year-olds. As a result, there are now tales of consumerism and living the good life. At the same time, call center employment is viewed as a site of exploitation (such as "cyber-coolies" working the night away in IT sweatshops) and moral decay (such as sex in the call center).[37] *Coolie,* for example, is a term used to describe poorly paid baggage handlers at train stations in India. Although call center employees earn a relatively high wage, it is commonly known that their American counterparts earn far more for doing the same work, hence the term *cyber-coolie.* At the same time, the industry is blamed for moral decay because of the social camaraderie associated with the call center environment, especially as it relates to men and women hanging out at night together.

Some argue that although call center employment provides some young people with a chance to be part of a global work environment, the monotony of the job can lead to burnout. Concerned citizens, such as Father John, a thirty-seven-year-old Catholic priest who is known for speaking about the effects of call center employment on young people, believe that creativity is sacrificed for high salaries. According to Father John:

> Also, see, there's no creativity. You just have a headphone, there's no creativity. And youth at this age are the most creative-feeling. I have a strong feeling if this

goes on for a long time, sitting with earphone, night, without lack of sleep and other things, it's going to affect their minds in the long run. So, psychologically, emotionally, the whole thing of no creativity is something which I am very sad about. The youth are the best, their creative minds should be channelized.

In addition to describing the monotony of call center work, some interviewees felt that the job itself was not necessarily conducive to expanding their career opportunities. Although fielding phone call after phone call through the night was viewed as dulling the mind, the constrictions on a worker's career path were more specifically related to the fact that other industries do not always consider call center employment to be "proper" work experience. Meanwhile, Nilesh, an industry consultant for one of India's first call centers in Mumbai and Gurgaon, deflected concerns about monotony and future career prospects by stating that call centers not only provide what he considers low-level customer service work, such as airline reservations, but also high-level customer service work, such as million-dollar collection accounts for major corporations.

Although in some instances the income from call center employment was viewed as a catalyst for economic empowerment, the flip side was stories of workers racking up debt at record levels. Parag, the owner of MedCorp, which provides medical transcription services for U.S. firms, observed that young people with previously limited or no income—such as students—accumulate credit card debt after joining the BPO industry. This phenomenon emerged as students began earning salaries high enough to qualify for credit schemes.

In dismay, Parag described how his own general manager did not understand the cost behind credit card debt and was paying 36 percent interest. He paid off the debt on behalf of the general manager, who is now paying him back. Concerned that the younger generation was becoming accustomed to the higher wages associated with the industry, he said, "In the USA, the economy is large and the population is low. Plus there is social security. Such does not exist in India. What will happen if these global companies leave? What will fill the void?" Although parents and critics of the industry also expressed similar concerns, this was not a theme mentioned by employees.

Despite the attention given to the relatively high salaries that call centers provide, Rekha, an eighteen-year-old employee at Mindspace in Malad, pointed out that call center employment came with hidden costs that she had not anticipated. Once every three months her company arranges a trip for the team. Employees bear the cost of the trip, which can run upwards of Rs 2,000 (US$44). According to Rekha, not attending can affect an employee's performance review because he or she is perceived as not being a team player. Just as companies view the money spent to entertain potential clients as the "cost of doing business," Rekha believes that, in order to get ahead, workers must take on certain company expenses as the cost of having a job. Although this was not a prevalent theme throughout the study, Rekha's situation was not unique. Employees of a major computer firm in Bangalore also mentioned the costs they incurred, such as initiation rites that involve buying Starbucks coffee for their group—no small expense—in order to become a "part of the team."

Despite safety concerns related to young women such as Rekha working at night in a call center, a 2006 report commissioned by the National Commission on Women deemed the call center industry to be the provider of the most security for its female workforce. This study was based on a sample of 272 women working in various night shift positions in industries such as hotel, medical, and textiles. Mira, a call center manager in Bangalore, agreed with the findings of this study and argued that call centers are far safer than local industries because they are held to higher sexual harassment standards.[38] At her company, a Fortune 500 computer firm, both men and women, she said, received sexual harassment training. She contended that this kind of training and notices are not provided in local industries and suggested that because the call center industry—particularly captive call centers such as the one she works for—is under such scrutiny by the media that they are far more conscientious about the rules.[39]

For individuals who were able to convince their families to let them work night shifts, opinions surrounding how hard or how easy it is to get a call center job varied.[40] During preliminary research in 2005, interviewees from Bangalore stressed the difficulty of getting a job. Hetal, a twenty-four-year-old employee, stated that of the five hundred people who applied for her position, only twelve were accepted. During fieldwork in 2006, employees in Mumbai suggested that there was a job surplus and it was considered relatively easy to get a call center job. The difficulty lay in gaining entry into top companies such as J.P. Morgan and 3 Global Services.

For those who make the cut, both managers and trainers pointed out, attrition is high, particularly during the training process. Shailesh, the trainer mentioned earlier, stated that his company has the following training schedule:

Voice and accent training	2 weeks
Process training*	4 weeks
OTJ training	2 weeks

(*This refers to training for the actual account that an employee will service, such as credit card, airline, and so forth.)

Shailesh explained that he handled employees at the OTJ training stage. His batch, at the time of this study, consisted of thirty-six employees. From previous experience he had learned that if they survive OTJ, they will, for the most part, stay with the company. Out of a hundred employees who make it to OTJ training, he estimates, thirty to forty drop out. Depending on the company, OTJ training is referred to as "the Nursery" or as "Care and Development."

Reflecting what I heard from other interviewees, Anjali, sent me an e-mail laying out the following four points about how call center employment is viewed:

1. The entry level call centre jobs are not considered very highly. That is the actual call associate job. Other managerial and training positions are considered by other employers as credible because it does give you a lot of people experience.
2. Credibility is suspect because these jobs are still low on employee discipline, organizational experience and commitment, professional ethics, and skill development and yet pay a lot in Indian standards, making young people feel it is a substitute to hard work.
3. Call centre jobs were viewed till recently as transition jobs, especially for qualified youth like engineering students, IT students, MBA students, etc., so they themselves preferred not to mention it on their resume. Like I didn't mention it anywhere.
4. The job of taking calls will be viewed for a long time as a low-skill job unless you rise beyond it to senior positions of handling teams, HR, customer service manager, etc.

Add this to the perceptions about night shift work and call center employment appears to be a questionable job choice. One aunt labeled her niece "completely mad" while another interviewee's parents wanted their daughter to be "a normal human being." Three respondents pointed out that their parents' dismay stemmed from having higher aspirations for their daughters. Ms. Paul, a mother in her early fifties, said, "Maybe I was wrong but I thought she could do something much better than work in a call center, because she did pretty well in college. So I thought, 'you can do something better with your brains.'"

From an executive standpoint, a major concern is the shortage of *quali-fied* workers.[41] In contrast to other global labor pools that are viewed as "disposable," or easily replaceable—as is the case with maquiladora employees in Mexico and factory employees in China—call center employees are in such demand that the *Wall Street Journal* reported that these workers have more leverage over their employers relative to other industries.[42]

In Ahmedabad, a city ramping up to compete with other IT cities in India, the shortage of workers intersects with class and education. Parag, the owner of MedCorp, began his company in 1999 with 60 employees and now employs 250. He pointed out that he could have easily doubled his current workforce due to the demand for services but was unable to because of the lack of a qualified workforce *willing* to take this sort of job. Daksha, the human re-sources executive assistant at WebCorp, felt that her company faced similar challenges. In the future, when they need to recruit "a big batch" (say, fifty employees), they will hold hiring sessions in distant towns such as Surat, Ra-jkot, and Baroda. In order to hire fifty "suitable workers," she estimates, they will need to interview at least two hundred people.

This disconnect is directly related to class and education. Parag explained that it is mostly those from the middle- and upper-class strata of society who are sought by call centers and BPOs. These families have the money to send their children to private schools where English is the primary language. In contrast, English is traditionally taught only after the eighth standard in pub-lic schools.[43] When public school students graduate, they lack the English lan-guage skills needed to work in the industry. According to Parag, this narrows the labor pool that companies such as his can draw from to less than 5 percent of the population. Out of this amount, very few want to join the industry be-cause they often (1) go to the United States for a professional job, (2) take over their parents' business, or (3) attend a professional college. Given their higher class status, joining the BPO industry is, to some extent, considered beneath them. The lower income groups that would most benefit from employment in this industry—starting salary at MedCorp is Rs 7,000 per month (US$155)—are shut out because they lack English skills.

Parag also brought up the gender-based education differences at his own company. During a discussion of the fact that 90 percent of his employees are college graduates he commented, "Even engineers are taking this job!" Anna, the human resources manager who also participated in the interview, said that engineers are good transcribers and that of the thirty engineers they employ, twenty are women. Parag expanded on this by saying that they are able to hire more female engineers because women are not given a chance in their own field.[44]

In addition, the fluency of English that is required to work in this industry is not only in reading and speaking, but also in accent acquisition and grammar.[45] Linda, the executive of TYJ Corporation in Mumbai introduced in Chapter One, stated during an interview, "If an applicant is from Ahmedabad, we don't touch them. Their accents are untrainable. We tried before, but it just didn't work." According to Parag, even if a person can understand and transcribe English, this does not mean he or she has an understanding of proper grammar. He also found that graduates of public school are generally weak in conversational English. His concern about grammar was reflected in a company e-mail that Irene, a thirty-two-year-old training manager in Mumbai, shared with me. With the subject heading "Pathetic English," this e-mail disseminated by her coworker complained about the quality of written communication between Indian workers and U.S. customers:

> I apologies in reference to the adjustments fiasco happened on the [Company B] side
> (I APOLOGIES too for the grammar fiasco)
> Yes sir i am too ready for this task. . . .
> (And we are TOO sorry for the English here)

The disparity between the supply and demand of qualified workers that Parag describes is not an isolated concern. During my fieldwork in Bangalore, a backlash against the "English Imperialism" associated with the BPO industry—meaning its demand for an English-speaking workforce—emerged as lawmakers grappled with an ordinance that would remove English as a language taught in the public schools and require teachers to teach only in Kannada, the local language of Bangalore.[46] Proponents of the law viewed it as a way to fight "English imperialism" while opponents expressed concern about how this law would affect Bangalore's ability to compete with other cities seeking to gain a foothold in the BPO industry.

As illustrated in this section, the opinions and concerns related to call center employment are quite varied. From terms such as *cyber-coolie* and *English imperialism* to anxiety about young people entering a site of moral decay that dulls the mind, to beliefs about how hard or easy it is to get a call center job, to executives worried about a shortage of qualified workers, to the disconnect between individuals who would most benefit from call center income and those who have the qualifications to join the industry, reaction to this industry has by no means been singular. Clearly the relatively high wages associated with the industry stem from the global demand for a night shift labor force, and this demand intersects with gender, class, and education in ways that are complex.

Wrap-Up

The night shift requirement of the call center industry spotlights the role of geography in defining gendered conceptions of work. Literature on the feminization of labor tends to look at the actual content of a job and uncover how it is imbued with stereotypes, such as women are better at sewing clothes in a factory because they have nimble fingers, and men are more equipped to handle brain surgery because they have exacting minds. The transformation of day shift work into the night shift, and the subsequent increased participation of men, demonstrates how "ladies work" is not only about the actual content of the work, but also about the space and time it occupies.

The idea of a modern-day labor force that goes from female to male is rare in comparison to the integration of women into historically male-dominated positions such as clerical work and pharmacists.[47] As jobs deemed "pink-collar" move into developing nations and men join their ranks, their increased participation provides an opening for thinking about how women's work becomes defeminized, or remasculinized, when labor processes move it into the night and men gain a foothold. At the same time, the de-skilling of the job from college to high school level provides another avenue by which men increasingly become involved in the industry. All of these emerging trends have significant implications in terms of women's incorporation.

Clearly, as the opinions of interviewees indicate in the following chapters, call center employment does provide some women with the opportunity to expand their social and economic mobility in ways previously unavailable to them, even as it constrains others. Instead of viewing transnational call centers either as sites of Western imperialism, dens of moral decay, or spaces that liberate women from traditional gender roles, one begins to see in the interplay between these competing beliefs that call center employment has the potential to reshape individuals' perceptions of themselves and of the community that surrounds them.

3 Mobility-Morality Narratives

Call center job equals call girl job!
What kind of work are these females doing at night?
She's too bold!

In Bangalore I interviewed a twenty-four-year-old man who referred to the night shift as "the hooker shift." His comment revealed how attitudes surrounding night shift employment intersect significantly with social and temporal constructions of gender. Women's physical mobility and access to urban areas are regulated by a timescape that limits their presence during the evening and night, particularly if they are going out alone. Women who break the "rules" are marked as sites of transgression and, in lay terms, considered bold.[1]

As Indian women enter the global labor pool, particularly its nightscape, they also experience the negative, gender-based reaction of "What are these females doing in the night?" regularly given to prostitutes and bar dancers. Such comments provide a context for thinking about women's access to night shift employment opportunities. As the first section of this chapter illustrates, this is not a new phenomenon; indeed, historical discourses on the safety and protection of women have frequently been used in the past to legally segregate women from night shift jobs. This historical context provides insight for the second section of the chapter, which explores how *mobility-morality narratives* are today recodified in ways that allow some women to traverse the nightscape in order to meet the U.S. demand for 24/7 workers. In the third section I delve into the sexual impropriety that is associated with call center employment and look at how the industry seeks to counteract this reputation. In the fourth section I explore the anxiety that both families and society in general have about women stepping out into the city, especially at night. Finally, I examine the use of the mobile phone as a form of mobility control that serves to keep track of the "mobile woman," whether day or night. I argue that even though night shift employment has the potential to reshape women's physical mobility, they continue to experience regimes of surveillance and control from which their male counterparts are relatively immune.

Working at Night: Historical Overview

In some respects, British colonial rule liberated women from traditional forms of bondage by outlawing *sati* (widow burning) and child marriage. British rule, however, also brought legal restrictions on a woman's right to work. The cotton mills that emerged in Mumbai during the 1850s ran on a twenty-four-hour basis and employees often worked thirteen- to fourteen-hour days. Under the guise of protecting women, the Factory and Workshop Act of 1891 allowed women to work night shifts but had a provision that stated that this applied only to factories "where a proper system of shifts had been adopted."[2]

Amendments to the Factory and Workshop Act, such as the Indian Factories Act of 1911, went on to restrict women from working before 5:30 A.M. or after 7:00 P.M. By 1929, the Bombay Maternity Benefit Act was enacted to provide maternity leave for women.[3] To avoid tightened legal restrictions on women's employment, cotton mills in Mumbai summarily fired their female workforce and replaced them with men.[4] Although the Indian Factories Act of 1911 and the Bombay Maternity Benefit Act were enacted under the guise of *protecting* women, in reality these laws resulted in removing women from the workforce. Put another way, the social construct of the nightscape as a male domain and as a space of exclusion for women was elevated to a legal construct.

The most recent legislation on night shift employment, Article 66(c) of the Indian Factories Act of 1948, states that no woman shall be required or allowed to work in any factory except between the hours of 6 A.M. and 7 P.M.[5] In March 2005 this act was finally amended, albeit with provisions:

> Provided that where the occupier of the factory makes adequate safeguards in the factory as regards occupational safety and health, equal opportunity for woman workers, adequate protection of their dignity, honour and safety and their transportation from the factory premises to the nearest point of their resi-

dence, the State Government or any person authorised by it in this behalf may, by notification in the Official Gazette, after consulting the concerned employer or representative organisation of such employer and workers or representative organisations of such workers, *allow* employment of woman workers between the hours of 7 P.M. and 6 A.M. in such factory or group or class or description of factories subject to such conditions as may be specified therein.[6]

Instead of re-envisioning women as individuals who have an inherent right to work whenever they see fit, this law focused on the ability of industry to employ women at night while also ensuring that provisions for their protection would remain in place. *Allowing* women to move about in ways that are considered an inherent right for men reflects that women remain tethered to a patriarchal framework that dictates what a woman can and cannot do. The "dignity and honor rule" inadvertently marked women as outsiders and spatialized the factory as a site where undignified and dishonorable behavior is a norm from which women must be protected.

Although the amendment provided a means for women to gain entry to nightscape employment, it did not address the gendered hierarchies that shape women's employment opportunities. For example, the amendment mentions "equal opportunity," but it does not mention equal pay, a key issue for women. Also, the behavior of male factory employees, who arguably are responsible for creating an unwelcoming environment for female workers, is not subject to scrutiny. Instead factories are expected to accommodate women in an environment that is accepted as hostile to them.

On the surface, a law giving women access to work spaces that were formerly off-limits illustrates that women are being legally integrated into male-dominated spaces. Yet, below the surface, gendered norms of how women must be protected within male-dominated environments endure and can have repercussions on women's employment opportunities.

Mobility-Morality Narratives

Indeed, gendered norms about what women can and cannot do—as well as where it is acceptable for them to go and where it is not—continue in the contemporary era. This "mobility-morality narrative," as I call, it, continues to mark women's bodies as the site of family honor, purity, and chastity, even if legislation dictating mobility has been amended.[7] Its impact ranges from what constitutes proper attire for women (as in "What kind of girl would wear such a short skirt?") to the type of work they engage in (such as prostitute or housewife).

From a geographical standpoint, linking morality to women's bodies generally has an immobilizing impact on their lives. Numerous historical examples point to this observation. Corseted women, for example, were unable to exert themselves without suffering shortness of breath. The "ideal" shape that upper-class European and American women of the eighteenth and nineteenth centuries were expected to acquire was, intentionally or not, a means of inhibiting their movement, although it left the legs and feet unencumbered. Actions such as foot binding in China also served to limit women's physical mobility, by rendering their feet inoperable. Other practices, such as female genital mutilation, led to extreme sexual pain. This practice remains prevalent in certain parts of Africa, particularly in villages, and is another means for confining a woman's physical and even sexual mobility. All of these physical actions in turn encumber women's social and economic mobility, which results in both physical and symbolic isolation.

The underlying message of these immobilizing regimes is that a *proper* woman's body is contained, and those who venture beyond the moral confines of household and family obligation are prostituting themselves.[8] The control of women's bodies as a means of demonstrating social status is a pervasive practice that cuts through various cultures and a range of class strata. These regimes also tell us how women who transgress gendered notions of place fare when they attract the attention of various "gatekeepers of morality," from family members to state-sanctioned rules of law (such as those of the police and the courts).

A clear example of a mobility-morality narrative in India was the historical practice of *purdah*. Purdah was not a uniform institution; throughout the country there were variations based on class, caste, region, and religion.[9] In general, however, this practice entailed the seclusion and veiling of women and was a reflection of power relations in both the public and the private spheres. Purdah also indicated socioeconomic status and was a means to maintain family honor. The ability to confine a woman to specific areas of the home and forbid movement in the public sphere illustrated that the male head of the household had the financial means to support the family without female participation. It also indicated the control men had on women's physical mobility.

In essence, purdah was a defining force in deciding who should have a presence in public spaces and who shouldn't. It was primarily women from the lower castes who had a presence in the public sphere, because their husbands or fathers could not afford to have them stay at home, whereas confinement of upper-caste women was a symbol of highly prized attributes such as chastity and virginity.[10] Purdah demonstrates how caste and class attitudes and the naturalization of economic relations (as in man as breadwinner, woman as homemaker) operate through sexism in a covert manner. Instead of a naked economic bias in the form of blatant violence toward upper-caste women who earn their own money, negative judgment of a woman's moral character and sexual prowess emerge when she does not stay at home. Thus the practice of purdah provides a historical understanding of how in the past mobility-morality narratives were used by society to immobilize Indian women, and how such narratives continue to operate today, albeit in different ways.[11]

Indeed, current mobility-morality narratives link gender to the globalization discourse in ways similar to how the "women's question" was linked to colonialism.[12] Purdah, for instance, became a contentious subject in the nineteenth century because colonists viewed the modernity of India through the status of its women. Colonial discourse constructed India as backward and primitive because of its customs, such as child marriage, sati, and purdah.[13] Yet postcolonial research points out that the "women's question" was used by colonists to rationalize their own hegemonic behavior. British women, for example, used issues such as purdah and child marriage to step outside the confines of a woman's place at home in England and to participate in the colonizing mission of India through public work such as teaching and nursing.[14]

Similarly, the call center industry can be viewed as a "globalizing mission" that frees individuals, particularly women, from the immobilizing regimes and narratives of traditional society:

> Women employed in call centers are no longer bound by the traditional patterns of family control over daughters. Financial independence provided by employment in call centers has empowered women to be assertive and independent in their outlook, attitude, and career choice. The gender-neutral and international working atmosphere in call centers has the potential to further female empowerment.[15]

This modern sentiment recycles the logic used to present the "colonizing mission" as a positive force in improving the lives of women and still relies on the "women's question" to justify the inequality inherent in it. The notion that when U.S. companies provide jobs in developing nations they free women

from traditional forms of bondage is problematic. Regarding American hegemony as the new global power that liberates women, Agnew states,

> American hegemony can also liberate people from the hold of traditions that
> disempower various groups, not the least women, whose independent sub-
> jectivity (as citizens and consumers rather than solely as mothers or potential
> mothers) and parallel participation in society as individual persons have tended
> to increase with its spread.[16]

Conceptualizing globalization as a force that liberates women from local traditions is tricky because it can inadvertently be used to disguise and rationalize the exploitation on which this "liberation" is based. This is not to suggest,
conversely, that globalization always increases exploitation.

Thus, in order for women to manufacture respectability, mitigate risk, and
maintain their reputations, they must abide by a mobility-morality narrative
that requires the presence of a male counterpart to justify a woman's presence
in the urban nightscape. Shilpa, a thirty-eight-year-old employee in Bangalore, was initially scared about going out at night. She linked her fear to how it
felt odd getting into a cab at 9 P.M. because she was worried that her neighbors
would think she was a call girl. Purvi, a twenty-four-year-old collections agent
in Mumbai, spoke of how her neighbors had wondered if she was a bar dancer
when she first started working at night. In Ahmedabad, Nilima reported that
in her neighborhood the perception of a woman working at night was that
"she's too bold," and neighbors assumed that such a woman "is doing something illegal, but not prostitution like [in] Bombay."

Ashini, a twenty-three-year-old employee, explained that when she joined
Company A her father was furious. It was her first job ever and her father's
response, "call center job equals call girl job!" left her shaken. Despite his ti-
rade, she joined the industry and currently gives her father Rs 2,000 (US$44)
a month to support the household. During in-depth interviews and focus
groups, I learned that female call center employees have also dealt with the
stereotype that they are doing drugs, drinking, smoking, and partying, and
that they are "not a family person." Kriti, a twenty-one-year-old employee, explained that her father had gotten into heated arguments with his friends over
her job because they told him, "The crowd is not very good. They all smoke."

Smoking as an "immoral" practice came up frequently. Amee, a twenty-
two-year-old employee, has been in the industry for two years and contends that male employees "develop bad habits" such as smoking. According

to Amee, "They become chimneys." She observed that far more men than women smoke, and explained that men smoke to relieve tension and stress. Amee said, "If a boy smokes it feels normal now because so many smoke." In contrast, if a woman smokes she is marked as "a bad girl."

Another theme that emerged during the study is that of the nosy neighbors. In some areas it is believed that when a woman leaves her house in the middle of the night she compromises her own reputation and that of her family. Certainly no middle-class neighborhood wanted to be seen as the one containing "those types of women." Mina, an eighteen-year-old employee who resides in Juinagar, an area of Navi Mumbai, has worked in the industry for approximately fifteen months. Currently working a 6:30 P.M. to 3:30 A.M. shift, she explained that when she first started this shift, her neighbors created problems for both her and her family. She spoke of how, for example, the society (term for *neighborhood*) she resides in "misunderstood my character" and she was thus required to produce for the authorities of her society a certificate proving she worked at Company A. Thereafter the police were sent to her home to question both her mother and their community watchman. In addition, while riding the shuttle to work Mina had to show her employee ID to the police, who proceeded to interrogate the driver. Mina contended that her night shift travel and her work would not have been the subject of such scrutiny had she been a man.

Mina's experience makes it clear that patriarchal regimes of surveillance and mobility-morality narratives remain entrenched. Calling the police on the girl next door for being outside at night sends a loud and clear message that women who traverse the nightscape are "out of place." There are also subtle yet equally compelling messages that women received about being out at night.

"People look at you," said Priya, a resident of Santa Cruz, a suburb of Mumbai. She recalled that a group of young men leered at her while she walked by, asking among themselves, "Where is she going?" Similarly, older men stared in a way that said, "You're a girl. You're not supposed to go out." Valerie, a twenty-seven-year-old resident of Bandra, a suburb that she describes as largely Catholic, explained that in her particular neighborhood there are a lot of non-Catholics, and initially "they would look and wonder." She found this to be extremely irritating but said, "They don't say anything. They dare not and now they don't bother." In frustration she pointed out that if she were a man going out at night there would be no reaction. Underlying her comments was the belief that Catholics are more open-minded compared to Hindus and Muslims.[17] In Ratna's Ahmedabad neighborhood, working at night is considered a big deal because women are not allowed to go off the premises after 8 P.M. Her night travels surprised neighbors who decided it was their right to know, "Where are you going after 9 P.M.?"

In addition to stares, questions, and police involvement, the practice of gossiping or "keeping names" is another means of tarnishing the reputations of both the worker and her family. Ms. George, a fifty-three-year-old mother whose daughter, Elizabeth, works for Company A, explains:

> MS. GEORGE: They [referring to Punjabis who are the majority of occupants residing in her building] keep names like, girls should not go out in the night shifts and all that. It's not good. They take it the other way. You know how these people are. They don't know what it is. And now most of them know what a call centre is, they have gone there . . . safety like . . . nothing like that.
>
> REENA: So what are reasons you found that people would make comments that girls shouldn't work the night shift?
>
> MS. GEORGE: Haan, girls they take objection. Some, they don't want.
>
> REENA: And why would they take objection?
>
> MS. GEORGE: They will say then . . . they don't like, like, people keep names around and all. And then, then marriage times and then have problem. So, they think that way. So I feel this is a Punjabi way, I want Punjabis here only, na. They keep a lot of names. But most of them, they, only their daughters do all these things.
>
> REENA: Tell me more about the names.
>
> MS. GEORGE: "Hamare main toh" means "[among our kind] they don't like girls working in the night shifts and all. Now, I've got one friend of mine, they also stay in BJ-7, her daughter's now in London, see. She is working in London, see. But that also, the old . . . old people, they are cousins, they used to keep names, "You know what she is doing there, that, this," that they use to keep names and all that. So . . . I think without seeing you should not tell, spoil anybody's name, no, "what she is doing. . . . " Gossip, they do.

"Keeping names" is a source of concern for parents because gossip about staying out all night reduces a woman's worth, a key priority in the family unit.

A woman's bodily worth is degraded when she is marked down to "that kind of girl."

In all but one case, interviewees were the first women in their family to go out at night on a regular basis, and working the night shift represented a dramatic change in their temporal mobility. However, in order to maintain respectability, female employees, for the most part, self-regulated their mobility in terms of when they went out, where they went, and how they dressed. According to Poonam, a thirty-two-year-old woman, "If you are careful and don't send the wrong signals, no one is going to try anything." Working in a contained office environment till 4 A.M. was becoming acceptable; donning a miniskirt and tank top in order to party at the trendiest discotheque was certainly not.

It is so important for women to conform to gendered notions of place that Shilpa Phadke discusses how women will actually risk their safety in order to maintain their reputation and family honor:

> One young woman living in a predominantly Gujarati Jain building on Malabar Hill told of how her boyfriend used to drop her some distance from her building since her family did not know she had a boyfriend. She would then negotiate the distance of about 100 metres on foot, however late it was at night. The discourse of sexual safety demanded that she value her reputation over actual safety.[18]

While attending the anniversary party of Company A in Navi Mumbai, I saw firsthand how gendered notions determined when a woman could be out and where she could go. The party, held on an expansive terrace, had approximately three hundred attendees. Prizes, dinner, a fashion show, and dancing were held between 9 P.M. and midnight. Early in the party, the crowd was a mix of both men and women. By 11 P.M. the party consisted primarily of men. On the dance floor, approximately seventy-five to a hundred men rocked out to Queen's hit "We Will Rock You" and sang along, "Fuck you! Fuck you!" Only a sprinkling of women remained and I was left wondering where the women had gone. Even my contact who had gotten me into the party had left by 10:30 P.M. Her father's driver was not in town to pick her up, and her parents—whom she describes as very protective—did not want her out late even if she was on company property and the company was providing transportation to employees. In her case, working the night shift was one thing, but partying at night was another.

A few weeks later I was invited to attend the going-away party for a call center manager. It was held at the Orchid restaurant in Chembur, a suburb of Navi Mumbai. At night this restaurant transforms into a bar with music. There were five women and ten to twelve men in our group and the bill came to approximately Rs 1400rs (US$31) for food and Rs 15000 (US$333) for drinks. One aspect that stood out was how masculinized the space was. All of the restaurant employees were men, and I noticed that after 11 P.M. there were fewer than ten women in a crowd of approximately eighty to a hundred customers. Unlike their male counterparts, who have more leeway to hang out, many women conform to societal pressures on where they belong at night and retreat to their homes, leaving the men to hang out with one another.

The self-regulation that women place on their physical mobility and the surveillance they face from nosy neighbors, leering men, and "keeping names" relates to the way the city seeks to *protect* the urban nightscape from "women of the night" and the moral decay they supposedly bring. Mona, a twenty-five-year-old employee at Company A, described how the police approached her while she was waiting for her shuttle pickup and questioned her about why she was out alone. She was petrified because "the ones you really have to worry about are the police." She said that if the police had wanted to bring her back to the station she would have refused because it would not have been safe.

In another instance, Manisha, an employee at Company A, was pulled over by police while riding a company shuttle. The police ignored the driver and requested Manisha's identity card. She felt harassed because "the police would know the difference between a decent woman and a prostitute." If they had tried to take her to the police station she would have refused because "those people are not safe." This attitude also emerged among respondents during a focus group. In their view, police officers were potential rapists because they think women who go out at night have "bad character."

The police who question a woman out at night reflect state-sanctioned conceptions of who belongs in the urban nightscape and who doesn't. At the same time, it emerged during interviews that even when women are the victims of crimes, they do not necessarily turn to the police for help. Smita, a twenty-six-year-old former call center employee, was the only person in this study to describe experiencing violence. Because she lived only a five-minute walk from her previous call center job, many nights Smita walked to and from work. At the finish of one of her 4 A.M. shifts she was assaulted and robbed on her way home. "They took everything," she explains. When I asked about contacting the police, she said she didn't bother because it would be "a waste of time." In her opinion, the police are "useless."

Sexing the Nightscape

Although interviewees said that the call center industry provides relatively high wages and great office facilities, this is not enough to protect the worker or the industry from the belief that night shift employment equals bad character. This theme emerged throughout fieldwork in Mumbai, Bangalore, and Ahmedabad. As a result, employers utilize a variety of strategies to counteract misperceptions about the industry. But then again, during the course of fieldwork it became evident that call center employment provides some workers with a venue for behaving in ways that previously were more difficult to access, particularly at night.

To counteract the perception that call centers are containers of moral decay and sexual impropriety, some companies have "family day" so that an employee's family can tour the grounds and see the work culture. Ms. Mehta, a forty-five-year-old mother, stated that her impression changed after attending this event: "The people are normal and good . . . the area is good . . . the team leader is middle class." This came as a relief to her twenty-three-year-old daughter, Nisha, who was thoroughly frustrated by her mother calling "a thousand and one times" to check on her. "No one else's parents call this much!" she told her mother during a family interview.

Other companies, as part of the recruitment process, will have a manager or team leader visit a potential female employee's home to discuss employment with the woman's family and convince them that the working conditions are safe and proper.[19] Human resources managers in companies with this practice pointed out that they do not have to do this for male recruits. Ajay, a twenty-something manager of a top firm located in Mindspace, takes an innovative approach to this matter. When someone new joins his team, he takes their picture and mails it to the employee's parents along with an introduction letter. He said it gives parents a good impression of the company and makes team members feel special.

Although the call center industry has received media attention about being a den of sex and sin, this theme did not emerge during interviews with employees.[20] During my preliminary fieldwork in 2005, however, Linda, the American executive at TYJ Corporation in Mumbai, a top-ten call center, began our meeting by commenting that she'd never seen so many people messing around on each other. As a result, the company had to implement various forms of surveillance on missing employees. She said, "We have to keep an eye on the med unit" because they found that an employee would feign sickness, then a "friend" would go to check on him or her and they would end up "getting busy." Similarly, security guards were dispatched to the shuttle vans parked out in the dark, to look for missing employees who were romancing the night away. Of the sixty-four female employees interviewed, only one spoke of having a dalliance while on the job. In an e-mail correspondence, Irene, the thirty-two-year-old training manager mentioned in Chapter Two, who is in the midst of a divorce, wrote:

> Well, it's kinda sorta weird!! I was in the ladies loo and he was in the men's— across from each other and we were on the phone and kinda got off like that . . . then there was this other time where the floor was empty and we were in one corner and I was under the table.

The night represents darkness, desire, and sex. At the same time, the global nature of this industry brings new ideas about romance to India's younger generation. Vast office spaces hold upwards of a thousand eighteen- to twenty-five-year-old men and women, many of whom, particularly women, had previously been segregated from access to intimate relations with the opposite sex. Yet call center employment is viewed as a middle-class work environment, and this view intersects with class distinctions about sex and desire. It's one thing when lower class or working class women are "up to no good," but a middle-class woman is supposedly "not that kind of girl" and needs to be protected from a "polluting" environment that will tarnish her reputation.

In discussions with individuals who expressed dismay toward the industry, they inferred that call center employment contains a "sexscape" that women who work in supposedly proper nine-to-five jobs do not encounter. The implication was that women who claim to work all night are up to no good. It is unknown whether sexual impropriety would be associated with the industry if it operated during the day. I contend, however, that integrating hundreds of young people into a collegial work environment, away from the eyes of family and nosy neighbors, during the day or night, is bound to bring forth latent desire. And given the relative lack of access to private spaces for sexual encounters, the use of semipublic spaces—be it a med unit, company shuttle, or under a desk—reflects how space is strategically deployed to serve individual desires.

Stepping Out into the City

Nisha, the twenty-three-year-old employee, who resides in Lokhandwala, an upper-crust suburb of Mumbai, said, "This is not a culture for women to go out at night." Although Mumbai is considered one of the more women-friendly cities in India, Nisha's statement reflects that gendered notions of a woman's place remain. When Kriti joined Company A, her mother was scared about "sending a girl out in the night." Sunita, age twenty-one, said that prior to working in a call center she was never allowed to spend a night out of the house and always had to be home by 11 P.M.

The primary concern for families regarding women working the night shift was safety. During the course of this study I became interested in how women's bodies were used to define how "safe" a city really is. Time and again, employees raised in Mumbai would tell me how safe their city was, especially compared to New Delhi. Yet not all the Mumbai-based employees in the study held this view. Anita, for example, migrated to Mumbai from Jabalpur with her sister to work in the industry. During our interview she recalled that moving to Mumbai was scary at first because she was not from a big city and big cities were "risky for women." Although she pointed out that she had not encountered any problems, she also believed that "in Mumbai, you can't trust anyone."

When I asked why Mumbai was safe for women compared to other cities, the "proof" I was given was that women in Delhi faced far greater danger in relation to violent crimes such as rape. In the eyes of Mumbaikar women, Delhi was often viewed as a lawless city where men were allowed to behave in any way they liked. Delhi, in fact, was even defined as the rape capital of India by one of the nation's prominent newspapers.[21] According to Jyoti Puri's research on sexual violence against women, Delhi alone accounts for 30.5 percent of the rape cases reported in India.[22]

Although concern for women traversing the urban nightscape was generally presented in the framework of protection and concern for women's safety, it became apparent that the underlying concern for women going out at night came from the "What will people think?" narrative.[23] This form of manipulation was not lost on some of the employees I interviewed. Kavita, a twenty-two-year-old in Navi Mumbai, stated outright that family concern for young women working the night shift is less about physical safety and more about how a woman's presence in the urban nightscape will negatively affect a family's reputation. Anxiety about a woman staying out all night is not only about risking her physical safety against bodily violence, but also about risking her social safety in the larger community. When a woman stays out all night, she risks rupturing her own reputation and that of her family, which are key concerns in communities where "keeping names" can make or break one's social and marital opportunities.

The "What will people think?" narrative inhibits women from going out as freely as their male counterparts, and this narrative demarcates where a woman can and cannot go in the city. Going to a mall with friends in the early evening is okay; unwinding at a bar after a long night of work is not okay. This narrative also requires women to look proper. Before stepping out of the house, a woman must scrutinize how she is dressed in relation to the time of day and where she is going. Unlike her male counterparts, her choice of attire comes from remaining aware of how patriarchal regimes of surveillance perceive her bodily existence—whore versus homemaker—and reflects how far some men believe they have a *right* to go—from unwanted gazes to rape—when they consume a woman's body. In some instances, women are required to inhibit their bodies (such as not passing a group of men hanging out at a paan shop) if they wish to avoid harassment. In other cases, they are expected to exhibit their bodies (such as when entering a trendy nightclub) if they want to fit in.

Although there appear to be more women in Mumbai's urban nightscape than in Ahmedabad's or Bangalore's, of the four distinct public spaces of Mumbai in which Shilpa Ranade mapped women's mobility, no more than 28 percent of the inhabitants were women.[24] Despite the modernity associated with Mumbai and its women-friendly reputation, the mobility of Mumbaikar women continues to be marginalized compared to that of their male counterparts. As a result, women continue to face sexual harassment, as illustrated in *Do You Know How We Feel? Aaaaaaargh!* a documentary produced by the Girls Media Group.[25]

In Ahmedabad, Seema, a twenty-four-year-old employee at WebCorp said, "People here are conservative and don't feel it's safe for a woman to be out." Prior to working the night shift she was not allowed to be outside of the house any later than 8 P.M. Now she can be out until 10:30 or 11 P.M. because her job has changed her parents' perceptions. She contended that "culture is changing in Gujarat [the state where Ahmedabad is located]," but also pointed out that men don't face similar restrictions: "My colleagues can turn up at 2, 3, 4 A.M.; generally, guys don't have issues." Middle- and upper-class residents I spoke to in Ahmedabad considered it "the safest city for women," but this was because women were not permitted to be out at night by themselves. Residents I spoke to emphasized that a woman could go out alone in the middle of the night and nothing would happen to her because Ahmedabad is so safe. At the same time, women explained that their families would not allow them to go out at night.

The Mobile Phone and Physical Mobility

The mobile phone has changed how women negotiate the nightscape while also helping to stymie some of the mobility-morality narratives that have emerged as a result of working at night. In many instances, the mobile phone is a technology women use to *gain permission* to travel at night. In fact, not one female employee in this study was without one. The mobile phone allows women to remain connected to regimes of surveillance, such as the family unit or the employing organization, and to stretch the social codes that deem it unacceptable for them to go out at night. If the mobile phone had not existed during the emergence of this night shift industry, it could be argued that women's participation would have been minimized. From this perspective, the mobile phone represents a revolutionary turn in regard to expanding some women's access to night shift income (even if it also adds to a sometimes false sense of security).

At the same time, the mobile phone, in and of itself, is not an agent for change. This technology is certainly mobilizing female employees and getting them out of the house, but the demand for night shift workers also intersects with economic globalization, the feminization of labor, and national policy, to name just a few influences. According to Donna Haraway, "we are not dealing with a technological determinism, but with a historical system depending upon structured relations among people."[26]

Mobile phones play a role in recodifying gender relations. On the one hand, they keep a woman *within reach* and accessible to those who claim control over her life (such as family). On the other hand, as a tool for maintaining family connections, mobile phones provide some women with the means to get out of the house and thus expand their mobility. This expansion, however, does not come from re-envisioning women as individuals who have an inherent right to move about as they see fit. Instead, technology merely provides women with the means to create an existence for themselves outside the household while remaining within the constraints imposed by the household.

The mobile phone is also at times a private portal to intimate spaces, such as making plans for a rendezvous with a boyfriend kept secret from one's family. In cases where parents keep a watchful eye on how often their daughter is talking on the landline phone or who she is talking to, for example, the text messaging feature of the mobile phone provides a means to communicate with one's friends or boyfriends incognito. Simultaneously, the mobile phone recodifies sexual harassment. An article by Yatish Suvarna in the *Times of India*, for instance, uncovered that men are using their mobile phones to photograph women without their consent—such as taking a picture up a woman's skirt or of her cleavage—and posting them on the Internet.[27] According to Suvarna, "The Indian public space is today stalked by boys and men who enjoy recording inescapable exposures of just about any woman."

When some women go out at night, the mobile phone provides them with a sense of security in terms of being able to call for help should a problem arise. The necessity associated with having a mobile phone, however, is also intertwined with patriarchal regimes of surveillance that are based on keeping tabs on women. Although the mobile phone is viewed as a protective measure, it is also at times a device for furthering the harassment that women experience. These varying issues reflect that the mobile phone simultaneously serves to increase some women's mobility while at the same time serving to reenact the inequality they experience in other facets of their lives.

Wrap-Up

The varying forms of harassment and temporal segregation that some women in this study experienced illustrate that women have to justify their existence in the urban nightscape. Despite the fact that working the night shift disrupts notions of a woman's "place" and transforms individual physical mobility to a certain extent, female call center employees continue to be subjected to stricter regimes of surveillance than men. Family members and society use safety concerns as a way to regulate and control women's mobility.

During the process of getting out of the house and "going global," women use the technology of the mobile phone to show their families that they will remain accessible, if only hypothetically. In other words, the mobile phone provides some women with a means to go out at night and at the same time conform to the regimes of surveillance that govern their mobility. As a portal to the home space, the mobile phone also reflects how technology is used to connect women back to the domestic sphere, even when they are working the night shift.

In closing, female call center employees must balance both safety and surveillance. To address concerns about "What kind of work are these females doing in the night?" they are armed with identity cards and mobile phones that allow them to justify their existence to the nosy neighbors, the police, and anyone else questioning their activity. This dynamic illustrates that the societal structures in place supposedly to protect them (that is, family, police, and neighbors) instead become a site of judgment in a variety of settings. From nosy neighbors who "keep names" to police suspicious about why a woman is out at night, women experience disdain when they move about in ways deemed transgressive.

4 Traveling at Night

This is not a culture for women to go out at night.

— *Nisha, call center employee*

I dominate my vehicle!

— *Dipti, on dealing with company transport*

To address concerns about women's safety during their travels, trains in Mumbai offer a ladies-only compartment. Public buses also have seats designated for women. Segregating women is seen as a way to keep them safe. Those who want to have room to sit while traveling or to stand without experiencing the trampling crush of desperate passengers trying to get on and off trains have the option to purchase entry into a first-class, ladies-only compartment.

Access to the city meets with class concerns about not being around "those kind of people" (the dirty and lower class) and gendered conceptions of a woman's place. In turn, beliefs about who belongs out at night and where they belong are complex. Location, for example, plays a role in shaping how women who go out at night are viewed, and one's class status informs how individuals experience the urban night. Reaction to women not being at home at night is by no means uniform and employees provided varying responses to the question of where it is considered acceptable for women to go and where it is not.

I begin this chapter by exploring how the mobility-morality narratives described in the previous chapter are intertwined with how companies transport their workers and how the varying transport options provided by companies was a deciding factor in where some women opted to pursue employment. I also discuss how passenger safety during the night is a source of concern for women night shift workers, in terms of both "reckless" driving and "reckless, harassing" drivers. Finally, in a discussion more widely related to violence against women who are out at night, I explore why the 2005 Bangalore rape and murder of one call center employee garnered worldwide media attention while a spate of murdered maquiladora employees in Mexico went ignored for years. By looking at this situation from the perspective of the class difference between these two industries, I discover how beliefs about *worthy and unworthy victims* shape the concern for and value placed on working woman who traverse the urban night. Call center employment certainly leads to new forms of temporal mobility for women workers because it provides them with a legitimate reason to get out of the house, particularly at night. At the same time, I found, regimes of surveillance and control continue to affect how and where women travel.

Location, Location, Location

According to Irene, the training manager introduced in Chapter Two, "Location plays a role in how those around you perceive women out at night." During a focus group interview, Michelle, a twenty-eight-year-old employee, explained that in Juhu, an upper-class suburb of Mumbai, it is not a problem for women to work at night. Her husband, however, suggested that it also depends on the area of Juhu the woman lives in, because "behind the Chandan side [a neighborhood in Juhu] it would not be OK if working at night."

During a discussion with Roshni, a twenty-eight-year-old resident of Juhu, I learned that, in addition to Chandan, it would also look suspicious for a woman to be hanging around SV Road going toward Juhu junction, and near Juhu Tara Road turning toward the Sea Princess Hotel, because of the brothels in the area. In addition, the entire stretch from the Juhu petrol pump to the police station is a problem for women to traverse because, as Roshni described, "up to the police station has these women soliciting."

Michelle said that going out at night in Andheri is acceptable in neighborhoods in and around the parish because that area is modernized, but outside that area it would not be considered appropriate. The focus group in which Michele participated consisted of Catholic employees and from their point of view, areas surrounding Catholic churches represent a site of modernity while nearby Hindu and Muslim neighborhoods are restrictive and provide women with less leeway to travel at night. In addition to linking perceptions of women out at night to religious sects, Parvati, a twenty-five-year-old Gujarati employee who lives in Thane, a suburb of Mumbai, also linked the perception of women out at night to the type of society (that is, neighborhood) in which they reside:

> I stay in a very cosmopolitan society and there are a lot of people around my area who work in call centers. It's pretty fine, they don't care. But some of my friends have problems because they are coming from a very conservative society. And like I told you, no, a lot of people don't see this as a serious job.

Meghna, a twenty-one-year-old employee in Ahmedabad, lives in the type of conservative society described by Parvati. She explains that no one else in her society "is doing this type of work." She explained that other women who want to work in the industry but are forbidden to have spoken to her about how "they appreciate" that she is able to get out and have even told her, "Your parents are allowing you to go, that is good."

Devaki, also twenty-one years old, said that five years ago it was unacceptable for women in her suburban Navi Mumbai neighborhood of Vashi to go out at night. It used to be that no women in her building worked at call centers. In the past six months, however, there had been a drastic change and now five or six women in her building work in the industry. In Bangalore, Shreya contended that in the past five years there had been a significant improvement in the acceptance of women going out at night. A resident of the area for twenty years, she believed that call centers played a role in making some areas of Bangalore more accessible to women.

Working at night not only provides some women with access to areas that were previously deemed off-limits, but also represents a change in *when* some women are working. In terms of *where* they go after work, women traverse the evening and late night in ways that reflect gendered notions of place. For example, the *dhaba*, the equivalent of a truck stop, is the only recreational space in Bangalore in which to hang out after a work shift, because city laws shut down restaurants, bars, and nightclubs at 11 P.M.[1] Mira, the call center manager for a Fortune 500 computer firm introduced in Chapter Two, said that the men went to the dhaba after their shift, but women were excluded. She repeatedly asked to join in; her boss refused at first but finally *allowed* her to go, and some men from the team brought her there. Describing the dhaba as dirty and lower class, she said, "It was not a place for women."

Although her middle- and upper-class male counterparts had the option to "climb down" the class ladder when looking for a space to unwind after a long night of work, for the majority of women the dhaba remained a space of exclusion and they retreated to their homes. Mira's case illustrates that awareness of gender differences in access to night spaces is not only about counting and mapping the number of men and women out at night, but also about understanding how women experience night spaces deemed off-limits to them.

Although the presence of men in the urban nightscape is common, just the sound of women outside at night is a source of discomfort in some neighborhoods. Irene, for example, was appalled to receive the following e-mail notice from her call center's administration department in February 2007 regarding "chitchatting ladies":

> Dear All
> There was a police visit today at 1.45 A.M. [T]hey have instructed that no agents will stand outside the office premises because they have received the complain[t] of chitchatting of ladies from local public. All agents are requested not to go out until they get the vehicle for drop.
> Regards

Just as location plays a role in determining where it is acceptable or unacceptable for women to work and hang out, especially at night, mobility determines access to paid employment. Scholars have found that some women are spatially entrapped in shorter travel journeys to which their male counterparts are immune.[2] This disparity is linked to the responsibility placed on women to maintain the household, and it limits the distance a woman can travel to work. Working at night further complicates how women experience spatial entrapment, because of the danger associated with going out at night, along with the expectation that a *decent* woman should not be out when it is dark.

Call center employment disrupts assumptions about *when* women are supposed to work outside the home. One theme that emerged during interviews was the role of location in taking a job. It would be expected that earning a relatively high wage in an industry marked as "pink-collar" would be considered a boon for women and their families. Add to this the availability of free private transportation that allows women to circumvent rickshaws and public transportation, and surely families would support a woman's desire to pursue call center employment. This is not the case.

The night shift requirement remains a source of dismay for family members. Manisha, a twenty-six-year-old employee in Navi Mumbai, and Hansa, a twenty-one-year-old employee in Ahmedabad, explained that women need approval from their family or husband, if married, to work in the industry. According to Anna, a human resources manager in Ahmedabad, working the night shift is not the norm for single women because "society doesn't allow [it]." Thus, during in-depth interviews, employees said that one of the reasons they were able to convince their families to let them out of the house at night was that the call center was close to home. Kriti, the twenty-one-year-old introduced in Chapter Three, for instance, said her parents allowed her to take this job "because it was only fifteen minutes away."

Riding the Shuttle

Because the call center industry falls under the governance of the Shops and Establishments Act, it is able to avoid the provisions of the 1948 Factories Act that forbid women from working the night shift. As a result, the burgeoning demand for night shift workers has helped to create a new industry as many call centers have outsourced their transport demands to local providers. Yet dignity, honor, and safety issues have remained concerns that both the employing organization and its female workers have had to address.

The availability of transport has clearly been key to bringing women into the industry. Reshma, a twenty-three-year-old employee in Bangalore, believed it is dangerous for women to drive cars at night and said she would not have joined the industry if transport had not been provided. The availability and type of transportation also influence at which call centers women prefer to work. There are two basic means of transporting employees. The first is picking up and dropping off employees at home and at the office. At Company A, this service consists of vehicles carrying six to eight employees and can take up to two hours each way, depending on where the employees reside and whether they are one of the first or one of the last to be dropped off or picked up.

The second form of transport involves a mix of individual and company strategies. Going to work, employees are required to meet at a central point and from there are transported in private buses to the employing organization. If an employee is not at the central location on time and misses the bus, she is responsible for getting herself to work. On the return trip, the bus again transports employees to a central stop. From there they are dispatched on four- to six-passenger shuttle vehicles scheduled to go to specific residential areas. This type of transport deters some women from seeking employment in the industry because they do not feel comfortable traveling on their own to the central stop at night, or their families will not allow them. Santhi, a thirty-two-year-old married employee who has been in the industry for six years, said, "If I had to go for a central drop, I wouldn't have gone for this industry." She explains that she lives in a remote area and if there were a problem during the night, the neighbors would not be helpful. Although nosy neighbors are a source of harassment, for women like Santhi, their lack of support is also considered a problem.

The pick-up and drop-off service is considered the highest level of transport available. Women whose families were difficult to convince about their taking a call center job looked specifically for companies that provided this type of transport. Jyothi, a twenty-five-year-old manager, explained that her parents would not have allowed her to work in a call center if it had not offered pick-up and drop-off transportation. Despite women's preference for this type of transport service, companies are moving away from providing it and are instead providing only one-way transport in order to reduce operational expenses.

In these instances, when an employee works a 10 P.M. to 6 A.M. shift, she is picked up before her shift but is responsible for her own transportation in the morning. An employee on an 8 P.M. to 4 A.M. shift is responsible for getting to work at 8 P.M. but is provided transport for the journey home. When explaining why Company A continued to offer pick-up and drop-off, Samir, vice president of operations, emphasized while pointing to the floor, "I want my workers here!" Picking up employees at their home ensures that they will reach the office on time.

Interviewees spoke of both the positive aspects and the challenges of traveling at night and company transport. Heena, a married thirty-three-year-old employee, stated, "Traveling at night is much more peaceful. The daytime is crowded and polluted." This theme emerged throughout the study. Despite the fact that the nightscape was often constructed as a space of danger, in many instances it was actually viewed as quiet and calm.

Numerous employees reported that company transport was faster than public transport. It was also reported, however, that various waiting times and the order in which a worker was picked up and dropped off sometimes made the journey and the workday much longer. Devaki lives about two kilometers from her office, and when she worked the 6:30 P.M. to 2:30 A.M. shift it would take approximately fifteen minutes to get home. But her shift had recently changed to 5:30 P.M. to 2:30 A.M., making it one hour longer. On top of that, changes in the transport schedule meant she now often waited up to two hours to get a ride home and did not reach her house until 4:30 a.m. Despite working only two kilometers from home, what used to be a nine-hour workday, including transportation to and from work, was now more than twelve hours, and the long hours were affecting her sleep.

Dipti, a twenty-five-year-old employee at Company A, said that another challenge is that some workers are slow to leave their house and the rest of the passengers end up waiting for them. In addition, the order of pick-up affects the transport time. The last in, first out pickup scenario is considered the best option. The employee who is picked up last on the home-to-work journey will be the first one dropped off on the work-to-home trip. Dipti originally had this scenario and said her travel time to work was one hour. The schedule recently changed, however, and the same journey now takes one hour and forty-five minutes. Expressing frustration about employees who run late during shuttle pick-up and create delays, she explained that one has to be aggressive in dealing with fellow passengers, stating, "I dominate my vehicle!" More formally, Company A, in response to such complaints, implemented a policy in which the vehicle waits for five minutes and then leaves, with or without the worker.

In another example, Nina, a thirty-five-year-old employee, said she is the first employee picked up from home for her call center position in Bangalore. With traffic and the waiting time of picking up coworkers, the journey takes one-and-a-half hours. In contrast, when she comes home at night the same journey is thirty-four minutes. In addition to the transport time, the work day, interviewees reported, is sometimes elongated beyond the set eight- to nine-hour shift because some companies require employees to be at the worksite a half-hour prior to their shift, and then, because of meetings with team leaders or phone calls that run over their shift end time, they have to wait another half-hour after their shift to get a ride home.

Safety on the Shuttle

Regarding passenger safety, Daksha, the human resources executive assistant, pointed out, "We don't stuff people in a vehicle." During a focus group of eight participants, concern was expressed about passenger safety because of accidents caused by reckless drivers. During in-depth interviews, six others also expressed similar concerns. Of the forty-two employees interviewed in Mumbai who took shuttle transport, three had been in accidents. Denise, a twenty-three-year-old former employee, said:

These drivers are reckless, like really bad at [CYC Corp]. In the car, I was in an accident and I had a lot of friends who came across accidents. They drive really fast, but it's because of pressure that is put on them also. I know of about four accidents that have taken place . . . at the time I was in an accident it was totally our fault. It was a rickshaw, so not much damage was done. The rickshaw was totally smashed, but we didn't get that banged because we were in a car.

Drivers were purported to be reckless because they are under tight timelines for transporting employees. In another case, Michelle explained that on company transport to her call center in Andheri, their vehicle was hit by a van. She was thrown from the back seat to the front and injured her hand. She was sent home that day, went for an X-ray the next day, and had to be back at work that night. Despite not being well, she was given only one day off because the call center was short-staffed. She said, "Even if you are sick, you have to go and do your work."

Purvi, the twenty-four-year-old collections agent introduced in Chapter Three, recalled that she was in a rickshaw accident on her way to work. She was not on a company transport because it was the start of her shift and her company provides transport only one way after 10 P.M. The accident put her out of work for one month. The company paid her medical bills, but she was not paid leave because she was a new hire. During interviews in Ahmedabad, no accidents were disclosed, and during interviews in Bangalore, one out of eleven interviewees, Nina, reported an accident. She explained that although rash driving does not happen very often, in this instance the driver fell asleep at the wheel. Both of her legs were injured, although she is fine now. The driver now walks with a limp.

Accidents on the road are an issue worthy of concern. Throughout the interviews, however, reckless drivers and accidents were not discussed. Instead of presenting this issue as a problem that was rampant throughout the industry, interviewees said it was limited to specific companies with inadequate worker safety and transport practices. Interestingly, the two companies whose employees referred to them as having problems with reckless driving were the same companies that employees at other firms cited as the place to work in terms of prestige, pay, and working conditions. In fact, one of the companies is on NASSCOM's top-ten third-party call center list.[3]

Safety on the shuttle is isolated not only to the "recklessness" of the driver, but also to the belief that drivers pose a threat to women's safety in the form of sexual harassment. Thus, concerns about female passenger safety were also addressed by placing a security guard onboard the vehicles. At Company A, for example, if all of the employees on the transport are female, then, in addition to the driver, a security guard is onboard. If one of the employees is a male, then a security guard is not required, but the male employee is the last one dropped off. Employees from other companies reported having the same policy. In companies where this is not a required policy, some men take it upon themselves to do this. For instance, Daksha explained that at WebCorp in Ahmedabad there is no policy that requires men to be the last ones dropped if a woman is on the shuttle. Instead, she explains, men do it out of courtesy.

Despite various policies on how women are to be protected when they travel at night, according to some interviewees policy is not always practiced. Devaki said, "At times there are a few females in the vehicle and no males." Kriti said that two to three times a month she is the last one dropped off, without a security guard present.

Company A, to whose employees these two incidents occurred, was not aware of this. In Devaki's case, she did not complain because she was not uncomfortable being the only woman in the vehicle. Although Kriti also did not complain about being the last one dropped off, she recalled that one night she was the only one who had to leave for her neighborhood at 4:30 A.M. Refusing to go alone, she reported this predicament to her team leader and he arranged for three men in her department to accompany her and then return to the office.

The policy of having a security guard onboard the vehicles that contain only women stems from concerns about harassment by men who are out at night and see a car full of women, and by the transport drivers themselves. Denise, described driver harassment in the form of "trying to chat me up." On the one hand, it was believed that drivers are likely to be lecherous because they are of a lower class. Purvi contended that women also bring harassment onto themselves because of the way they dress, whereas "if you hide yourself, driver will not see." On the other hand, it was also believed that drivers will not dare to harass female call center employees because they understand them to be of a higher class. From this perspective, class is a buffer that regulates sexual harassment because drivers would receive far more attention and scrutiny for bad behavior toward a so-called "decent woman" than if they treated a woman of their own class in the same fashion, particularly if she was a sex worker.

In closing, the idea of having one man (such as a security guard or fellow employee) in a confined space to protect women from another man (such as a driver) is an example of patriarchal regimes of protection in which it is believed that adding more men—the perpetrators of the problem to begin with—will protect women's bodies and reputations from harm. As with rickshaws, trains, and public and private buses, there are no female drivers to provide company transport services. The informal policing of men by men attests not only to male power but also to the curtailment of male power, albeit by men. The assumption in keeping more than one man on the shuttle until all of the women are off is that the men will police each other. Yet this by no means guarantees the women's safety. Because it is groups of men who engage in everything from "Eve-teasing" (a term used to denote sexual harassment and assault) to gang rape, expecting men to be a self-surveilling force in the behavior of other men does not always have a protective effect on women's lives, especially when it is believed that a woman is behaving in ways that mark her as "asking for it."

Rape and Capital Penetration

When I spoke of my interest in call center employment in relation to women's safety in the urban nightscape, a few respondents brought up the Bangalore rape case. On December 13, 2005, Pratibha Srikanth Murthy, a twenty-four-year-old employee of Hewlett Packard, was raped and murdered en route to her call center position in Bangalore. This case garnered worldwide media attention. Scrutiny emerged in relation to Hewlett Packard's role in the crime because Murthy was murdered by a man posing as her company's transport provider.

Call centers in India offer transportation to their employees because (1) there is no reliable transport in place during the night and (2) providing transport is a key to recruiting employees, particularly women.[4] Nilesh, the industry consultant who helped launch a call center in Mumbai and Gurgaon, said, "We ended up becoming our own bus company." In doing this they were also expected to secure the safety of employees during the journey. The cost of this service is far from negligible. Linda, the American executive with TYJ Corporation in Mumbai, pointed out that transportation is one of the top three expenses for call center operations, the other two being labor and IT infrastructure.

In relation to what Edward Herman and Noam Chomsky term *worthy and unworthy victims*, I became interested in the fervor and media attention given to the rape and murder of one woman in Bangalore compared to the attention given to the rape and murder of hundreds of women working in the maquiladoras of Mexico.[5] Beginning in the 1990s, a spate of brutal murders and rapes occurred in Ciudad Juarez, Chihuahua. In fact, the homicide rate for women in Chihuahua quadrupled during the emergence of its maquiladora industry in the 1990s.[6] As of 2007, hundreds of women remain missing and approximately three hundred women have been found murdered and mutilated.[7] According to Ginger Thompson, "their bodies [were] tossed like garbage in the desert. All along the border, the land, the water and the air are thick with industrial and human waste."[8]

When I posed this issue to scholars who focus on labor issues related to class and globalization, they said that the Murthy case received attention because call center employment is considered middle class while maquiladora employment is viewed as working class. In essence, sewing clothes in a factory is considered working class whereas speaking English and taking on an American identity is viewed as closer to middle class, or at least represents how Indians are gaining ground in the global value chain.

Murthy's death was deemed *worthy* of outrage because she was working in a *proper* (that is, middle-class) job where such violence is not supposed to happen. It is generally expected that middle-class jobs will be safe (code word for *dignified* and *honorable*) for women. Melissa Wright, in contrast, finds that violence toward working class women is normalized to a certain extent.[9] Viewed as one of the hazards of working among "those kinds of people," acts of violence, harassment, and degradation become constructed as part of a maquiladora woman's livelihood. She also found that workers who refute the perception that they are disposable are labeled as abnormal and out of place.

In addition, Murthy's murder occurred within an industry that is a catalyst of the "India Emerging" discourse.[10] Women such as Murthy are supposed to exemplify that economic globalization has the potential to propel developing nations such as India out of poverty and thus contribute to the rise of the middle class, a key market for the U.S. companies. It's certainly not supposed to lead to their rape and murder, especially considering that in some cases they represent the future customer base of some of the very companies for which they work.

By associating call center employment with the middle-class and wanting employees to work all night—in contrast to working *proper* day shifts—this industry has also disrupted the timescape standard that middle-class status is supposed to bestow on individuals. In other words, it is one thing when a poor person works all night, but quite another when the middle-class person does. To mitigate this requirement, companies are expected to provide a good working environment and to make securing the safety of workers in the nightscape a priority. Providing transport is also a means to deflect the perception that call centers are nothing more than IT sweatshops where cyber-coolies work the night away. Surely a sweatshop wouldn't be nice enough to transport its workers in private vehicles.

Rather than taking a hands-off approach to Murthy's demise, the industry responded by implementing various protective measures to prevent this from happening again in the future. In Mumbai this incident had a ripple effect on the industry and, relative to transport, a few women spoke of going to work "before and after Bangalore." Kriti explained that she had never been keen on being the first woman picked up on the home-to-work journey. But prior to the Bangalore rape case she had not expressed her discomfort to her employer. Afterward, she informed her team leader that she wanted to be the second person "on the pick-up" because the usually bustling market area they passed was closed during the night. Driving through an area where no one was around, and with only her and the driver in the vehicle, was a source of anxiety for Kriti. In addition, when being dropped late at night, she requested that the driver wait five minutes, until she was inside her building.

Although some of the drivers at Company A were switched out for more professional drivers, little changed in the actual transport policy because both employees and managers pointed out that they already had secure processes in place. At other companies there were drastic shifts. New policies were adopted, such as that a woman must not be the last one dropped at home, and that a security guard must be onboard vehicles that contain no male employees. Other policies included the following: (1) every twenty minutes the company calls to see if a woman has reached home or where she is; (2) women are not allowed to sit in the front seat; (3) employees have to sign in before getting into a shuttle and when getting out; (4) employees are provided with the cell phone numbers of both the driver and the transport manager; and (5) if the vehicle is more than five minutes late arriving at the office, the transport manager contacts the driver.

Despite the uproar surrounding this case, only two women I interviewed in Mumbai referenced it during discussions about safety, violence, and harassment. It was not presented as the "hot topic" among the participants in this study. Some employees also believed that the case was blown out of proportion. Amish, the industry consultant introduced in Chapter Two, said, "Women get raped in college. Does that mean we should not send them to school?" Ashim Ahluwalia, director of the 2005 call center documentary *John and Jane*, thought that the Bangalore rape case was being used as an excuse to again prohibit women from going out at night. He also pointed out that if a woman was ever found to be working in a call center and as a call girl at the same time, that example would be used as an excuse to further drive women out of the industry. Parents, after all, would not want their daughters associated with an industry that is linked to sex work.

There are numerous reasons the industry responded the way it did, ranging from how worker safety might affect future IT policy in India to anxiety that downplaying this incident would give the impression that global companies do not care about India's middle class. The industry response to this matter was swift; they did not want to risk losing a section of the labor pool, namely women, because families would refuse to let them out at night. For instance, during a call center workshop that my colleague Mathangi Krishnamurthy and I held during the November 17–18, 2006, Women Run ICT Enterprises Conference, Parul, a forty-something participant, said that after the Bangalore rape case she forced her daughter to quit her call center position in Chennai out of concern for her safety.

Given the shortage of qualified workers that some companies face, workers are in high demand.[11] Although men's participation in the industry is significant—in part due to the relatively high wages combined with a night shift requirement that is less of a contentious issue for them—the recruitment of women is vital to the continued growth of the industry. Gopal, an industry consultant, said that concern for the safety of women working in call centers—unlike the attitude toward their maquiladora counterparts, who are deemed disposable and replaceable—is a matter of economics: companies need to be perceived as a safe place to work so they can attract and retain employees.

Class dynamics indeed informed how the Bangalore rape case was received in society. I also contend that this case demonstrates how gender is infused into geopolitical relations and reflects the friction that emerges in the power play between nationalism and globalization. My argument is based on the premise that rape operates under the rubric of perceiving a woman's body as property to be seized. In general, rape is considered an act of violence on a woman's private, bodily space; or in the framework of a woman "belonging" to her husband or family, on private property.[12] This perception is destabilized as violence against women slowly becomes more public in nature. In terms of geopolitical relations, Jennifer Hyndman contends, women's bodies are being transformed into a "public site of violence on which constructions of the nation and its boundaries take place. . . . "[13] In making this statement, she points to the June 1996 International Criminal Tribunal for the former Yugoslavia, in which rape, for the first time, was prosecuted as a weapon of war and a "crime against humanity."[14]

Although India is not in the middle of war, the politics surrounding the worldwide media attention given to the Bangalore rape case reflect what some historians and feminists consider to be a framework in which the Indian female body is considered to be a representation of the nation-state (as in Mother India) and in which "intrusions" from outside the boundary of the nation-state, such as globalization or colonialism, are represented as masculine.[15] From this perspective, women become the bodily site on which the virtues of the nation-state are to be asserted in opposition to the polluting forces of globalization.

Rupal Oza finds that by linking gender to the nation, different groups in India formulate a critique for or against globalization.[16] Drawing from the debate surrounding the 1996 Miss World beauty pageant held in India, she illustrates how opponents constructed the nation as a symbol of desexualized motherhood that had to be protected from the polluting forces of globalization. In this case, resistance to globalization is based on a re-inscription of control and suppression of women's sexuality.[17] Alternatively, proponents in her study argued that the pageant demonstrated to the world that India is an advanced, liberal nation. Yet even within this framework, the pageant used raising funds for children's causes as a means to detract opponents. By linking contestants to motherhood and compassion, women's sexuality was performed within acceptable boundaries. According to Oza, "women's bodies and sexualities became the material and discursive sites where nation was performed, values were contested, and border and boundaries were policed and controlled."[18]

The demand for female night shift workers disrupted notions of a woman's traditional place at home. Similar to Oza's research on how women's bodies are used as a site of proclamations for or against globalization, the Bangalore rape case provided a specter for the night shift debate. This is not to belittle the importance and outrage worthy of such a crime, but instead to consider why the global corporation received so much attention when rape occurs at all levels of society.[19]

If Murthy's Hewlett Packard call center position in India had taken place during nine-to-five work hours and she had been raped and murdered on her way to work, it is quite possible that this crime would not have received worldwide media attention. Companies such as Hewlett Packard would not have become intertwined with issues of rape and murder because conducting business during the daytime places the onus of public safety and security during the home-to-work journey on the individual and the local government, not on the global corporation.

Opponents of the call center industry use Murthy's death as a platform to decry the hazards of the industry, particularly as it relates to the well-being of women. In this context, the Bangalore rape case operated under the rubric of women representing the identity and morals of a nation-state, which must be "protected." It also reflects how some stakeholders use women's bodies, when it's to their advantage, to critique what J. K. Gibson-Graham terms the "penetration of capital" script. This script frames workers as rape victims who are powerless to the dominant forces of multinational corporations. Gibson-Graham urges us instead to consider ways of "making globalization lose its erection."[20]

Nationalism

When I presented the section on rape and capital penetration to the South Asia Institute in April 2007, it was suggested that interpreting the bodies of middle-class women as a site upon which national anxieties are played out is a weak argument because, unlike in previous eras, such as the early and mid nineteenth century, the "women's question" is no longer front and center in the national agenda. Instead, the focus is on IT and economic development, nuclear arms, terrorism, and ongoing strife with Pakistan. The real situation, however, is more complex as gendered discourses disguise themselves in subtle and nuanced ways.

During colonial times, for example, there was a decline in the attention given to the "women's question" in Indian nationalist discourse. The assumption was that this decline occurred because other issues, such as sovereignty, became more important. Partha Chatterjee offers an alternative understanding on why the status of women received less attention: "The reason lies in nationalism's success in situating the "women's question" in an inner domain of sovereignty, far removed from the arena of political contest with the colonial state. The inner domain of national culture was constituted in light of the discovery of 'tradition.'"[21] Put another way, the "women's question" did not merely fade away. Instead it was resituated from being a public concern (as in politics) to being a private one (as in tradition) within the nationalist movement. Women became the bodily site for advocating a return to the "good ole days" of pre-colonial tradition and culture.

Fast forward to twenty-first century India and one can witness a backlash to the "India Emerging" developments. The liberalization of the economy in combination with the rise of the *Shiv Sena*—a conservative Hindu right-wing group founded in the 1960s by Bal Thackeray—has created a dramatic shift in Mumbai's economic and political scene. Economic liberalization has propelled the material and commercial wealth of this city. From shopping malls to upscale movie theatres, middle- and upper-class Mumbaikars are accessing new forms of recreation and entertainment on which to spend their money.

At the same time, the Shiv Sena's conservative political front has gained ground as it has sought to assert its xenophobic vision of the city, particularly as it relates to ridding the city of Muslims. By 1992 this conflict reached a boiling point that turned Mumbai into a riot zone. In 2006, concerns about another riot emerged when a statue of Thackeray's wife was desecrated. I was in Ahmedabad at the time and was told not to return to Mumbai until order was restored because it was dangerous to be out. The fear of riots shut down many parts of the city because people were afraid to leave their homes. In addition to looting, a number of cars and a train were burned. In the midst of these competing events, Mumbai has become more conservative and anti-outsider.[22]

During these events, the livelihoods of middle-class women were certainly not considered important. Inspired by Chatterjee's work, I contend that it's not because the "women's question" became less important in nationalist discourse.[23] Instead, it enters through various backdoors and constitutes a backlash that is fueled in subtle but compelling ways. Consider, for instance, that it is expected that women will continue to maintain and reproduce some of the ideals embedded in nationalism, such as family values. Under the rubric of family values, women are expected to put family first, even at the expense of their own dreams and goals. As some women gain increased access to the paid labor force, anxiety emerges about such women becoming too "bold" and not being "a family person."

One of the backdoors used to quell such anxiety is academia. In 2003, the University Grants Commission in India renamed all women's studies departments to women and family studies. Although this may not appear to be an overt move to oppress women, Saraswati Raju found it to be a means to reconnect women to the sphere of domesticity.[24] Linking women back to the household in the midst of angst about their place in society, particularly as it relates to their iconic status (as in Mother India) and their role in nationalist movements, is not new. Consider, for instance, the emergence of home science education in India during the 1920s and 1930s.[25] This type of education was a means to increase the respectability of middle-class women and their worth in areas such as arranged marriage. In the nationalist discourse, however, it also served as an apolitical channel for addressing feminist concerns such as access to education while simultaneously not disrupting the belief that a woman's primary focus must be her home.

When the highest echelons of education co-opt such a message, they reinforce an ideology that no matter how far a woman goes, her place, her existence, must remain connected to domesticity. It also reflects the underlying ways in which women, even when they physically step outside the domestic space, whether to work, hang out, or shop, remain tethered to it.

Wrap-Up

On the one hand, India's position as a key player with a labor pool capable of providing global services addresses national concerns related to economic development. On the other hand, the "colonization of time" embedded in this particular type of development intersects with anxieties about women losing touch with traditional family values, particularly as they relate to going out at night and sexual impropriety.[26]

Reactions to such concern are not necessarily overt, as in legally forbidding women's right to abortion or placing curfews on how late they can be out at night. Instead, anxieties about women "getting ahead" are manufactured through narratives about how dangerous it is for them to be out at night. They are also produced through performances such as the choreographing of who gets on and off a shuttle van, where, and in what order. And when it takes women such as Devaki more than two hours to get home, despite living only two kilometers from work and despite the rickshaws available outside her building, it speaks volumes about how some women experience temporal constriction in their lives.

Under the guise of protecting them from "those types of men" lurking in the darkness, women are rendered immobile relative to their male counterparts. As illustrated by the experiences of the women who contributed to this chapter, these narratives become mobilized in ways that subject women to strict regimes of surveillance, in spite of the fact that night shift employment disrupts notions of a woman's "place" and recodifies individual temporal mobility. Although they break new ground by staying out all night, their safety—a code word for *their reputation*—is kept by segregating themselves, via company transport, from the other women of the night such as bar dancers and call girls. Their safety and reputation (of being a good girl) is also protected through the presence of a male security guard or male employees who serve as their escorts during the night.

In this chapter I have argued that the attention that companies pay to women's safety needs during the journey to and from work is dictated by class expectations. Middle-class women are viewed as worthy of protection whereas working class women are not. This differential is illustrated in the fact that the murders of working-class maquiladora employees in Mexico were ignored for years whereas the rape and murder of one middle-class call center employee in Bangalore received immediate widespread attention. Call centers in Bangalore and Mumbai responded swiftly by instituting varying forms of protection. These included company rules that do not allow women to sit in the front seat of a vehicle—for fear of a lecherous driver—and that monitor the whereabouts of vehicles on a regular basis. The result is a society that monitors and protects some of its women. This protection, however, is had at the price of continuing to expect these same women to mind their place.

5 Fast Money, Family Survival, and the Consumer Class

You can make out they are working in call centre by their dressing style. The youth today have got style, smile, and mobile.

—Father John, thirty-seven-year-old Catholic priest

Fast money—this is the term used to describe the income made from call center employment. Yet during interviews, focus groups, and participant observation, a more nuanced understanding emerged of how this "fast money" actually relates to family survival and consumerism. This chapter investigates the various reasons women pursue employment in an industry that, on the one hand, provides them with a relatively high level of income while, on the other hand, marks them as fast, loose, and not smart enough to get a *real* job, and occasionally makes them the target of remarks such as "That poor girl. Her family doesn't have enough money, so they have to send her out late at night."

One fact is clear: the economic mobility that results from call center employment is a key driving force in why women choose to work in this industry. Time and again employees stated, "I cannot make this money in another industry." Simultaneously, call center employment is often defined as a stopgap job or temporary employment while on the way to a better career, higher education, or marriage.[1]

Examining call center employment beyond simplistic notions of fast money and stopgap employment provides a more complex understanding of what draws women to this industry and what can keep them there well beyond the one- to two-year time frame that executives such as Linda label "a good run" in regard to employee retention. The experiences of the women I discuss here demonstrate that financial stability and upward economic mobility intersect with women's lives in unexpected ways. Surely the income from call center employment represents both empowerment and exploitation.

Why Work for a Call Center?

Why would someone work for a call center given the night shift requirement, job stress, health concerns such as sleep disorders and digestive problems, and the underlying social disdain for the industry? This section examines the myriad of reasons that women join the industry despite stereotypes that call center employment requires little skill or intelligence, and where the "fast money" is by no means easy.[2] I have identified six key themes: (1) family survival; (2) "Because I want to!"; (3) money for spending, saving, and venture capital; (4) the great escape; (5) the single woman's life; and (6) join the airlines.

Family Survival

Dependence on women to maintain the economic livelihood of their families and communities represents what Saskia Sassen terms the *feminization of survival*.[3] Despite the rhetoric about call center income as an agent fueling the emergence of the consumer class, there is a push-pull in terms of how women experience the economic mobility such income provides. Some are certainly able to use their income to start a business or travel extensively. For many women, however, call center employment provides the means to keep their families fed and clothed and protects them from economic disaster along with the ensuing drop in class status that such disaster would bring.

In particular, call center employment allowed two single women in this study to be the sole supporters of themselves and their widowed mothers. Manisha, the twenty-six-year-old employee introduced in Chapter Three, was able to purchase the flat where she and her mother live.[4] Similarly, Elizabeth, a twenty-four-year-old senior customer service representative, supports her mother, Ms. George (introduced in Chapter Three). Elizabeth's father passed away when she was a child and Ms. George struggled for years to raise her two children on a teacher's salary.

After two interviews with Elizabeth at Company A, I was invited to interview Ms. George at their two-bedroom flat in Navi Mumbai. During a discussion about household expenses, Ms. George explained that their monthly maintenance fee and electricity bill cost approximately Rs 3,000 (US$67) per month. Without Elizabeth's income—approximately Rs 24,000 (US$532) per month after taxes—Ms. George would be destitute; her teacher's pension pays only Rs 1,200 (US$27) per month. Before Elizabeth went to work at the call center, money had been a source of acute tension and stress for her. In addition to the basic living expenses that she was barely able to meet, Ms. George had more than Rs 35,000 (US$776) in outstanding property taxes that she was unable to pay. At the time of our interview, Elizabeth's income not only supported them but was also being used to pay down their outstanding debts.

In contrast to the spendthrift stereotype of call center employees, Elizabeth and Ms. George's livelihood was carefully budgeted. They did not eat out, Elizabeth did not purchase branded clothes or the latest fashions, and neither of them took vacations. At the same time, there were clear improvements. Instead of going to the market, they now purchased vegetables and other household provisions at the Center One Mall in Vashi. Elizabeth pointed out that this is a step up because the mall is clean and the produce there is better than at the market. Ms. George said, "There are lots of changes. Since she's started working means, all my tension and problems, solved, like. I can bear the outgoing [going out and expenses], because in pension . . . umm . . . 1200 [rupees] nothing could be done."

Ms. George beamed with pride when she spoke of her daughter's ability and willingness to take financial responsibility for the household, but she also expressed remorse that their financial situation does not provide Elizabeth with the opportunity to pursue her dreams. When asked on three separate occasions what some of the positive aspects of call center employment are, her responses were negative:

REENA: What have been the positive impacts for both you and Elizabeth of her working in a call center, working in the night shift?

MS. GEORGE: Night shifts means when she works, I feel lonely like, in the night staying back. I don't get sleep. Keep waiting when she'll be back [*laughs*]. . . . Just waiting. Sitting at the window. . . . I don't get sleep. When she is there then, I feel relaxed, when she is at home.

REENA: So one of the downsides is that loneliness, not having your daughter around. What're some of the good things you think about in terms of Elizabeth working at these night shifts. Or is there anything good?

MS. GEORGE: Good about her means she is only her job and her home and nothing else firstly. I don't like.

REENA: So what about some of the good things? Any opinions you have. Do you want Elizabeth working in a call center?

MS. GEORGE: [*sigh*] At present like, since, because of, she has to run the
house, that is why . . . there's no one else no. Otherwise, I don't want my
daughter to work, actually.

REENA: And what do you rather her be doing?

MS. GEORGE: I wanted her to do whatever, means, her wishes were like she
wanted to do some further education, she wanted to continue. Then she
says, "I want to become bigger, study abroad there and earn so much for
you and make a house of my own."

Although call center employment provides the income necessary to support
the household, Ms. George was clear about how it negatively affected her
daughter's life. It kept her out at night, restricted her options, and forced her
to forgo higher education. In contrast to Elizabeth's assertion that she worked
in a call center because she wanted to, her mother defined it as the choice
when there is no equal or better alternative. The most Elizabeth could earn
outside this industry is approximately Rs 3,000 to Rs 5,000 (US$67 to US$111)
per month. Furthermore, employees know that other businesses do not equate
call center employment with job experience and they would have to start at
entry-level again if they left the industry. In this context, call center employment is a site of both constriction (that is, reduced entry into other industries)
and opening (that is, high wages).

Ms. George's concern that her daughter's life was only about work was
not an isolated response. This theme surfaced throughout the study. Denise,
the twenty-three-year-old former employee introduced in Chapter Four, explained that her parents hated call center employment more than she did. Her
mother, Ms. Paul, a woman in her fifties, provided the following reasons she
did not want Denise working in a call center:

Because the timings are very, very irregular. There were no fixed timings. And
no proper sleep. The only thing she used to do when she was in a call center was
go to work, come home, eat and sleep, get up, get dressed, and go to work. That
was the only thing she used to do!

As Ms. Paul watched her daughter's life transform from day to night, she was
clearly unhappy with the shift. Yet her willingness to accept her daughter's
decision was understandable when she recalled the constraints that she herself
had endured in her lifetime:

When I think in terms of my father, he would have a fit if I thought of working at night. He would really have a fit. He wouldn't let me. My father belonged to the old school and wouldn't let me do anything besides become a teacher, but nowadays we give them freedom to choose what they want to do and every girl works on shifts.

For Nivedita, a twenty-five-year-old single mother who has been in the industry for four months, working the night shift has provided a means to support her five-year-old daughter and maintain her autonomy. Nivedita is experiencing bad times financially because she is in the middle of a messy divorce from her husband, who has money but refuses to support their daughter.[5] Despite the relatively high wages, she explained, her mother's primary response to her job, particularly the night shift requirement, was, "What will people think?" Nivedita lives on her own and her parents reside in Mahabaleshwar, approximately six hours from Mumbai. Given her twelfth standard education with only a few correspondence classes in psychology, the Rs 10,000rs to Rs 14,000 (US$222 to US$310) starting salary at Company A is well above the salary of her previous job. With her call center income, Nivedita rents a small flat and has hired a full-time maid, whom she described as "old and from the village," to care for her daughter.

In contrast, Mina, the eighteen-year-old employee introduced in Chapter Three who was harassed by neighbors for going out at night, lives with her younger sister and mother. Her parents are in the middle of a divorce and her father lives in Saudi Arabia. She cited three key reasons for taking this job: (1) to help her mother pay bills and the housing loan; (2) to provide support for her younger sister; and (3) to fund her college education. She said she didn't want her parents, in particular her mother, to bear the burden of educating her.

When asked about her family's response to call center employment, she stated that her mother did not react. Her father initially objected to her working the night shift and commented that "a girl might get spoiled if earning her own money in college," but he eventually came around. Concerns about women becoming *spoiled* from earning their own income parallel attitudes toward women who defy gendered notions of place and space, be it going out at night or entering a Hindu temple during their menstrual cycle. Physical descriptions such as spoiled, devalued, and polluted are part of the backlash that women face when they challenge traditional notions of their societal place.[6]

Call center employment income also intersects with pay scales that formerly were attainable only in white-collar professions. Nisha, introduced in Chapter Three, currently works for a top-three call center in Mindspace. During our initial interview in May 2006, she explained that when she started working approximately eighteen months before, the starting salary at her company was Rs 11,000 (US$244) per month. Every six months there was an appraisal that ultimately brought her current monthly salary to Rs 20,000 (US$443) per month. In addition, she received a Rs 25,000 (US$554) bonus. She explained that the starting salary for new employees is now Rs 15,000 (US$333) per month. Nisha's mother, Ms. Mehta, a housewife, also participated in the interview. She commented that her brothers—one an architect and the other an engineer—earn similar salaries. Nisha has an arts degree from Bombay University but earns an income that is on par with her uncles, who spent years studying. This represents a dramatic shift in the salaries available to young people who are fluent in English.

In a follow-up interview six months later, I learned that Nisha's father had died unexpectedly, leaving this middle-class family in turmoil. During our initial interview, Nisha had explained that her family did not rely on her income for the maintenance of the household. This changed with the passing of her father. Nisha resides in a joint family living arrangement consisting of twelve individuals living in two flats (apartments). Nisha now gives money to her mother as well as to her elder cousin. In addition, she has fixed monthly expenses, such as her mobile phone and transportation to work because her company provides only one-way transportation. After outlining her key expenses, she contended that the "big money" associated with call center employment really isn't big:

Money to elder cousin	Rs 6,000 (US$133)
Money to mother	Rs 5,000 (US$111)
Transportation charges	Rs 800 (US$18)
Mobile phone charges	Rs 1,000 to Rs 1,500 (US$22 to US$33)

Despite the perception that call center employment provides its workers with enough money to hang out at the latest discotheque, drink all night, and party till dawn, this is not the case, Nisha argued, for those whose families depend on their income.

Amish, the industry consultant introduced in Chapter Two, pointed out that "people will now pay 100 bucks [US$2] for a film, which five years ago was unheard of." Such was the case with Shivani, a twenty-two-year-old employee, who said that she can now afford to go to movies once a week whereas before she went once in six months. The disposable income left over for women such as Nisha, however, is minimal when the increasing cost of entertainment in the city is combined with supporting a parent over the long term. Instead of enabling her to leapfrog into a higher income or class strata, the income from her call center employment simply allows Nisha's family to stay afloat.[7] Nevertheless, her ability to contribute to the family unit speaks volumes in a society where there is little in the way of catching those who fall onto hard times. Nisha's case demonstrates that instead of being viewed as a financial drain on the household, in the form of practices such as dowry, some women contribute to the economic sustenance of their families in ways that were previously unavailable to them.

Outside the family unit, provisions such as social security, welfare, unemployment, and Medicare are nonexistent for the majority of the population. Given such constraints, every little bit helps. The economic mobility associated with call centers does provide some women with the opportunity to migrate to urban IT hubs. Not only does the income generated by this emerging migration trend reshape the lives of the worker's family, but interviewees also spoke of the confidence and independence they gained from moving to new cities.

Born and raised in Jabalpur, the capital of Madhya Pradesh, Anita and her older sister made the twenty-hour bus journey to Mumbai to work in the call center industry. Since migrating almost two years ago, Anita, now twenty-one, has worked at three call centers. Both she and her twenty-two-year-old sister were able to secure employment and a temporary place to live prior to arriving in Mumbai because the growing demand for 24/7 workers has led some companies to recruit workers from distant towns such as Jabalpur and to provide dormitory housing upon arrival.

When Anita was a child, her father passed away unexpectedly and her mother was left with five young children to raise. Anita recalled that they went from being a middle-class family to being a poor family. Often her mother could not afford to buy clothes for them. Anita's call center income has since improved the impoverished status of her family.

Her first job at TYJ Corporation paid Rs 10,000 (US$222) per month, which she called "a lot of money." Anita's salary steadily increased over the next two years. She provided me with the following breakdown of her income:

80 percent to mother

10 percent to savings

10 percent to living expenses

Sending 80 percent of her income to her mother is a source of pride for Anita. She views her two younger brothers as her responsibility and the money helps to support them. During the interview, she reminisced that as a child she couldn't afford the dresses her friends had and she recalled the feelings of shame and inferiority this gave her. She said that now "it feels good because I can afford to buy for my mom, brother, and sisters."

Despite the fact that call center income had improved her family's livelihood, Anita's mother was completely against the idea. Anita explained that it was her uncle who convinced the family to send her and her sister to Mumbai, because he wanted them to have the opportunity "to know the world." Their move was a source of angst in the household. For two young women to move to a distant city, particularly fast-paced Mumbai, with no male counterpart and work the night shift was unprecedented in her family. In addition, prior to joining the call center industry, Anita was never allowed to leave the house past 7 P.M. Although call center employment had clearly improved the life of Anita's family and although she likes that she can now go out at 9 or 10 P.M. without facing family restrictions, the transition to Mumbai has not been easy. With tears in her eyes, Anita spoke of the sorrow and anguish she felt because she had not seen her mom in more than eight months.

The individuals who contributed to this section are clearly varied. Nisha's story illustrates that call center employment can provide a financial net that can hold a family together when a breadwinner passes on. Anita's childhood, in contrast, illustrates what happens to a widowed mother and her children when there is no financial net between middle-class and poor. Nivedita's story shows how the breakdown of a marriage leaves some women to bear the responsibility of raising a child alone. In her situation, working the night shift has allowed her to maintain a sense of personal dignity and autonomy despite perceptions of her as "that poor girl, her husband doesn't want her."

In India, the desire for boy children remains firmly entrenched because they are perceived as "social security" for parents while girls are expected to marry and leave the home.[8] Elizabeth and Manisha defy this expectation. Their cases illustrate the contribution that women make to the support of their parents, particularly widowed mothers, who continue to be subjected to second-class status relative to that of widowed fathers.[9]

For women such as Anita who don't have the economic means to pursue higher education or other job opportunities, call center employment is arguably the most viable alternative. But defining Anita as "that poor girl, she had to move to Mumbai to support her family" is problematic. It casts women like her as primarily a bodily site of capital accumulation.[10] It does not give enough consideration to the depth of their journeys, nor does it provide an understanding of the sense of accomplishment that women experience when they rescript gender roles—whether consciously or not—in the family unit. Instead of such women being viewed as pioneering spirits traversing new lands and breaking through traditional constraints governing a woman's place, they are presented as migrating because they have to.

"Because I Want to!"

When asked why she worked for a call center, Elizabeth, who has been employed in the industry for three and a half years, responded in exasperation, "Because I want to!" She responds to being described as "that poor girl" with "I'm not poor!" and she is irritated by the judgment and disdain placed on call center employees, including the idea that call center employment is not a proper job. The prevailing attitude is that salary and occupation should correspond to education. An individual with a college degree, for example, is expected to earn more money than a high school graduate. Call center employment disrupts this expectation.

Despite the high wages, however, call center employment is marked as an easy job that anyone can get because it does not come with an education requirement specific to the content of the job. As a result, "people who are educated don't support you," Elizabeth said. In contrast, she pointed out that her apartment building security guard was very excited, supportive, and interested when she told him about her job.

Elizabeth's situation illustrates that the upward economic mobility associated with the call center industry does not necessarily bring with it respect or acceptance. This is particularly the case among the educated, middle, and upper classes, where the industry initially sought recruits. Despite earning a relatively high wage and supporting her widowed mother, Elizabeth and women like her do not receive support and praise for stepping up to earn the family bread. Instead, they are viewed with pity by the larger community. Underlying all of this is the night shift requirement. Working all day to support one's family is one thing; working all night is another.

Armed with a bachelor of commerce degree, Elizabeth brings home a monthly income of approximately Rs 24,000 (US$532) after taxes, a salary that is on par with or higher than that of an entry-level white-collar professional.[11] Women like Elizabeth not only disrupt the spatial and temporal limits placed on their gender by staying out all night, but they also undermine the notion that a woman's income is secondary to that of the male head of household. Elizabeth, for example, has a brother who works in the call center industry. Although the traditional view is that sons take care of aging parents, her single brother was the one who left home and he does not provide financial support to the household.

Unlike Elizabeth, Irene, the training manager discussed in previous chapters, is in the middle of a divorce and lives alone. She rents a one-bedroom flat in Bandra, a suburb that is home to film stars and night clubs. When asked what keeps her in the call center industry, she cited both job satisfaction and money as the most important reasons. Similar to nineteen other women in the study, Irene has familial bonds that allow her to pursue other career options. Although she does not view call center employment as a long-term career, Irene explained that she has stayed in the industry for five years because it challenges her and on two occasions provided her with the opportunity to travel to the United States for business.

Diya, a twenty-nine-year-old employee at WebCorp in Ahmedabad, has worked in the BPO industry for six years. Although she has the opportunity to pursue higher education with the support of her family, she has remained in the industry because of the relatively high wages. In addition, she prides herself on being the "only kid doing something different and weird," because her brother has a daytime job and her sister is a doctoral student. When asked to explain what constitutes "different and weird," she cited the global nature of the work and the work hours that connect her to off-shore customers.

Diya is also the only one in this study not to be the first woman in her family to stay out at night on a regular basis. Describing her family as very progressive, she spoke of how at one point her mother worked six hours away from where they lived and would come home on the weekends. Diya's grandmother took care of the home while Diya's mother was away. This was considered unheard of in her mother's time. Diya also mentioned having an aunt who worked at a hospital and thus was used to night shifts.

Valerie, introduced in Chapter Three, is a graduate of Xavier College, a premier institution in Mumbai. Her highly prized education provided her with the competitive edge needed to gain entry into one of the major advertising firms in Mumbai. To the shock of friends and family, she transitioned into the call center industry after three years in advertising. This was viewed as a step down.

Her reasons for joining a call center were not only because it pays more money, but also because she wanted more time for herself. She described the advertising industry as very stressful and call center employment as easier in contrast because "you know what you are doing for a fixed amount of time and you can't take work home." Another reason was linked to her desire for a master's in business administration (MBA), for which the call center she works for would pay. Valerie does, however, miss her advertising days, especially the parties to which her job gave her access. Her long-term goal is to return to the advertising industry after she gets her MBA.

Anan, a 30-something married senior quality assurance manager with two young children, does not need to work. She works out of a desire to be independent. Anan pointed out that she currently earns a yearly salary that took her mother, who worked outside the home for nearly six decades, fifty years to attain. For many women, as is further demonstrated in the next chapter, a vision of independence and freedom was paramount to their decision to pursue call center employment.

Money for Spending, Saving, and Venture Capital

Consumerism in India's major cities gained momentum in the mid-1990s but exploded in the twenty-first century.[12] When I asked employees what impact the income derived from call center employment had on their spending habits, women whose income was not necessary for family survival pointed to their ability to shop for their family and themselves. The liberalization of the Indian economy has flooded the market with brand-name fashions that previously were accessible only to those who traveled or had connections abroad. Some of the women, for example, had a preference for branded clothes such as Guess and Tommy Hilfiger.

A few interviewees linked changes in their spending to the fact that working the night shift changed not only their economic mobility but their physical mobility as well. For Seema, the twenty-four-year-old WebCorp employee introduced in Chapter Three, working the night shift means she "can roam around" starting at 6 or 7 P.M. and be at the office by 10 P.M., whereas before she was forbidden to go out past 8 P.M. She uses this newfound time to hang out at the mall and shop in the bazaar.

The increase in income has also brought with it an increase in spending. Supporting one's family, paying tuition, buying junk food, traveling, and shopping for clothes, mobile phones, and household items were the primary ways in which participants said their money was spent. Although the increased income was often linked to gaining a sense of independence, Karen, a twenty-four-year-old employee, had a different reaction. Stating that call center employment has "spoiled my life," she expressed concern about becoming more of a spendthrift: "I'll spend a thousand bucks [US$22] in a day and think no worries because I have 40,000 [US$887] in the bank."

At first I was confused by Karen's conception of *spoiled*. Did she mean that her life had been ruined by her job? As we discussed the issue further, it became apparent that *spoiled* meant that life was easier because she no longer worried about not having enough money. Shilpa, the thirty-eight-year-old employee in Bangalore introduced in Chapter Three, does high-level outsourcing work for a Fortune 500 company. She did not express concern about becoming a spendthrift. Instead, she said she finally had the financial security to make major purchases, such as a scooter for herself and a motorcycle for her husband. She commented, "What is Rs 40,000 [US$887]? I can buy that."

Devaki, the twenty-one-year-old employee introduced in Chapter Four, stated that compared to her coworkers' parents, hers placed little restriction on her mobility. Prior to joining the industry she would go out two to three times per month and be home by 2 A.M. This pattern remained, but because of her increased disposable income, she now hangs out at more expensive venues such as the Velvet Lounge in the Renaissance Mumbai Hotel in Powai and the Provogue Lounge in Bandra.

The private shuttle transport provided by call centers has also reshaped how some women want to travel during their off-work hours in that they opt for more expensive forms of transport. Devaki explained that she is now spoiled by taking a private vehicle and doesn't like to ride the public bus anymore. Kriti, introduced in Chapter Three, said her mother asked her, "Why are you taking a rick?" Her mother was surprised that she was now taking rickshaws to get around and not the cheaper public transport she had used before.

Mona, the twenty-five-year-old Company A employee introduced in Chapter Three, comes from a family that does not require her income. She purchased her first home at age twenty-three, bought a used car the following year, and takes yearly vacations. Among her colleagues at Company A, she is a role model of success in terms of how women use the income from call center employment to achieve economic independence.

In fact, a few participants used their income to start their own businesses. Of the seventy-two employees who participated in this study, three employees—two women and one man—used the money they saved from call center employment in this way. In 2002, Anjali (see Chapter Two), then twenty-three years old, spent eight months working at night for a call center in Powai. She recalled sacrificing her sleep during the daytime in order to network and explore ideas for her future venture. Similar to Parvati (see Chapter Four), Anjali comes from an upper-middle-class family that does not require her to contribute financially to the family. Although her case is not typical, it is an interesting one. Earning Rs 15,000 (US$333) a month, she used her capital to start a nonprofit organization that provides entrepreneurial and leadership skills to young people as well as workshops on individuality and freedom, diversity, and the culture of democracy.

Since then, Anjali has partnered with the World Bank and the United Nations to hold workshops for young people as well as to organize youth projects. When we met, for example, she was in the midst of putting together a globalization and identity workshop sponsored by the BBC and the British Consulate. Although she makes clear that other industries would not provide the pay package that the call centers do, she also stated, "The business is transported, the work ethic is not. The kind of hours and the requirements beyond that is not something that developed countries would do. They push workers to do hours that they wouldn't do in the U.S." This comment reveals that some employees sense they are held to a productivity standard from which they perceive their U.S. counterparts are immune.

Kriti also took the plunge to start her own venture. Our first interview was conducted at Company A in February 2006. In a follow-up interview at the Center One Mall in Vashi in October 2006, I learned that she was laid off a few weeks after our initial meeting. Kriti had worked at Company A for one year and was able to secure employment with another company. Her new company, however, is not located in her hometown of Navi Mumbai and her commute is now an hour to an hour-and-a-half each way. During the interim phase between these two jobs, she made plans to open a boutique carrying her own clothing line. By November, Kriti was working full-time in a call center, enduring a nearly three-hour daily commute, and running her business during the day. Her goal is to leave the call center industry once her daytime venture becomes profitable.

In contrast to Anjali, Kriti joined the call center industry because her family needed the money. Because her middle-class family is economically stable again, the earning members of her nuclear family (that is, her father, her brother, and herself; her mother is a housewife) pool a certain amount of their monthly income for household expenses and she is left with Rs 15,000 (US$333) to spend or save as she sees fit. Kriti emphasized that she enjoys working at a call center because of the work and the office environment, not just because of the money.

Anjali and Kriti's choices illustrate that the economic mobility associated with call center employment does not always transform into irresponsible spending or consumer debt, a concern voiced by critics of the industry. It's important to point out, however, that both women come from families that did not require a large portion of their income to support a household. Additionally, they were not subject to stringent controls on how their income was to be spent. In Anjali's case, this was due to her sheer force of will to move out of her parents' home at age nineteen and seek her own independence. Kriti remained in the family unit and her decision to start her own company was supported by her family. Still, despite this support, the sections on marriage and living arrangements later in this book illustrate how social and family pressures continue to restrict how Kriti and other women use their economic mobility to assert their individuality.

Additionally, some participants reported that their spending and day-to-day living expenses had actually decreased since joining the call center industry. Denise explained that the one-way pick-up provided by her company reduced her transportation expenses, and that taking a rickshaw home at 6:30 A.M. was cheaper because she shared the fare with her coworkers. If she were to take the same route during the day, she would be stuck in traffic, which would make the journey arduous and, according to Denise, more expensive in some instances. In addition, such participants suggested that they spend less because when they have a day off or come home from a shift, they want to sleep.

According to twenty-three-year-old Maya, "Spending reduces because you do not have time to go out." Valerie said that she is saving approximately Rs 4,000 (US$89) a month because she does not have time to hang out. Previously she had worked in advertising earning Rs 8,000 (US$177) a month and pointed out that "it was hardly nothing to make ends meet."

Sariya, a married thirty-four-year-old employee, resides in a joint family household of seven people (husband, mother-in-law, father-in-law, uncle, and her two daughters, ages four and ten). They share a two-bedroom, seven-hundred square-foot flat. Because the household depends on her income to cover its day-to-day living expenses, the opportunity to save or to spend for personal consumption is unavailable to her.

During my preliminary fieldwork, I suspected that night shift employment may constitute a form of temporal entrapment.[13] By working through the night and inevitably sleeping through the day, employees become further excluded from social and economic opportunities within the larger community. Indeed, in the case of women such as Valerie, Maya, and Sariya, the temporal entrapment resulting from working all night prevents them from indulging in the spendthrift behavior with which call center income has become associated in the media and in popular society.

None of the women I interviewed reported having credit card debt, a key concern among opponents of the industry. This does not mean, however, that some employees are not mired in debt. Debt was perhaps not something an interviewee wanted to reveal, because it could be a source of embarrassment, particularly given the negative perception that workers currently face. But employees were forthright in discussing how they were able to place a portion of their income into savings. Of the thirty-nine participants who discussed their finances in depth, twenty-four were either the primary support of their household or gave a portion of their income to support their family. Although the relatively high salary from call center employment allows some workers to increase their conspicuous consumption in ways that were previously beyond their reach, my observations and my discussions with participants didn't reveal enough about the spending habits of workers or the level of debt they incur to make any conclusive statements. Suffice it to say that surely this was a problem for some female workers, but it was not a pervasive theme that emerged during the course of fieldwork.

The Great Escape

Though it was not always admitted outright during initial interviews, in follow-up interviews it emerged that call center employment also provided some participants with a legitimate reason to leave the house at night. Concerns about promiscuity and bad character were deflected by linking employment to skill acquisition. Also, in contrast to working as a prostitute or bar dancer, the night shift aspect of this industry is also tempered by its collegial work environment and its connection to the global economy.

With access to a new timescape, a few women reported that they would "bunk off" without informing their family and use the time instead to go out with friends or meet with a boyfriend they were secretly dating. But in terms of their access to the city—hanging out at bars they previously wouldn't frequent or going to parts of town that were previously beyond their reach due to financial and familial constraint—more than half of the call center employees who discussed this topic did not report experiencing any change. Kriti explained that, in her experience, night shift work makes it difficult to find time to hang out.

As I analyzed the varying responses that women gave about not going out, three key factors emerged: (1) for single women, the strictness of their family made it difficult for them to get permission to leave the house; (2) for married women, their responsibility to the household in combination with working all night kept them homebound; and (3) both sets of women were just plain exhausted from working all night.[14]

Still, for those women who reported a change, all were single and either lived in families that were not particularly controlling or had the will to defy their parents and just sneak around. Mona said her current work schedule gives her about five to six hours of free time and her parents don't mind if she goes out to a disco. The income from call center employment allows her to go to pubs, movies, and restaurants and to shop on Linking Road, a popular spot in Bandra, all of which were previously out of her reach.

In terms of sneaking around, Ajay, the twenty-something manager introduced in Chapter Three, described a female employee who called in sick. The company received a panicked call from her parents in the middle of the night because their daughter was not home when they expected. It was explained to the parents that the company didn't contact them about their daughter's whereabouts because they assumed she was at home sick. It was soon discovered that "she bunked to go out with her boyfriend." Lopa, a twenty-two-year-old employee who has worked in the industry for four years, also uses her call center job as a means to sneak around, and so far she has not gotten caught. On days off she will pretend to go to work and instead hang out with her girlfriends or fiancé. Similarly, Valerie spoke of how on some days off she will pretend to go to work and instead spend the night at her boyfriend's place.

Although using call center employment as a means to get out of the house at night was a theme that emerged throughout the course of the study, employees for the most part were not forthright about whether and how they used the night shift requirement to sneak around themselves. First-time interviewees, for instance, would speak of how "a friend" or "someone in their office" was caught with a boyfriend or bunked to go out with friends. Interviewees who maintained contact with me during the course of the study and even after I returned to the United States made it clear, however, that the night shift requirement of the industry was a draw for women who were looking for a legitimate reason to get out of the house at night.

The Single Woman's Life

A few months into this study, a theme of single women wanting to experience living on their own emerged. Indeed, call center income provided some women who didn't support families a means to live on their own, and some of those I interviewed followed this strategy. Income from call center employment also allowed some single women to experience life in a whole new way, from traveling beyond the confines of the typical family vacation to saving money to purchase their own flats. Parvati earns Rs 20,000 (US$443) per month working for a call center near her home. She is completing her master's degree in political science and is also one of only two women in the study in the telemarketing and collection side of the call center industry. Although the work is harder, according to Parvati, this area has a higher status and is stereotyped as a man's field because it requires aggression and a strong will.[15]

In contrast to the twenty-two women in this study whose income directly supported the family unit, Parvati does not connect her work to family survival, confidence building, or skill acquisition. Nor does she use her money to buy branded clothes or the latest mobile phone, a chief complaint from opponents of the industry. Instead, Parvati takes monthly vacations. From the temples of Hampi in South India to various hill stations in Maharashtra, Parvati has traveled throughout India with friends from work and college. Vacationing every month is a deviation from how society would expect a call center employee, particularly a single woman, to live. Although Parvati was the only participant to have such a lifestyle, she was not alone in using her income to take vacations outside of Mumbai. Nine other participants also mentioned that their call center income provided them with the means to travel.

According to Winifred Poster, call center employees have a rigid schedule that doesn't provide much in the way of respite or downtime.[16] Despite this, Parvati's upper-middle-class status, call center salary, and work schedule allow her to travel beyond the boundaries of Mumbai on vacations ranging from four days to one week. I was fascinated to learn that one could simultaneously pursue a master's degree, work full-time, and vacation every month. Parvati explains:

> I get two holidays in a week, so I would work at a stretch and take four holidays the next week and I am allowed to take two scheduled leaves in a month. Of course it's based on the T.L.s [team leaders], but if you make your sales targets, they don't care and you can take leave.

Parvati's experience illustrates how working in positions that are generally viewed as "a man's job" allows for increased flexibility and autonomy. Feminist scholars find that, from factory work to data processing, labor that is deemed feminine is subject to stricter surveillance and control over the worker's time.[17] Furthermore, positions in telemarketing and collections have the potential for higher wages because some companies provide bonuses and commissions on the basis of performance. Purvi, introduced in Chapter Three, for instance, has a base salary of Rs 17,500 (US$388) per month. Yet as a collections agent, she also receives a commission that brings her monthly after-tax salary to an average of Rs 34,000 ($US754) a month. An employee who is not in the management ranks, she was the highest paid person in this study. In fact, her earnings surpass those of many team leaders, whose salaries range between Rs 20,000 and Rs 26,000 (US$443 to US$576) per month.

In contrast to Parvati, Purvi has used her economic mobility to build a life for herself. She emphatically stated, "Call centers help women come up in life." Her case is compelling because she is an only child whose parents are deceased. She moved to Spain for one and a half years to live with an aunt who offered to adopt her, but she discovered upon her arrival that her family primarily wanted her to do their housework. This state of servitude, combined with a dislike of the Indian community in Spain, led her to return to India.

Currently she has no relatives in Mumbai, rents a 460-square-foot flat in Navi Mumbai, and is planning to buy her own flat.

Purvi is empowered by her success and said, "I have been the leader of myself." This contrasts with the exploitative perspective presented in Sonali Gulati's documentary film, *Nalini by Day, Nancy by Night.*[18] In the film, Avni—who goes by the alias Anne Scott—speaks of working as a collections agent for General Electric. Despite achieving a million U.S. dollars in credit collections for General Electric, she is paid the equivalent of US$7 per day for her work. Avni is aware of the unequal global labor relations that allow her to earn a salary that is relatively high by Indian standards but does not compensate her in a manner equal to that of her American counterpart. "You've been giving me peanuts" is how she describes the salaries of call center employees relative to their output. In Avni's view, "they [companies abroad] are minting money in hand." Nevertheless, Purvi, despite also being aware of the inequity of the system, still sees call center employment as a golden opportunity given the lack of options available to her.

It is important to note that of the thirteen single women who lived outside a joint or nuclear family unit, six were already living on their own prior to call center employment. In these instances, call center employment did not serve as an impetus to move out. Instead it allowed those who had already gone through the social and family stigma of living alone to maintain and, in many instances, improve their lifestyle.

For instance, Irene pays Rs 15,000 (US$333) for her one-bedroom flat in Bandra, an up-and-coming Mumbai suburb. Compared to the living standards of the average employee, her rent was considered exorbitant. During the interviews at Company A, colleagues regarded her lifestyle as unique because she smoked, lived alone, and was in the midst of a divorce, and it was known among her inner circle at work that she was dating a coworker.

For women such as Irene who could afford to live on their own and had addressed the hurdle of it being considered inappropriate not to live with one's family, access to housing itself was a challenge, particularly for single women who work the night shift. They are viewed with suspicion in that some landlords do not want to rent to single women, whom they suspect to be bar dancers or prostitutes.

During the course of my fieldwork, I learned that the three primary housing options for single women are hostels, paying guests (PGs), and to rent or buy a flat. Anjali has lived in hostels, PG accommodations (see next paragraph), and rented flats. She found hostels to be the worst option because of the strict rules and monitoring that women must endure there. The documentary film *Freedom Before 11* shows that women living in hostels are subjected to stricter surveillance in comparison to men living in hostels.[19] Particularly telling is when one manager refers to the women in her hostel as *inmates*, as are discussions in the film about the fact that women who live in hostels are viewed as having "bad character."

A PG rents a room in a home. This kind of housing is also difficult for single women, especially if they work at night, because in some PG accommodations restrictions are placed on women's mobility. In her quest to find housing, Reshma (introduced in Chapter Four), for example, was informed by one owner, "If you come back after 10 P.M., we will not let you in." Similarly, Poonam (introduced in Chapter Three) was forced to move out of the PG room she lived in because the landlord objected to her coming and going late at night.

In general, women are expected to remain with their parents until marriage. An exception to this would be to pursue studies in a different locale. Women such as Anjali who defy their parents by moving out of the family confines are not the norm for the urban middle-class. In fact, with the exception of Anjali, participants who expressed a desire to live on their own said it was not an option for them, despite the fact that they could afford it.

Kriti's eyes lit up while she spoke on this topic and she exclaimed, "My dream is to live in a hostel and work at 3G in Mindspace. The building is beautiful and it's a great area to work." With its sleek buildings and indoor waterfalls, and surrounded by the latest malls and movie theaters, Mindspace is considered, in the eyes of many call center employees, the premier place to work in Mumbai. Kriti's job provides her with enough income to afford such a lifestyle and she could easily obtain employment in Mindspace given her current work experience. Family pressure, however, has deemed it unacceptable. "What would people think?" was a common theme that emerged during interviews with single women who wanted to use their call center income to live on their own. Kriti explained that if her family lived outside of Mumbai it would make sense if she moved away. But as a resident of Mumbai, "It would appear strange to live away from home."

Join the Airlines

During a focus group session with six employees at a Catholic church in the suburbs of Mumbai, I learned that other industries generally do not consider call center employment a viable work experience. Call center employment does, however, provide a competitive edge for those seeking entry into the airline industry. According to the articles "A Supersonic Boom" in the *Times of India* and "Elephants do Fly" in the *Economist*, the increased air traffic in India has fueled the demand for flight attendants.[20]

Sapna, a human resources manager of a call center in Mindspace, found during exit interviews that more and more women were using call center employment as a stepping stone into the airlines. She explained that call center employees are in demand because they are "polished" and because their voice and accent training is seen as useful. Denise, the former employee, noted that her eight months of work experience at a top-ten call center gave her a competitive edge when she applied for a flight attendant position. At the time of our interview she was in the middle of training for Airline A, a premier domestic carrier in India, and she spoke at length about the training regimen. As part of their training, flight attendants must follow a strict regimen of three hours of daily exercise. Body measurements are regularly scrutinized and, according to Denise, an attendant can be grounded without pay if she shows up for work with a pimple. This company emphasizes the sublime sexiness of its flight attendants, which requires them to walk a fine line between "see me, I'm sexy" and "no, I'm not that kind of girl."

Denise's experience shows that some women are required to embody their labor practices in ways that mark them as feminine. The occupational segregation that emerged in relation to working in the call center industry and in the airline industry continues to reflect that traditional notions of a woman's place endure. Women are on the call center floor but not in the boardroom; they serve drinks on the plane but they aren't in the cockpit.

Airline A, owned and operated by an Indian national, has managed to avoid negative media publicity regarding its questionable employment practices. In fact, this airline is considered a model company in terms of customer service. Danny, a twenty-nine-year-old call center manager, confided that it's his dream to one day fly on Airline A because unlike its budget competitors, flying on Airline A is a status symbol of success.

The lack of media attention or public outcry regarding the questionable employment practices of this domestically owned airline contrasts sharply with the strict surveillance of transnational call centers. Although the unfair labor practices of multinational corporations in developing countries are the subject of scrutiny, domestically owned and serviced companies are at times able to get away with discriminatory practices that global companies cannot. Transnational call centers, for instance, are subjected to various forms of scrutiny over employment practices such as night shift work and masking the identities of its employees. Yet when an Indian-owned airline company subjects women to outright discriminatory practices, a similar sense of outrage does not surface.

In contrast, Sonia, a twenty-six-year-old call center employee for a major U.S. computer company, said that women are treated better in the transnational call centers than in local industries because "all eyes are watching." Imagine the uproar if call centers were to require female employees to use a coquettish "come hither" voice when speaking to American consumers making airline reservations or processing credit card payments. The scrutiny placed on the behavior of global corporations in some instances holds them to a higher standard than Indian companies. This is not to suggest, however, that call centers are void of dubious practices. According to Poster, facial expressions are considered part of the voice and accent posing.[21] She observed that even though call center customers cannot see employees, managers pace up and down the aisles shouting at employees, "Smile and dial!"[22]

Wrap-Up

The relatively high income associated with call center employment is a windfall for eighteen- to twenty-five-year-olds who are fluent in English. It has become apparent, however, that looking at call center employment as primarily a source of fast money is problematic. This belief disguises the myriad of factors that draw women to the industry and limits our understanding of how women experience earning their own money. Indeed, women joined the industry for a variety of reasons, such as family survival, escaping the chains of immobility, changing their spending and saving habits, gaining capital to start their own business, and embracing the single life.

Without a doubt, call center income has brought forth spending and saving patterns that were previously beyond the reach of employees. In addition, a sense of independence is garnered from finally being able to get out of the house at night on a regular basis, something that was previously off-limits for the women who participated in this study. This escape has provided ways for women to sneak around at night that were previously beyond their reach. Some women, however, did not report a change, and this was related to factors such as strict parents, responsibility for maintaining the household, and sheer exhaustion.

Regardless of whether or not the economic mobility associated with call center employment transformed an individual's physical mobility and spatial access, the speed with which workers attain a relatively high income—income that in many instances took their parents decades to attain—disrupts the timeline for *paying one's dues*. Thus this shift has brought with it upheaval and confusion. Society seeks to make sense of this shift not only in terms of the fact that it dramatically increases some women's earning potential, but also because some high school graduates now have the potential to earn an income that is on par with entry-level white-collar professions.

As workers benefit from the cash and flash associated with call center employment, an undertone of jealousy emerges in comments such as, "She's bought a house. She doesn't deserve it." At the same time, labeling call center income as merely fast, easy money serves to justify harsh perceptions of irresponsibility, laziness in terms of finding a *real* job, and lack of direction. Combine the perception of fast money with staying out all night—working "the hooker shift"—and it is on the backs of women that stereotypes of "bad character" and poverty (such as "that poor girl, her family has to send her out at night because they don't have enough money") are engendered.

From landlords not wanting to rent to single women who work at night to parents believing that a daughter who earns her own money in college will become spoiled, views about women who work outside the home are complex. When a "good girl" starts working the hooker shift and goes from earning a low wage to earning a high wage, which in turn is viewed by society as nothing more than "fast money," pity, envy, scorn, and moral condemnation are just some of the reactions that emerge as more and more women gain economic mobility as a result of working the night shift.

Although participants certainly pointed out that call center income gave them a sense of independence, for the most part the money did not buy them the right to move out of their homes. It was still considered taboo for a single woman to live away from her parents, especially if they lived in the same area in which she worked. In the context of parental control, lower-class women who migrate to major cities for call center employment and live on their own experience less surveillance on their mobility compared to middle-class women who live with their parents.

Under the rubric of equating modernity with the freedom to move about as one sees fit, this difference disrupts the class narrative that generally demarcates middle-class Mumbaikar women as more modern compared to the city's lower class migrant women. This disruption provides a framework for rethinking how women are the bodily site on which class narratives are constructed: a middle-class girl (that is, a good girl) stays with her family whereas a poor girl (who is seen as exploited) leaves because she has no choice.

6 On the Home Front

Doing something for the sake of exploring your youth is scandalous.
Independence is not acceptable or preferred.

—Anjali, former employee

According to Mona Domosh, geographers in general do "not move past the front stoop" when it comes to looking at the household as a geographical space from which one could learn.[1] Indeed, whether the home even constitutes a scale of analysis worthy of intellectual merit, as opposed to studies focused on a global level, is a subject of debate. On the one hand, the home is viewed as a "relatively stable background structure[s]."[2] On the other hand, it is believed that the construction of gender relations within the household provides a powerful understanding of how both public and private space remain gendered.[3] In fact, scholars such as Sylvia Chant define the household as a "geographically and historically dynamic social institution in which gender is embedded and negotiated."[4]

Instead of viewing household space as neutral or in the background, this chapter begins by examining how household relations generally fare when women become employees of call centers. To illustrate how this process plays out in intimate ways, I focus on two life histories to demonstrate how wife-husband relations in the home shift as a result of economic mobility, particularly as it relates to women who both work at night and earn an income that outstrips that of their husbands. Next, I discuss how some parent-child relationships fare when daughters join the call center industry. Without a doubt, the effects of night shift employment on household relations vary significantly. I would argue, however, that it is in these variations that we begin to understand why income and education alone do not always transform gender roles in the household.

The Shifting Household Dynamic?

In response to women earning relatively high levels of income from call center employment, Amish, the industry consultant, exclaimed, "Women don't put up with shit anymore!" Yet during participant observation and in-depth interviews, it was apparent that this is not always the case. During a breakfast visit to the home of Gita, a forty-three-year-old manager, her husband barked to her "Serve food!" in front of their seventeen-year-old son, thirteen-year-old daughter, and me. Although Gita's husband earned far less than she did and her earnings allowed them to purchase the home they live in, the husband dominated their household.

Similarly, Anan explained that despite her success as a senior quality assurance manager, she is expected to awaken every morning before her husband, a mechanical engineer, to get his clothes ready, prepare his tea, and get their three-year-old son ready for preschool. Anan lives in a joint family arrangement (that is, resides with in-laws) in which her husband is the only son and has been pampered all of his life. She said that having a husband who does not contribute equally at home and expects to be served by the women in the house is a common issue for many married women working in call centers. Although Anan earns a salary that is well above average, call center employment has a lower status compared to other fields, particularly engineering. In this instance, working outside the home does not translate into improved gender relations because notions of who has "the better job" impact the woman's status at home.[5]

Despite the apparent lack of change in gender relations, Anan worked full-time and participated in an MBA program because of the sense of independence it gave her. Vasanti, age twenty-three, also pointed out that for married women like her, the sense of independence derived from night shift employment meant "we can spend on whatever we want" and "we don't have to ask someone for money."

Single women also reported that the income from call center employment gave them a sense of independence on the home front. Prior to working in a call center job, Kriti received pocket money from her family on the basis of her expenses. She spoke of wanting a mobile phone and her father refused, citing that it was too expensive. She subsequently began working as a tutor for young children. For twenty hours of labor per month (one hour per day, five times a week), she earned Rs 1,000 (US$22), which she saved to buy herself a mobile phone. She said, "It felt great to buy for myself!" Now earning Rs 17,000 (US$377) a month as a call center employee, she said she has gained an even greater sense of independence from not having to ask her parents for any money.

During my fieldwork in Ahmedabad, employees suggested that there is a difference in what independence means for married women and single women. Amrita, a twenty-one-year-old employee, explained that for married women independence is more about having one's own income whereas for single women like her the sense of independence comes from getting out of the house at night. She explained that in her society "girls are not allowed to move out at night." Although she has yet to go out at night during a day off, Amrita said that her job has given her the confidence to do this in the future. She also emphasized that money and working at nights has helped her to become more "bold."

Throughout our discussions about relations in the household, it was apparent that call center employment income does not translate into a demand for change in gender roles at home. Women did not insist that their husbands, fathers, or brothers take up an active role in cooking, cleaning, child-rearing, and other forms of labor typically deemed "ladies work." As illustrated by the stories of Anan and Gita, some women are still held to the traditions of "Serve food!" and making sure the tea is ready in the morning.

Also, in many households, a mother or mother-in-law ends up attending to the day shift domestic front. This dynamic is interesting from the perspective of relations between young women and elderly women. At an age when they should be retiring and enjoying a matriarchal status, elderly women continue to be treated as unpaid servants or managers of the household.

Instead of equalizing gender roles in the home, then, the paid and unpaid work of younger women or the placing of domestic duties on the backs of elderly women enables men to benefit from the double income of women in the paid labor force. It is also why some women are able to gain entry to this night shift labor pool—because household responsibility is passed on to other women. Elderly men and young men, in the meantime, avoid the drudgery of housework under the excuse that it is "ladies work" and that to take on such work will emasculate them—another concern related to the "What will people think?" narrative.[6]

Thus, under the guise of economic development and women's liberation, the bodies of elderly women are used to fuel the career aspirations of some younger women. Put another way, in some families elderly women are used to maintain gender regimes in the household. As a result, the entry of women into a night shift labor pool does not translate into a substantive change in gender roles in the household.[7]

At the same time, there are also many servant-maintained households. Still, it falls on the women to manage the process and schedule their time accordingly. It may appear that having servants makes the lives of middle-class working women in India easier, yet this is not always the case. The amount of labor involved in cleaning and maintaining a middle-class household in the high-density suburbs of Mumbai (because of dust and pollution) is time-consuming and arduous. Anan has four servants in her joint household and each one performs specific tasks: (1) sweeping, (2) washing, (3) dusting, and (4) preparing chapattis. According to Anan, the housewife–working woman's schedule is based on when and if the maids show up, and she makes it a point to acknowledge that she is fortunate because she can count on her mother-in-law to manage the servants and be there to watch over them. In summary, I discovered that call center employment did little to shift gender roles dramatically in the household.[8] Nevertheless, as is demonstrated in the next section, the income garnered from night shift employment does bring forth substantive lifestyle changes for some workers and their families.

Wife-Husband Relations in the Household: Two Life Histories

The women who participated in this study continued to face constrictions, in one form or another, in their lives. At the same time, it is also important to consider the changes gained from night shift employment. To convey the mix of constriction and opening created by night shift employment, I draw from the life histories of two women: Shilpa and Poonam, both introduced in Chapter Three. Their lives, though divergent in many ways, reflect how economic mobility can, in one instance, transform gender roles beyond expectation and, in another, shift gender dynamics with little change to a woman's "place."

It is important to point out that although both women work at night, their positions constitute a higher rung of outsourcing that intersects with customer service, sales, and engineering. Employed in positions that have more prestige, they work directly for a top U.S.-based IT company on the Fortune 500 list. Although the actual content of their work does not fit the profile of an entry-level call center employee, their cases illustrate that even as women continue to advance in this rapidly emerging nightscape labor force, conceptions of a woman's worth can change drastically while at the same time remain the same.

Shilpa: Money, Marriage, and the Male Inferiority Complex

Shilpa, a thirty-eight-year-old employee with an engineering degree, doesn't hold back when talking about her career, her marriage, and how she manages her husband's sense of inferiority in light of her success. In 1989, at the age of twenty-one, her first job paid her Rs 800 (US$18) a month. Seventeen years later she earns upwards of 10 lakh (US$22,171) a year. Her story follows:

> Born and raised in Bangalore, Shilpa said that she never considered a love marriage because her father is very strict and would have never allowed it. When it came time to marry, she was also told not to be demanding in terms of finding a husband with the her level of education because there were not as many men in her community that were on par with her. Her parents arranged her marriage to a man with a diploma and after the wedding they moved to Calcutta for his job. Within a year they returned to Bangalore and she describes her time there as lonely, miserable, and as a period in which she cried a lot.
>
> She moved in with her in-laws, which she termed a nightmare. The household consisted of seven people: brother-in-law, sister-in-law, father-in-law, mother-in-law, an unmarried aunt, her husband, and herself. She found the family to be highly possessive, particularly the aunt who had raised her husband and his two siblings while Shilpa's mother-in-law worked. After the birth of their first child, Shilpa was disturbed by how possessive the aunt was over her daughter. She pointed out that at times she felt that her husband and daughter were not hers but common property over which his family held domain.
>
> Describing her own household as one in which "my brother and I were treated the same," she quickly found that in her new home the rules were quite different. For starters, she was not allowed to eat all the food that was served at the table. In shock and dismay she learned that the nonvegetarian food was appropriated for her brother-in-law. Although her husband was sometimes allowed to eat nonvegetarian, the women were strictly denied. In addition to enforcing food segregation, her in-laws controlled her dowry of jewels and would gift them to other people. In some instances the aunt would pressure Shilpa to give a particular necklace to a relative who had taken a liking to it. Although the

intention of dowry is to provide women with a form of material independence when they enter their new household, in Shilpa's case, as in many others, the dowry became common property.[9]

The dire economic situation that Shilpa and her husband experienced on their return to Bangalore made matters worse. Shilpa worked as a teacher from 7:30 A.M. to 2:30 P.M. and her starting salary was Rs 1,200 (US$27) per month. She remained in teaching for five years in order to be home in time for their children. She was given a Rs 50 (US$1) salary increase on a yearly basis and by the time she left she was earning Rs 1,400 (US$31) per month. Her income combined with her husband's income was no more than Rs 3,000 (US$67) a month, of which they gave Rs 2,000 (US$44) to the family to cover household expenses. Her in-laws would make disparaging remarks about their income and she was unable to buy things for herself because of the family scrutiny. As a result, she would attempt to keep her purchases a secret.

Describing herself as plump when she married, Shilpa said she became thinner and thinner because of the stressful dynamics in the household. People around her saw what was going on and directed comments such as "She was such a nice girl, what have you done to her?" toward her in-laws. With the help of jewels from her dowry, Shilpa's parents intervened by providing a property in her name. This allowed Shilpa to leave her in-laws and start a nuclear home with her husband and children.

Shilpa decided to leave her teaching job and take a night shift job because it provided her with the career opportunities she was looking for and a much higher salary. Her monthly salary has steadily progressed from Rs 7,000 to Rs 12,000, then to Rs 30,000 (US$155, US$266, and US$665, respectively) to a current salary of Rs 50,000 (US$1,109). She receives bonuses that bring her annual income to approximately 10 lakh (US$22,171) per year. In addition, her company awarded her a four-day all-expenses-paid trip to Malaysia. Her husband has worked steadily in the newspaper industry and currently earns Rs 20,000 (US$443) per month.

Shilpa is fully aware that she manages her husband's ego in relation to her success. She has an engineering degree but he has only a diploma. It would take him more than four months to earn what she does in one. She speaks of his condescending manner toward her when they first married, that he would pick on her about obscure things and put her down in front of other people with comments such as "You're an engineer. You should know this." As her salary progressed through the years, she worried about what would happen to their relationship when her earnings outstripped his.

Instead of the worst, she has found that her husband is now very proud of her and, according to Shilpa, "With money, a strained relationship became good." Her income is held in a common account that he manages. In discussing how they came to this arrangement, she explains that as a child she watched her mother hand over her earnings to her father. Similarly, she gives her money to her husband and it is not lost on her that "it makes him feel good because he has an inferiority complex."

In terms of managing the household, her husband is in charge of the finances and buying provisions. She tells him, "Whatever rotten vegetables you buy, I will cook." When asked about her husband's role in the education of their children, she said he does not look after them. He believes that studying with children is ladies work. In fact, when Shilpa had her second child, her mother was against it because she knew her son-in-law "would not cooperate" and her daughter would bear the responsibility of raising the child. Her mother's hesitancy also stemmed from the hardships she faced raising two children while working and she thus felt it was better to have only one.

At the close of our interview, Shilpa recalled that she didn't need money growing up because both of her parents worked and took care of her. On the basis of her experience living with her in-laws, she said, she now understands the importance of money and believes that it is equally important for the mother to earn an income. Although she initially took less challenging and lower paying jobs so she could be home in time to attend to her children, she believes that as her children grow, she too must grow as an individual. In other words, some women are able to interpret unequal demands and expectations in ways that nonetheless offer them a sense of empowerment. Finally, she makes the following point about arranged marriage: if there is a problem with the marriage, it is the fault of the parents because they chose the spouse. If she had found someone on her own and problems ensued, then she would be blamed for making a bad decision.

Poonam: From Day Factory Worker to Night IT Career

Poonam is a thirty-two-year-old employee with a degree in civil engineering. In seven years her salary has increased almost twentyfold as she has gone from earning Rs 2,000 a month to earning Rs 5,000 a month (US$44 to US$111) to earning approximately 1 lakh a month (US$2,217). Confident and self-assured, she has refused to be hampered by the idea that a woman must always follow her husband wherever his career takes him. Married for ten years, she moved to Bangalore two years ago to pursue her own career goals. Her story follows:

> Born and raised in Chennai, Poonam's first office job out of college earned her Rs 5,000 (US$111) per month. Married at the age of twenty-two, she relocated to Madhya Pradesh with her husband, a college professor, and found work as a civil engineer in a cement factory.[10] Her salary decreased to approximately Rs 2,000 (US$44) a month, an income she terms negligible. Describing her experience working in a factory of more than a thousand employees, she said, "That was really tough because it used to be totally male dominated so they couldn't really accept a female who would come in and tell them what to do. . . . I was the only girl in the plant, basically." In time the laborers "came around" and she spoke of how she enjoyed the work because of the level of respect she had gained for taking on such a job.
>
> A year-and-a-half later she became pregnant and decided that civil engineering would not be a viable career over the long term. She turned to the IT sector because she considered the work to be easier. Of her time as a civil engineer she said, "It was nice when it was just my husband and I, but [then I] got pregnant and had a kid and realized it won't work. I didn't want to go back to it because it's very tiresome, but it was fun while it lasted."
>
> She returned to Chennai to stay with her parents and give birth. Thereafter she refused to return to Madhya Pradesh because she decided—and her husband agreed—that it would be better for her career to work in Chennai. This led to friction with her parents. After three or four months of living at home, her parents were pressured by their peers with comments such as "When are you going to leave her at her husband's place again?"
>
> Befuddled by her decision to stay in Chennai, her parents told her, "What will people say? What will society say? You can't stay with us!" To appease them, she visited Madhya Pradesh to "show face," to prove that everything was fine, and then immediately returned to her parents. Upon her return, the tension only grew worse. She took IT classes as a means to gain employment, which was viewed as irresponsible because it did not constitute a proper job. While spending one month working on a class project from her computer at home, Poonam recalled that her mother would constantly scream at her, "All the time you are sitting at computer. You don't do anything else. You don't take care of your kid!"

But after her class project was written up in a national newspaper, their views changed. She spoke of how proud her parents were after that, but they remained adamant about her not living with them. Knowing that her parents would pressure her to return to Madhya Pradesh if she did not find a job, Poonam secured employment with an IT company in Chennai. Thereafter her husband also secured a position in Chennai and the family was reunited.

Although her parents and in-laws assumed them to be "settled," Poonam was recruited to work at a Fortune 500 IT company in Bangalore. She accepted the position two years ago and moved to Bangalore on her own. Meanwhile, her in-laws in Chennai took care of their child. She explained that the reason her husband did not join her is because she was unsure if she would continue with the job.

Her husband expressed full support for her decision, but both friends and family members were appalled. A mother leaving behind a five-year-old child to pursue her own career goals was unheard of. "You can't do that. You cannot leave your child and go," was the response from her parents and in-laws. Her friends in Chennai called her crazy. Her coworkers would tell her "it's not worth leaving your family and doing this." When asked what kept her going in spite of detractors, she said, "It's just that I was convinced that what I was doing was right, so that's why I kept on it."

Upon her arrival in Bangalore, she moved into PG accommodations with a rent of Rs 3,000 (US$67) per month. Her stay was short-lived because the owners did not like her coming home late at night. Thereafter she rented a house and lived alone, an experience she describes as "good." "In fact, I liked living alone! [*Laughter*] I mean, you know, you are not answerable, right? I've not done anything in the morning, just have my coffee. Otherwise, if I were to live with my husband and kid I would probably have to do other things in the house."

Poonam lived away from her family for approximately twenty-one months. She would visit Chennai every other weekend, a journey she deemed stressful given the travel required and the demands of her new job. Three months prior to our interview, Poonam's parents and son, now seven years old, moved to Bangalore to live with her. Her husband remained in Chennai. Poonam purchased a flat with her own income, which is currently in excess of 10 lakh (US$22,171) per year. As she reflected on her lifestyle, she pointed out that she loves her job and garners a great deal of satisfaction in her career, but also recognized how working at night affects her family life. She said, "My kid is here and he likes to cuddle up to me, but I am not there. That is hard. He likes it when I read out to him. I miss out on a lot of things."

Throughout the course of this interview I was intrigued by what had led Poonam to pursue a life that runs counter to expectations of a married woman's place, which are (1) to be by her husband's side or at least in the same city, (2) to be at home to raise children or at least in proximity of them if one is working outside the home, and (3) to earn an income that supports a family, but certainly not enough for a woman to buy her own home and decide to live away from her husband. Her story is compelling because in contrast to women who migrate due to economic necessity, Poonam came from a family that did not need or, in the case of her elders, want such from her. A coworker who spoke in admiration of her remarked, "I could never do what she did." And unlike her male counterparts, who can migrate without being castigated as being bad fathers who do not care for their children, Poonam is viewed as an anomaly because her decision to be mobile does not fit the mold of where society expects a "good" mother to be.

Parent-Child Relations in The Household

By working at night and earning a relatively high salary, workers are also confronted with shifting parent-child relationships. The social stigma of working at night sometimes translates into contentious family dynamics in the household. Despite earning a salary that in many instances provides support to their families, some workers also face disdain and disregard in their households.

In addition to labeling women who work in call centers as too independent and bold, families view negatively the fact that they work at night. This dynamic illustrates how perceptions about women in the paid labor force extend beyond the actual work space. When women work outside the home, they disrupt their place in the household. In fact, call center employment *decreased* the social status of workers in some households, and a gendered narrative emerged as to why women who worked in call centers were looked down on.

Women perceived as sexually deviant, even if only by association (such as because they work in a call center), are viewed with suspicion. For parents who give precedence to the "What will people think?" narrative, the male-female camaraderie associated with the industry is a threat to the moral order to which they subscribe. Working in a call center gives the impression that their daughters are promiscuous, and this is viewed as marring the reputation of the entire family, not just the worker.

In some instances, call center employment has provided women with the means to assert their autonomy in ways that previously would have been unheard of. Karen, introduced in Chapter Five, spoke of how for years she'd had a rocky relationship with her father. After her mother passed away, her relationship with her father became even more tumultuous. Although she would not provide details on what led to their temporary estrangement, she spoke of how in a fit of rage and frustration she had moved out of her father's home and into a hostel. This was considered scandalous. She returned home after a few months and only after they had mended their relationship. While listening to her story it became clear that the income from call center employment had provided her with the financial means necessary to take a stand for herself.

During interviews and focus groups it became evident that the high salaries associated with the call center industry did not always buy women upward social mobility in the eyes of their parents or in social circles that judged such work as a job for the lazy and uninspired. This is not to suggest, however, that call center employment had a negative impact on all parent-child relationships. In some instances, it made them closer.

Elizabeth, the twenty-four-year-old who is the sole support of her widowed mother (see Chapter Five), pointed out that call center employment allows her to spend more money on her mom during the limited time they have together. Reflecting on the hardship her widowed mother endured as a single parent struggling to raise both Elizabeth and her brother on a meager teacher's salary, she stated, "I love my mom. I want to take care of her." This is significant because her brother does not help out. As Elizabeth's mother explained:

MS. GEORGE: I think she is gives me more support [*laughs*]. It's just opposite now [*laughs*]. She supports me. Always goin' [working], sometimes I go in depression. She says, "Why . . . why you're worried? I'm there, no . . . I'm your son, I'm your daughter, everything for you." So my son has gone, left na.

REENA: Yes, she had mentioned she had a brother and he works in a call center that's in Mumbai.

MS. GEORGE: So since he's earning now, he has separated. He's on his own.

REENA: Does he contribute to the household?

MS. GEORGE: Nothing. That is why he has left, no. He doesn't want to contribute [*laughs*] Haan . . . that's why she said no, "Don't worry ma, I'm there no, I'll do everything. I'll earn so much mama, don't worry . . . I'll take care, "Don't worry," she says.

In this situation, the economic mobility that Elizabeth gained from call center employment provided her with the means to take care of herself and her mother, whom she often spoke of in admiration. Elizabeth also made it a point to tell me she doesn't buy branded clothes or spend money hanging out with friends, because she is cognizant of how difficult life has been for her mother financially. Instead, she stated, she enjoys her mom's company and makes it a point to spend their free time together.

Prior to Elizabeth's call center employment, she and her mom would remain in the house or go for walks because they could not afford outside entertainment such as movies and restaurants. Although their life continues to be carefully budgeted due to previous household debts, Elizabeth beams with pride about how she now earns enough money so that "I can take my mom to whichever place she wants."

During a separate interview, her mother made the following comments regarding their relationship. Interestingly, Ms. George made it a point to connect their relationship to how she viewed Elizabeth's clothes and lifestyle in general:

REENA: How do you find that her job has impacted your relationship with her?

MS. GEORGE: No changes at all, no not at all. Just the same, as simple as ever. [*Laughs.*] Much more simple she has become, more. Always one plait. [I] always tell her, "leave your hair or tie a pony tail," No! Tight plait she wants to be!

Different she is [in comparison to other young women] . . . I always tell her short salwar kameez is in fashion, you also stitch no. "I don't like, mama. That will become out of fashion after someday. Long is always in fashion. That doesn't go out of fashion." Long salwar kameez's. Then, like any tops also she will wear no, she will not wear short tops, pant, jeans and all. She is very much conscious about her dressing, baba. That too at the trial wear [trying on clothes in a private dressing room] nothing should be seen. [*Laughs.*] Even if, even if I sleep next to her, by mistake if I touch her, she'll tell immediately, "You can't sleep properly, why are you touching?" [*Laughs.*] I'll tell her, "Then what you'll do when you get married? You will say to your husband same thing, I mean, "go!"?

Simple, *haan.* She has never worn sleeveless till now. She doesn't like sleeveless.

Even though Elizabeth is the primary breadwinner of the household and Ms. George is proud of her daughter for this, the night shift requirement of the job remains a source of contention. Ms. George wished her daughter did not have to work through the night to support them, and it was during a family interview at another employee's home that I gained an alternative understanding of why the night shift requirement is a source of angst for some mothers.

Nisha, the twenty-three-year-old whose father passed away unexpectedly (see Chapter Five), was one of the few employees whom I had the opportunity to interview at her home, among family. In fact, our meeting turned out to be happenstance. I had stopped her on the streets of Mindspace to ask for directions, and in conversing with her I mentioned my research. Without hesitation, Nisha gave me her phone number and invited me to her family's home for lunch on one of her days off. A week later, I spent the afternoon interviewing her and her forty-five-year-old mother, Ms. Mehta. Her nineteen-year-old sister also participated intermittently, along with their eighty-something-year-old neighbor, whom Nisha explained was like a grandmother to them.

When I asked Nisha about her parents' initial reaction to her taking a call center job, she explained that it was not a problem. Ms. Mehta began shaking her head in disagreement. Despite attending "family day" at her daughter's company and being impressed with the surroundings and the people, Ms. Mehta explained that even today she remains uneasy about Nisha working in a call center, because of the night shift requirement. Although she did not go into the "What will people think?" narrative that other employees complained their parents brought up, she did speak of receiving comments from neighbors such as, "How can you allow her?"

Instead of linking Nisha's job to concerns about her daughter being seen as promiscuous or as marring the family's reputation, Ms. Mehta described how uncomfortable it felt for her not to have her daughter around her at night. She stated, "When I sleep my daughter should be around me. This is how it was when I was growing up [in Rajasthan]." One of the ways in which Ms. Mehta deals with this is to call Nisha frequently to check up on her. During our interview it was made clear that this calling left Nisha exasperated; she complained about her mother calling her fifteen times in one night.

Reading some parts of this book, one might ascertain that the nightscape is generally a site of low-end labor positions that disrupt parent-child relationships on the home front and offer relatively little in the way of upward mobility. Although it is important to point out the constrictions that many women face, to ignore the openings it provides for some women leads to a skewed understanding of what the nightscape has to offer. Although she was an outlier to the scope of this research, Riya, a twenty-three-year-old college graduate, offered to provide such a perspective.

We met toward the end of my fieldwork on a train to Churchgate. Assertive, independent, and forthcoming, Riya took me to her grandparents' restaurant for a meal and shared her night shift aspirations with me. Riya is Rajasthani and grew up in Ahmedabad but moved to Mumbai for the job opportunities because, she said, if she stayed in Ahmedabad she would "just loaf around." She lives with her grandparents, who migrated to Mumbai more than fifty years ago and opened one of the first Thali restaurants in the city. Unlike the parents of many of the women I interviewed, Riya's parents were keen to see her travel and live abroad on her own, similar to her sister, who lives and works in the United States and travels around the world. Riya's mother, in fact, even offered to pay for her to attend school in Nottingham, England, and then in Toronto, Canada. Riya declined because "It's cold over there!"

Riya spoke of how she had recently applied for a type of call center job. In her words, it's a higher level position than a customer service job because she would work as a trader for overseas accounts. The night shift requirement of this position is based on the timing of whichever overseas stock exchange market she would trade in. She currently works as a trader for a company in Mumbai and cites two challenges of working for a local company. First, in addition to working the daytime hours of the market, she is also required to make three appointments per day with current or prospective clients. The client's home or office can be as far as Vashi, and often she does not reach her own home until 11 P.M. She is the only woman in her office and her colleagues remark to her about the extensive travel and long work hours, "We're guys, we do it; you're a girl and you're doing [it too]?" Late hours are so common for her that when she came home at 8 P.M. one evening, her grandparents asked if she had quit. The second problem she faces is sexual harassment from her clients.

Riya provided three reasons for wanting to transition to an off-shore client. First, the company to which she is applying provides transport. Before 10:30 P.M. they provide buses from Dadar, an area close to where she lives. After 10:30 P.M., shuttle transport between the office and her home is provided. To get to the company's offices, located in Powai, by public transport would typically take a commute of more than two hours each way. In Riya's opinion, however, the transportation package the company offers combined with the fact that there would be less traffic to deal with at night made the travel required for this job far less arduous compared to her current schedule. Second, she would not be required to make client visits, which would eliminate her current challenge of dealing with sexual harassment. Third, of course, is the money. This particular company procures contracts that generally require twenty to twenty-five people on a team to service an account. Individuals are hired and sent to the country for which they will be trading. So for instance, if New York requires traders, they will be brought there, all expenses paid. Her friend went to London and spoke of how profitable it was because in addition to being provided with accommodations, employees were paid 65 pounds a day (US$129). Riya learned that employees can return to India with upwards of 2.5 lakh (US$5,543).

When asked what her family thought of her night shift aspirations, Riya explained that her grandparents and parents are fine with her working through the night in Powai because of the transportation. Reflecting on why some parents do not like the idea of night shift work for their daughters, she made the point that parents are generally worried not only about security but also because "if something does happen there is no justice. A person can just disappear, and the heartache this would cause a family." Because an overarching safety net (meaning police and local government) is not in place to secure a woman's right to be out at night, women are compelled to self-police their mobility, and parents are compelled to maintain a watchful eye over them. Should a woman not follow societal expectations of when and where it's acceptable for her to be, particularly at night, her behavior is coded as risky and she is marked as "asking for it" should she meet with violence.

Wrap-Up

Indian women are labeled subservient and homebound in comparison to their Western counterparts. Poonam's story illustrates that some "third world" women leapfrog into lifestyles that even for Western women—the supposed gold standard of progress—are unusual. Her story also vividly illustrates that the East-West distinction used to define women is problematic. Furthermore, conceptualizing "woman" as a singular category is incomplete.[11] As feminist scholars point out, when identifying similar experiences of subordination and success among women, one needs also to acknowledge that individual livelihoods intersect with race, class, education level, and citizenship.[12]

Re-envisioning the category "woman" in the global arena beyond the dichotomy of East and West—and its subtext of exploited versus empowered, traditional versus modern—allows for an understanding of how women such as Poonam constitute a global network of workers who use their economic mobility to disestablish notions of a woman's place.[13] At the same time, it is important to remain cognizant of how the complex relationship among class, citizenship, and the feminization of labor is a reflection of the structural inequality embedded in global relations.[14] Poonam is certainly successful beyond the imagination of those who surround her, and she represents the upward mobility that can be gained when women take on the nightscape. At the same time, the demand for her labor comes from a desire for a "third world" worker whose skills can be purchased on the cheap while her U.S. counterparts earn a salary that is four to five times higher.

Earning a high income does not necessarily buy women respect in the home, as illustrated by Gita's husband, who continued to see it within his domain to have a wife by his side ready to "Serve food!" Instead, they gain a sense of independence from earning money like men. These women no longer have to ask husbands or parents for money, and they often support their households financially. On the flip side, this independence is tempered by having to downplay their actual economic contribution in order to assuage the inferiority complexes of the men in the house. And little has changed in terms of men taking on the "dirty work" of the household; these responsibilities have merely shifted to other women.

In terms of parent-child relationships, it is clear that call center employment has led to disruptions. Some parents have difficulty adjusting to their daughters not being at home with them, despite having visited the call center premises and approved of the working conditions. For others, roles have changed in the household as parents have come to feel that their children are now taking care of them in ways the parents assumed were their responsibility. The effect of call center employment on parent-child relations clearly varies, and as Karen's situation illustrates, in some cases it leads to a daughter rebelling in ways that previously were unheard of.

In closing, rules of place remain embedded as women continue to deal with societal beliefs. Certainly exceptions apply, as illustrated in the case of Poonam, but she was not the norm of women who participated in this study. Instead, she represents the potential that both scholars and policymakers associate with upward economic mobility.

7 Social Mobility
Other Openings and Constrictions

The call center becomes our marriage pool!

—Drasti, employee

You have no other life other than call center, except for your holiday.

—Denise, former employee

When I moved to Mumbai, I did not anticipate that a suburban Catholic church would provide a glimpse into how the call center industry shifts the social fabric of its workers. Concerned about some of the rapid social changes taking place, Father John described the perceptible shift he had witnessed over the past few years. A youth group he ran in 2001 was composed of twenty-five to thirty individuals between the ages of eighteen and twenty-three. By 2003 to 2004, membership had dwindled to zero. When he reached out to the community to find out why this had happened, he learned that the majority of these former churchgoers had joined a call center. They no longer had time to participate in church activities because they were sleeping during the day.

Parents approached Father John after sermons complaining that their children, after joining the call center industry, had no time for family and treated them with less respect. He described a conversation with one distraught dad:

One father was telling, "Father, I got very angry with my son. I told him, what are you doing with the money? Have you put in the bank?" Then boy turns to the father and says, "Dad," He used the word *bak, bak, bak* [blabbering nonsense]. "Don't talk too much, if you need some pocket money, tell me, I'll give. But don't talk too much." This is what the boy said to the father.

That a son would not only earn more money than his parents at a young age but also talk back to them is considered shocking. This points to how the income from call center employment disrupts the parent-child hierarchy in some households, as discussed in Chapter Six.

In this chapter I examine how working the night shift recodifies the social lives of call center workers. I begin by exploring how employees create and experience new social connections and spaces associated with call center employment, from forging new friendships to experiencing distress about missing family functions that were once an important part of their daily lives. I then focus especially on the marriage prospects of call center employees and discuss this in relation to the social stigmas that women experience as a result of going out at night. As will be evident from the findings in this chapter, working outside the home and earning a relatively high wage does not always lead to upward social mobility.

Social Crossings

Amish, the industry consultant, told me that in many industries coworkers generally come from the same class or educational background. Using his own path as an example, he explained that he and his coworkers shared a standard education required of consultants (an MBA) and came from the same middle-class background. I was similarly under the impression that call center employees were predominantly recent college graduates who came from middle-class families. The collegial work environment of the industry, combined with mainstream media stories, also gave me the impression that call center employment was merely a transitional space for young people between college and a "real" job. This was not the case at all.

In fact, what was most striking was the range of individuals who were brought together, particularly at the entry-level stage of the industry. A theme that emerged time and again from employees was that they were meeting people they had not had access to before: an engineer worked alongside a college dropout, a single mother who had barely completed high school was in a training class with a law student. Employees described how the shared connections they had previously experienced (such as attending the same school or college, studying the same subjects, having a comparable family background, aspiring to similar career goals, and having social and cultural beliefs in common) changed when they entered the call center workplace. Indeed, call centers offered alternative social networks and social connections.

Swati, the twenty-six-year-old employee (see Chapter Two) with a bachelor's degree in commerce, described working beside a medical student and the friendship that developed between them. This friendship was significant to Swati because she never imagined becoming friends with a future doctor. Since joining Company A more than three years ago, Swati had found that she "got the bestest friends . . . they will remain with you." The expansion of her social network was linked not only to what her colleagues did outside the call center, but also to where they came from. She described meeting people her age who lived on their own in PG accommodations and who came from places she considered far away, such as Pune. This experience was new to Swati because previously her friends had come from the same neighborhood and socioeconomic strata as she did. Her experience illustrates that call center employment affords some workers the opportunity to forge friendships and social connections with cross-sections of society previously inaccessible to them.

During an interview with Indira, a twenty-seven-year-old with a college degree in chemistry, and Manisha, the twenty-six-year-old (introduced in Chapter Three) who is a college dropout from an English literature program, each described the other as her best friend. Both have worked at the same call center for more than six years. Indira uses her money for investments and shopping because her parents do not rely on her income. Manisha, in contrast, dropped out of college to be the sole support of her widowed mother. Although she was unable to save money like Indira, Manisha's salary had provided the means to purchase a home three years earlier.

During a group interview at Inorbit Mall in Malad, Neil, a twenty-seven-year-old electrical engineer employed as a team leader for a call center, introduced me to Smita, the twenty-six-year-old former employee introduced in Chapter Three. She has an MBA in human resources and she and Neil described themselves as best friends who met through the call center. Across from Smita sat Lopa, the twenty-two-year-old employee who has worked in the industry for four years and is now in a quality analyst position (see Chapter Five). She completed twelfth standard and does not have plans to attend college. Neil and Lopa met at the office and are now engaged. Halfway through the interview, two more of their friends arrived. One was a twenty-five-year-old manager engaged to a woman who is keeping him a secret from her parents; the other was a twenty-something voice and accent trainer.

What made this group meeting—along with the previous discussion with Swati, Indira, and Manisha—compelling was that it reflected the variety of individuals brought together as a result of joining the industry. Through their stories and descriptions of friendship ties, I learned that among these employees was a chemist who aspires to return to scientific research via knowledge process outsourcing, a college dropout who dreams of being a writer, an MBA graduate who hated working in a call center, an electrical engineer whose father is ashamed of his career path, and a high school graduate looking to join the ranks of upper management. All work under one roof and, in many instances, trained for the same entry-level positions. This occurred within a societal framework that generally believes a person should be employed in a position that is in line with his or her level of education.

The individuals just described, though divergent in many ways, reflect a melting pot of sorts in terms of the social camaraderie they formed while working in a call center. I do not use the term *melting pot*, however, to suggest that call centers are an egalitarian space void of structural inequality. Previous research and responses from employees in this study point to varying forms of inequality, ranging from occupational segregation to low wages relative to the actual output demanded of workers.[1] I use this term instead to describe how the call center, as a social space, provides some employees with the means to forge social networks outside of their familial and educational social circles.

For individuals who came from families who lacked access to or interest in mixing with those outside their community, or for those whose parents maintained strict regimes of surveillance and control over their lives, the opportunity to interact with people of varying educational, social, and economic backgrounds is generally seen as a bonus. Call center employees, despite their educational differences, work side by side, often as part of a team. In the entry-level space of a call center, a college dropout trains and takes calls beside an engineer. This setup is different from other workplace hierarchies that, for example, place the high school graduate in a secretarial position for the engineer. This type of spatial setting is a twist on boss-worker relationships that use individuals' educational or class status to define their place in a workplace hierarchy.

Responses to the social aspects of this industry reflect the individual's background. Kriti, the twenty-three-year-old who opened a boutique with her call center income, attended a women's college and had little opportunity to interact with men. The call center drastically changed that. "There are more boys than girls," said Kriti. As a result, she found herself forming more friendships with men. Describing herself as shy, she recalled that working at a call center gave her more confidence. This theme emerged throughout the study as women who described themselves as shy and introverted used terms such as *confident, bold,* and *outgoing* to illustrate how working in a call center had changed them.

Valerie, the Xavier College graduate discussed in Chapter Five, joined the industry despite the opinion of her peers that working in a call center was a step down. She explained that her previous social network was through the college and she didn't like it because it was mainly rich people, whom she associated with name-dropping and snobbish behavior. In contrast, she viewed the friends she had made via the call center industry to be "down-to-earth and simple."

Smita had quite a different opinion and did not hold back when asked what she thought about call centers, "I hate those call center people!" She related the industry to Maslow's hierarchy of needs, a popular psychology theory on what motivates individuals, and stated that call center employees were stuck at the bottom because there was no creativity in the job and the work was monotonous. She said, "The work is not for the brain." In contrast to women who spoke of liking the job because they were exposed to an array of people outside their previous social network, Smita viewed her former colleagues, with the exception of her friend Neil, as "a different breed of people" who lack direction and focus in their lives because they get caught up in the money they make. This again points to the divisive class relations that sometimes emerge in the call center environment.

Hanging Out, Hanging Back

Just as call centers open up new social connections, they open up new social spaces as well. Indeed, some women reported using their call center income to hang out on nights off and on holidays. Yet the vast majority reported going straight home after work. Some companies, in fact, had regulations that shuttle drivers were not to drop off employees anywhere except their homes. After finishing a Friday night shift, employees faced with this company policy but wanting to meet with friends after work were not allowed to use company transport to be dropped off at a café. The inescapable delivery of women to their parents' doorstep not only was done out of concern for the women's safety, but also was a means to alleviate family anxiety about women socializing in inappropriate ways during the night.

The two places most cited by participants as the place for them to hang out on their nights off and on holidays were movie theaters and malls such as Inorbit in Malad, Center One in Vashi, and Phoenix Mills in Lower Parel. Linking Road in Bandra—famous for its roadside shoe vendors and array of faux fashion—was also mentioned. After that, cafés and discos were cited.

Call center employment certainly afforded some women the opportunity to hang out and socialize in ways that were previously unavailable to them. Employees who participated in this study pointed to the positive aspects of call center employment, such as meeting new people and working in a globalized environment. At the same time, they were aware of the constriction they experienced. Although the industry is associated with workers who have money to party and hang out, eighteen out of twenty-five women who discussed their social life in depth experienced confinement in this aspect of their lives.

The most common response to how call center employment affected one's social life was, "I hardly have time for family and friends." Saloni, a twenty-two-year-old, for instance, was saddened that the friends she used to hang out with on a regular basis had now transformed into "phone friends." She believes that employees sacrifice a lot to work the night shift, especially in their personal relationships. Denise, the former employee quoted in Chapter Four, stated, "You have no other life other than call center, except for your holiday." Elizabeth, who supports her widowed mother (see Chapter Five), stated that working in a call center had not changed her social life or night life, but she pointed out that it was becoming more acceptable in Mumbai for a woman to be out at night, whereas in places such as Goa, a holiday destination, it was still not as acceptable, she believed.

The trade-off for the constriction of time caused by sleeping during the day and missing out on social venues that were part of the pre–call center lifestyle was, Amish said, that call centers provide food, entertainment, transportation, and a social environment that would otherwise not be accessible to women. He described the call center environment as one that gave women a chance to be independent. Without a doubt, the "cool" work environment described by some employees was in direct contrast to the job opportunities previously available to them. Furthermore, the night shift requirement provided some women with the means to go out at night, whereas previously their families had prohibited this behavior. Surprisingly, however, Jyothi, the twenty-five-year-old manager mentioned in previous chapters, revealed that the independence associated with this industry was by no means uniform and absolute.

Earning more than 30,000 rupees per month (US$800) and raised in a family that did not need or require her to contribute to household expenses, Jyothi earned enough money to purchase clothes, eat out, take rickshaws, and go on vacations. In essence, she had the money to be mobile in ways that were beyond the reach of many of her coworkers, particularly those whose families depended on call center income for their livelihood. In addition, she was one of three participants who spoke of having relatives living in the United States whom she'd be welcome to visit.

Did her money and transnational connections translate into independence outside her work environment? Would it be fair to assume that earning one's own money leads directly to increased social and temporal mobility, particularly for single women who make a relatively high income and do not support a family? The answer in Jyothi's case is no. In fact, her social life was the most sequestered and controlled of the employees I met in Mumbai. Earning her own income did not translate into breaking free of the mobility-morality narratives that bound her to a strict work-to-home, family-centered lifestyle. She was occasionally given permission to hang out with call center friends on a day off, such as to buy clothes for a family event, but this permission had to be strategically negotiated, and under no circumstances was she allowed to stay out all night or crash at a friend's place. In fact, at the age of twenty-five, Jyothi had never slept away from her family. It was forbidden.

After years of working the night shift, Jyothi moved into her current management position and now works a 2 P.M. to 10 P.M. shift. Despite her previous night shift schedule, she was not allowed to go out after work and was expected to return home promptly. During an interview, as well as while observing her at the office, I noticed that she was at times harried and nervous about not missing the transport that would have her home within the time frame her parents demanded. When asked about this, Jyothi explained that her parents are protective.

Jyothi's story illustrates that upward economic mobility and temporal mobility, in the form of earning a relatively high wage and working at night, does not necessarily translate into increased social mobility. Certainly not all women in this study experienced the level of constriction that Jyothi did, and in some cases other women in her situation were more apt to take chances by sneaking around. But the ways in which Jyothi self-surveilled her mobility, such as keeping an eye on the clock so as not to be home even a few minutes later than her parents demanded, were things I observed throughout the course of my fieldwork. Some women, for example, were hyperaware of keeping to their time and place so as to avoid questions about where they were and what they were up to when not at home.

Marriage and Family

During the course of fieldwork it became apparent that gendered narratives are used to degrade both female and male call center employees, particularly in terms of their social capital in the marriage market. In fact, one of the more surprising findings, at least to this researcher, was the disdain that parents had toward the idea of their son or daughter marrying a call center employee.

Women working in call centers actually face a triple bind. First, the income itself is a source of anxiety to some families. This anxiety draws from the belief that women who earn their own money—and a high income at that—are too bold and lack family values. This does not bode well for their marital worth.

The second bind stems from the night shift requirement. Staying out all night to earn one's own money interferes with the day shift state of servitude that women are expected to embody and perform in the household. Vipin, a recently married twenty-five-year-old employee from Ahmedabad, said it would not be possible for his wife to work as he does because "it would interfere with her duties in the house." Prakash, a single twenty-four-year-old from Bangalore, called household labor "dirty work." Referring to arranged marriage, he said:

> She does not marry a guy, she does not marry the love of her life, she just marries into a family where she has to do the daily chores for in-laws. The women are coming out of this, but the guys are not comfortable with this.

Going out at night also mars a woman's sexual reputation, a concern among prospective husbands and in-laws searching for brides they believe to be chaste and "homely." The third bind relates to the fact that working at night to earn an income is a source of stigma that, combined with the *nature* of the job, marks women as low-skilled workers. This in turn does little to change a woman's marital worth, because her income, although perhaps vital to the economic survival of the family unit, is degraded as easy money.

In addition, women face cultural expectations related to their age. The women I interviewed in Mumbai generally stated that in their society it is expected that they be *settled* by the age of twenty-five. They also shared that their parents would much prefer them to be married by the ages of twenty-one to twenty-three. At the same time, the call center industry generally recruits employees from the eighteen- to twenty-five-year-old demographic. This practice directly intersects with a key rite of passage for women: marriage and having children.

Preeti, a twenty-five-year-old interior decorator I met on a train ride to Churchgate, told me that despite the drastic social changes that Mumbaikars have experienced over the past few years, many women her age are still compelled to ask a potential husband and in-laws, "Will I be *allowed* to work?" A similar sentiment was voiced during interviews with call center employees. Devaki, introduced in Chapter Four, had worked in the industry for thirteen months. The only child of a Sindhi family (the Sindhi are a socioethnic group that originally belonged to the province of Sindh, which became a part of Pakistan after Partition of India in 1947), she told me that her parents want her to marry by age twenty-two or twenty-three. She views this time frame as a problem for women, particularly in the arranged marriage market, because the groom and his parents may not want her to work. She was quick to point out that she would refuse such a marriage because she wants to work. Devaki is currently dating a man who holds a day job as an architect; he doesn't stand in her way of pursuing a night shift call center career. They belong to different religions and are currently making plans to marry. Their parents support her decision to pursue a career.

The right to work outside the home is not only about taking care of one's family. As illustrated in the previous chapters, it is also about garnering access to the dignity and esteem that one gains from being self-directed. Preeti and Devaki illustrate the challenges women face in pursuing a career outside the home and in dealing with ideologies about a woman's marital place. Both refuse to accept a marriage that requires them to be homebound. The fact that they not only voice such a desire but are also safe enough to assert their will reflects how far society has come for some women. At the same time, the fact that women continue to have to ask permission (that is, be allowed) to behave in ways that are considered the norm for men (such as working outside the home) reflects how divided gender roles remain. It also provides an understanding that patriarchal regimes of *who's the boss* remain a part of this society.

Yet men working in call centers also faced stigma. Even though call center employment is viewed as a way to gain upward economic mobility, the money does not increase an employee's worth in the marriage market. Among the middle-class households, the money from call center employment is negated by its lack of professional prestige. For women it is linked to the belief that they are promiscuous because they are out at night and mixing with men, whereas for men it is linked to the belief that call center employment is not a secure job.

Still, call centers were also viewed by some employees as an opening in terms of creating new avenues for young people to meet each other, perhaps reshaping the tradition of arranged marriage. During an interview about the impact that call center employment had on her family and her social life, Drasti exclaimed, "The call center becomes our marriage pool!"[2] She explained that her parents in Delhi wanted to arrange a marriage for her but were unable to because she was sleeping during the daytime hours in which she was expected to meet her prospective husband and in-laws. In this respect, call center employment provides a means for some women and men to reject the arranged marriage market, because they view this tradition as outdated. Also, according to Valerie, viewpoints about the marital worth of women who work in call centers are based on "weird logic."

With the exception of two women, both the men and women who contributed to this study stated outright that their families would *not* want them to marry a call center employee, even though they themselves were in the industry. Questions about marrying a coworker generally brought about hushed tones of "oh no." Others stated outright that their parents would throw them out if they did.

Diya, introduced in Chapter Five, lives on her own and was the only woman in this study to drive her own car to and from work. Employed at WebCorp for six years, she recalled that her mother's reaction to the possibility of her marrying a coworker was "[you] finally found someone like you, working night shift, a nocturnal animal." The other interviewee who reported the same parental response was Vanathi, a twenty-seven-year-old employee who lives with roommates. She said, "If I meet somebody at WebCorp, I can bring him home and they can get me married. They would be happy to give me a grand wedding."

Back in Mumbai, during an interview with Denise, I asked her mother, Ms. Paul, what she would think if Denise married a call center employee:

MS. PAUL: I hope not!
REENA: Why?
MS. PAUL: Because of the timings, obviously.
DENISE: Well, I think it's just because "Where's he working?" "Oh, he's working at a call center."
MS. PAUL: Yeah, people say. . . .

Ajay, the manager at a top firm in Mindspace (see Chapters Three and Five), explained that his fiancé is afraid to tell her father about him for the very reason given by Ms. Paul. Ajay stated that his future father-in-law, a colonel in the Indian army, will look down on him despite the fact that he has a college education, is in a management position, and earns a salary that far surpasses the salaries of managers in other industries. It is generally believed that money, in the form of financial stability, is an indicator of a man's marital worth, whereas a woman's sexuality, which is expected to be nonexistent prior to marriage, is the foundation of her worth.[3] Ajay's situation, however, illustrates that one's value on the marriage market is more complex. Money alone is not enough to buy him respect in his fiancé's family.

Interviewees revealed that some men don't want to marry a woman who works in a call center. Ms. George, the mother of Elizabeth, explained, "You know gents, how they are, suspicious they'd be. Some trust their wife fully, some don't. That's why they don't like the wife to go out." The night shift requirement and social camaraderie associated with the call center environment are viewed with suspicion and degrade the respectability of women in social spaces outside the call center.

Another reason some men don't want to marry a call center employee is linked to the belief that a man is supposed to be the primary breadwinner of a household, so the money women make in a call center is a source of anxiety. According to Prakash, the twenty-four-year-old from Bangalore:

If the guy finds out after this arranged marriage thing that, you know, the girl is not all that, the way she's supposed to be or the way he expected her to be, and she says, "I want to go and work," he would probably say yes first. Thinking about the math and all that, getting in the salary, double income, all that works, in a sense he might say yes.

Then what if she starts earning more? Then this guy is done for. He is over. He cannot digest that fact because what does this fellow know? He knows that he should be the primary breadwinner and if he cannot be that, that's it, that's the route. The reasons could be many [for why] he doubts his wife, that even can come up between the husband and wife. This guy could say, if she comes home late, he could accuse her of sleeping with somebody else. But all this is just, it's manifested out of basic breadwinner. The whole concept comes from that. If he is not able to be the primary contributor to family income, he cannot survive. His ego will eat him up.

Come marriage time, in fact, it was reported, some parents force their daughters to quit their job because they don't want them to be known as a "call center girl" in the arranged marriage market. Interviewees pointed out that this reaction is linked to a concern that a woman won't "get a *good* [my emphasis] guy" if she works in a call center. *Good* in this case refers to the socioeconomic status of the groom and his family, and it is also indicative of the fact that, just like women, men who work in a call center become marked as the *bad* guy.

During a group interview, Lopa reported that a friend of hers was forced to quit for this very reason. I was unable to interview an employee in this predicament, given the secrecy surrounding the matter. Also, if I were to pursue women in this situation and their families found out, I would cause more trouble than good.[4]

Karen, the twenty-four-year-old employee introduced in Chapter Five, predicted that in the future it will be vogue to marry within a call center. To date, accurate data on the number of married women who work in the industry are unavailable, but employees did report witnessing an increase in the number of married women at their offices. It was suggested that this was because employees were marrying their coworkers. Sheila, a training manager at Company A, pointed out that a common saying used to describe such couples is, "They come in a package deal." In an e-mail conversation she wrote:

> If one quits the other soon will too. . . . Even if one is sick the other one stays home. . . . Hugely annoying when you have both in the same process* or in my case . . . In the same training batch. I even had one couple say that they would quit if we didn't put them in the same process.

(*Process* means working on a specific account, such as credit card service, airline reservations, and so on.)

Some companies provide special provisions for married couples as a means to address their need for family time outside the office. At Company A, for instance, I was informed that all married people are given weekends off. Previously, as a means to accommodate them, married women could request one of the few coveted day shift positions and be given preference. That option, however, is no longer available.

None of the thirteen married participants in this study was wedded to a coworker. All of the women had been married prior to joining the industry, to men with day jobs. Usha, a twenty-something manager at TYJ Corporation, described her relationship with her husband as "ships in the dark." She and her coworkers joked about this being the reason they have no children (that is, no time for sex).

Heena, the thirty-three-year-old married employee mentioned in Chapter Four who has a diploma in engineering and instrumentation, has worked at Company A for four years. Previously she worked as a lab technician, then she got pregnant and stayed at home with their daughter, now ten years old. She described her years at home as boring and said she decided to give the call center industry a try because it was something different to do. She stated that she enjoys the work environment because she is around young, energetic people and her social circle now draws mostly from people in the call center industry. Heena was also the only married woman in this study to describe her husband helping out in the household. In contrast to Anan's husband, the mechanical engineer who expected Anan to prepare his tea and get his clothes ready, Heena's husband—the owner of a travel agency—wakes up early to get their daughter ready and take her to school. Although the call center represented a space of social camaraderie, Heena was also saddened that the night shift makes its impossible for her to spend quality time with her family during the week, and she misses out on family functions.

In contrast to Heena, who wanted to try something new, Michelle and Sariya, also married, joined the industry because their families needed the money. Yet they also pointed out that they could no longer attend the family functions that used to be a regular part of their lives. This was a common complaint that emerged throughout the course of this study. In regard to developing a social life via the call center, Sariya explained that her social life outside her family stayed the same after joining the industry. She described it as "There is none."

Anjali, the former employee who used her call center income to start a nonprofit organization (see Chapter Five), had an entirely different work experience. After living with roommates, she moved in with her boyfriend, whom she met at the call center, and they secretly lived together for four years. To avoid harassment and the risk of being thrown out, they lied to the neighbors and said they were married. She explained that she didn't have the courage to tell her parents, who also lived in Mumbai, because her behavior was taboo. Working in a call center and moving away from home was bad enough in the eyes of her family, so for them to discover that she was also living with a boyfriend from the call center would have sent them into hysterics. Put another way, she engaged in high-risk behavior that came with possible dire, long-term consequences.

When her parents visited, she would hide his clothes under the bed and "wipe out all trace of [the] man" from the flat. During our interview in October 2006 she explained that she had recently moved back to her parents' home. Her boyfriend had moved to Bangalore for work and they maintained a long-distance relationship. By December 2006, however, the relationship had come to an end.

The freedom to take risks is vital to creating a dramatic shift in the experiences women can access. This assertion draws from Shilpa Phadke's research on women's mobility in Mumbai.[5] She contends that in order to increase women's access to public spaces, what they need is not so much provisions for their safety but the right to take risks.[6] Although Anjali's experience does not represent the norm for women in this study, her story illustrates that call center employment can change the lifestyle of individuals who decide to behave in ways deemed reckless.

Disruptive Women: A Comparative Context

Degrading women who disrupt societal expectations is certainly not new. On the surface, it may appear that women experience censure primarily when they "behave like a man." Yet as is demonstrated in the following discussion of nurses in the United States, call center workers in India, and factory workers in Bangladesh, even when women take on jobs deemed "ladies work," they continue to experience social stigma. This in turn impedes the social mobility of both themselves and, in some cases, their families.

Sheba Mariam George's ethnographic account of Keralite women who migrated to the United States as nurses offers an insightful parallel to the experiences of female call center employees, particularly in terms of how women come to embody and experience social stigma when they work outside the home.[7] The migration pattern from India to the United States is viewed as one in which men come first. It is generally assumed that they are the carriers of a skill set that leads the way. *When Women Come First*, George's study of women who moved to the United Stated to work as nurses, reveals how gender relations fare when the opposite occurs. Despite earning a salary that was in many instances the sole support of their husband and children, and earning enough money to send remittances back to their family in India, the nurses in George's study faced disdain from the Keralite community, in both the United States and Kerala.

In addition to the nurses being labeled too independent and bold, their nursing work itself was viewed as dirty work. This attitude was linked to the Hindu custom of not touching random bodies, a rule that women are held to with stricter scrutiny. Under this rubric, women who work as nurses are "polluted." This gendered symbol for *womanhood gone awry* transformed into derogatory remarks. The women were labeled "dirty nurses" by the community, and the husbands of these so-called dirty nurses came to bear the label nurse-husband, an emasculating term. Nurse-husbands were viewed as taking a step back for staying at home while their wives earned a living. Even if they worked outside the home, nurse-husbands were snubbed because of the assumption that their wives provided the financial base of the family.

This dynamic illustrates that perceptions about women in the paid labor force extend beyond the actual work space. When women work outside the home, they disrupt their place in society. In turn, it is not only they but also the men connected to them who experience censure. During the course of this study, a term for the husband of a call center employee did not emerge, but George's account illustrates that perceptions about women in the workforce do not operate in a vacuum. Similar to the Keralite nurses, women employed in the call center industry face disdain despite earning a relatively high salary. For the most part, the disdain is less about the actual content of the job and more about women earning high salaries while traversing the urban night, a space generally considered off-limits to them.

Working as nurses also affected the lives of their children, particularly when marriage time came around. In the transnational marriage market, George found, parents would reject marriage proposals from the United States when it was discovered that the mother of the prospective spouse was a nurse. As stated by one of George's interviewees:

> When they were looking for a wife for my husband's nephew, they didn't want
> the daughter of a nurse. There was one proposal where the mother was a nurse
> and the family was outside India—very wealthy—and offered a lot of money
> as dowry. The girl was very well educated, but they said no because she was a
> nurse's daughter. And so there are still some people who don't like nurses.[8]

This case illustrates the point that money does not always buy upward social
mobility, particularly when it's the women who bring home the family bread.
India's transnational call center industry is relatively new and it is unclear
how the social stigma surrounding employment in this industry will play into
the lives of an employee and, in the future, her children. George's findings,
however, gives us insight into the fact that stepping outside the norms of convention creates long-term shifts that affect future generations. This conclusion is not to suggest that call center employment is bad for workers and their
families; instead it illustrates the possible effect that such work may have in
shaping the social fabric of future generations. On the one hand, the money
from call center employment bolsters a family's economic mobility. On the
other hand, the stigma related to working the night shift may impede social
mobility within the very communities that have been part and parcel of a
worker's life.

Although they were aware of the stigma associated with working in a call
center, employees did not report a personal sense of degradation, particularly
as it related to their martial worth. Instead they focused on the possibilities
that working in a call center gave them, ranging from the sense of independence they felt from earning their own money to their pride in being the first
one in their family to "do something different." Women also pointed out that
they didn't care "what those people think," because they were not interested in
an arranged marriage or, in some cases, in any form of marriage.

Such responses to the societal backlash that women face for going against
convention were similar to Nazli Kibria's findings on women employed in the
garment factories in Bangladesh.[9] The sexual reputations of both garment employees and call center employees were marred because of their work, primarily because garment labor is considered lower-class work and call center
employment required women to work at night. Call center employees refuted
the degraded sense of self-worth that society sought to imprint on their bodies
by pointing to the independence and money gained from working in this in-

dustry. Similarly, Kibria found that garment workers refuted notions of their "challenges" in terms of finding a spouse. As stated by one woman, "Because I am self-sufficient, I can go where I want and marry whom I want."[10]

Nursing also was not immune from sexual degradation. A Keralite man living in the United States refused to marry a nurse because they are regarded as proud, willful, and disobedient.[11] Another man links this disdain to the attitude toward nurses: "It is a sexual kind of thinking. You can get them for anything. They are loose."[12] In this case, "get them" refers to the belief that nurses are more accessible, whether as marriage prospects or as one-night stands, in comparison to other women.

Whether they work in customer service, garment production, or nursing, when women go against convention, their behavior is met with anxiety, even if the work they do is construed as "ladies work." Regardless of whether a job requires a college degree, as nursing does; a high school education at minimum, as call center employment does; or little to no education, as factory work does, when paid labor translates into women staying out at night, living on their own, or being the breadwinner of a family, they are viewed as a threat to urban, male order. This happens regardless of their education or class strata.

Wrap-Up

Social stigma is spatialized and mobilized in the lives of workers in ways that go beyond the actual work site. Furthermore, social mobility and social barriers, whether gaining entry into the latest club or no longer being considered a great catch in the marriage market, intersect not only with the amount of money one earns, but also with how it is earned. Anjali and her former boyfriend splurged one evening to dine at an upscale restaurant. When the owner learned that they worked in a call center, Anjali said they were snubbed as posers who lack real wealth and prestige. The owner chided them with comments such as, "Oh, so you work at the call center? You all are always wasting money and blowing it on entertainment." Of this experience she wrote:

> We did not feel like eating after that. For a lot of people it's an important transit opportunity and people are making the best of it and previously these kinds of employment options were not available. But somehow everything becomes a moral issue rather than a livelihood issue. As a society we are still there. In one

way there are checks and balances and some preservation of common values, but most of the time it's a hindrance.

In the end, then, call center employment, for the most part, did not increase the social status or mobility of employees. Furthermore, when women work in ways that disrupt gendered notions of place, they are perceived as degrading the reputation of themselves and their family.

Nurses, for example, experience scrutiny because they are seen as entering *those dirty spaces* that pollute their womanhood, spaces where unfamiliar bodies are in contact with each other, even if it is for healing purposes. Similarly, female call center employees experience scrutiny because they are seen as entering *those sexy spaces*, in that the urban night symbolizes deviance and sexual promiscuity, even if it is purely a time for working. In both cases they are marked as the *bad girl*. By entering those "dirty, sexy spaces," women bear the brunt of the mobility-morality narratives discussed in Chapter Three. Put another way, nurses are contaminated symbolically by working where bodies make contact, and call center workers are contaminated symbolically by working during a time that is constructed as off-limits to them.

In general, the high salaries of the industry, though considered a financial boon, do not buy women respect outside the office environment. Although interviewees reported that in the past three to four years it was slowly becoming more acceptable to work in a call center, the social stigma surrounding night shift work remained. Even as workers are introduced to a wider pool of individuals from a variety of backgrounds, they are also confronted with their own prejudices against groups that are different from themselves.

Sleeping through the day—a result of working all night—also interfered with some of the social obligations to which women were expected to conform, such as meeting potential marriage prospects and, once married, taking care of in-laws in the household. This was a source of concern to parents because call centers draw from a pool of women workers who are at their prime in terms of being of marriageable age. Instead of a woman's marital value increasing because she earns a high wage, she is degraded by working at night. This is significant in a society that views a woman's marriage prospects as a marker of her worth.

In closing, call center employment affects the social mobility of workers in a variety of ways. Although for some it is just a paycheck to support their families, for others it provides access to a social life that was previously beyond their reach. One thing is clear: the openings and constrictions associated with how call center employment affects workers' social lives are largely dependent on the positionality of the workers themselves. And despite labels that mark employees as primarily middle-class and college educated, it became apparent during the course of fieldwork that the individuals who fuel the growth of this industry hail from a myriad of backgrounds.

8 Conclusion

Geography is irrelevant.
—Sudip Banerjee, President of Enterprise Solutions at Wipro Spectramind[1]

Geography is history. Distances don't matter anymore.
—Raman Roy, Chairman of Infosys[2]

Although geography no longer matters to some company executives, the reality is that profits exist only in the realm made possible by geographical difference. The experiences of the women who contributed to this book also illustrate that geography is alive and well. Indeed, the hypermobility of multinational corporations roaming the globe in search of an accessible, cost-effective labor pool certainly creates new employment opportunities for urban, English-speaking women in India. Yet when a woman is chastised by her father for wanting to work at night—call center job equals call girl job!—it is a reflection of how the hypermobility enjoyed by twenty-first-century capital is not necessarily shared by the twenty-first-century global workforce. The geographic mobility of daily life—whether the right to leave one's house at night or the right to travel about as one sees fit—speaks volumes in terms of how women experience gendered notions of place, particularly when it comes to working the night shift and the stigma this entails.

Key Findings

By working in transnational call centers in India, women inevitably enter "the hooker shift." As suggested by changes in the gendered aspect of this industry (such as men's increased participation), when day shift work moves to night, men gain a foothold in jobs traditionally viewed as women's work, because going out at night is less of a contentious issue for men. In this respect, the night shift requirement of this industry is a barrier for women. Although the actual content of the work remains the same when it is exported, the gendered narrative on which it operates (that it is pink-collar work) is disrupted. Beliefs about night shift employment—and views related to who belongs out at night and who does not—play a role in determining women's participation in this industry.

For women who join the industry, the relatively high wages and global work environment are viewed by some as a means to challenge patriarchy. Amish, the industry consultant who exclaimed, "Women don't put up with shit anymore!" echoed the sentiment of scholars such as J. P. Pradhan and V. Abraham, who stated, "In India's patriarchal society, the emergence of call centers is nothing less than a social reform movement as far as economic, social and cultural empowerment of women is concerned."[3] As demonstrated in the lives of the women who participated in this study, call center employment does recodify the lives of women workers. The night shift requirement of this industry, in combination with a relatively high salary and the opportunity to work in a global environment, provides some women with a *legitimate* reason to get out of the house. This escape is garnered under the rubric of skill acquisition, working in an office environment, or contributing to the support of the family.

However, the night shift aspect of this industry also means that patriarchal regimes of surveillance are recodified, because women must move about in ways that are deemed transgressive. Instead of revolutionizing gendered norms of mobility and spatial access, women in general continue to be held to stricter regimes of surveillance. Access to the urban night—justified by being paid workers in a somewhat legitimate profession, as opposed to prostitution—certainly represents a dramatic shift in when some women work outside the home. Their entry into the urban night does not, however, draw from re-envisioning women as individuals who have an inherent right to move about in any way and at any time they see fit. This type of re-envisioning—"to travel like a man"—would be truly revolutionary compared to what has so far occurred with the rise of women working the night shift.

The changes in women's mobility brought about by transnational call center employment reflect a dichotomy that provides women with a means to step outside the household in ways not experienced by previous generations.

At the same time it is based on maintaining gendered access to spaces outside the home. Concern for a woman's safety, for example, is used to control her mobility, especially at night. Women who go out alone at night continue to be viewed as an anomaly because it is expected that they will be accompanied by a man. Given that women are generally not the ones accountable for creating a violent or unsafe environment, the irony of this situation is that it's their bodies that bear the censure.

As one fifty-four-year-old woman from Ahmedabad pointed out, "If a man goes out to rape a woman at 10 o'clock at night, no one asks questions; but if a woman goes out, she is suspect!" Her comment raises the question, What if the mobility of men had to be negotiated through the use of identity cards and the presence of a female security guard or a female counterpart to ensure their safety, maintain their social reputation, and justify their presence in the urban nightscape? This dynamic might not be viewed as a protective force, but rather as an unnecessarily restrictive one. Figuratively speaking, women's bodies are under siege, and those who step outside the coveted norms of a woman's place are marked as a disruptive force to the moral order of society.

From neighbors setting the police on a woman and her family because they see her out at night, to questions such as "What are these females doing in the night?" to keeping tabs on women via mobile phones, to questioning a woman's worth on the marriage market because she works at night, to expecting a working wife to play down her contribution to household finances, to forcing one's daughter to quit her job because of a rape that occurred in a different city, women continue to experience inequality in a variety of settings.

Without a doubt, the places that some women traverse—whether a Fame Adlabs movie theater on a Saturday afternoon or the Center One mall in Vashi on a Friday night—represent a shift in where women have historically spent their free time. Similar to how Hindu temples draw from gendered regimes of access (menstruating women, be gone!), the social spaces that young women access today also reflect gendered notions of space that will continue to change over time but at the same time will remain tethered to beliefs about a woman's place. For the majority of the women who contributed to this study, hanging out in malls and movie theaters was considered perfectly acceptable. Partying all night in a bar or club, especially if unescorted, was not.

Although transnational call center employment sends women workers out of the house at night and provides them with a relatively high wage that is viewed in some circles as an indicator of liberation, their work is degraded;

subsequently, women experience backlash. The actual content of their labor is demarcated as easy work, a job that anyone can get. The fact that this so-called easy job is done at night causes beliefs about women taking it easy, working the "hooker shift," to surface. Despite high wages and an upscale office environment, the snickers and stares, sympathy and subjugation, remain. As one interviewee's uncle pointed out, the chance to be independent and "know the world" does not negate women's responsibility for how staying out all night affects the family unit in terms of managing the household.

The "What will people think?" narrative came up time and again, illustrating the varying ways in which individuals are pressured to conform to ideals about their place in society, and subsequently, how these ideals are embodied. When a woman works in a call center and smokes, she is marked as a bad girl, whereas a man's smoking is seen as a way to relieve stress. When it comes to concern about how call center employment will affect an individual's worth on the marriage market, a gendered narrative emerges. For women, it's more about going against the societal expectation that a woman is supposed to put family first and be chaste and homely. For men, it is more connected to not having a secure, "proper" job in order to fulfill the societal expectation that they be the family's breadwinner. The underlying tone of sex and fast money associated with the industry is used to denigrate workers and is part of the backlash that workers experience for *not paying their dues* and instead achieving a salary level that was previously available to an even narrower segment of the population (that is professional, white-collar workers).

Backlash is but one example of how mobility-morality narratives are experienced. A *good girl* is expected to mind her place whereas a *bad girl* transgresses and doesn't play by "the rules." Every place—from a public bus to a kitchen—comes with regimes of surveillance. These regimes are both external and self-inflicted and stem from the pressures placed on women to maintain their reputation.[4]

The ways in which women both experience and respond to the mobility-morality narratives that shape their lives change as technology evolves. The mobile phone, for instance, can expand the physical and virtual spaces that women experience. Mobile phones also expand some women's social space by creating a private avenue for planning travel getaways and for meeting with a boyfriend kept secret from the family. So far, however, mobile phones have done little to dramatically shift the underlying tension between what constitutes a woman's place and what does not. Although women's entry into the urban night was abetted by the sense of safety and connection that carrying a mobile phone brought a woman's family, this shift was also achieved through presenting call centers as a safe place that provides a high wage and an upscale office environment. As such, the mobile phone is certainly a device that re-codifies the mobility-morality narratives that shape *when* women go out, but it does little to challenge the underlying framework that places women in a position of having to ask permission to move about in ways deemed accept-able for their male counterparts. In this context, the mobile phone acts as a surveillance device that families depend on to keep tabs on women.

During fieldwork, threads related to the "outliers" of the working woman's story certainly emerged. Although not considered the norm of the industry, the outliers demonstrated that the effect of night shift work on women's lives is rarely a linear outcome that can be predicted and set as the standard. From Irene, the nearly-divorced training manager who lived alone and was dating a coworker; to Anjali, who secretly lived with a boyfriend for four years and used her income to start her own nonprofit; to Parvati, who used her income to take monthly vacations; to Poonam, who moved away from her family to pursue her career aspirations; to Purvi, an only child whose parents are de-ceased and who relies on her commissions as a collections agent to save money to buy her own home, women's lives extend beyond how they experience mar-ital relations, household labor, and "family values." It is through the stories of these individuals that I began to realize that the tales of womanhood woven into popular culture are at times limiting, because they disguise the richness and depth of women's lives.

Finally, two underlying terms, *darkness* and *blood*, emerged time and again in the course of working on this book. Writing about women's access to sacred spaces in a book about women's employment in the call center industry may appear to be a stretch. In terms of mobility-morality narratives, however, it provided a parallel for consideration. Darkness, for example, has an immobi-lizing effect on women's lives because they are generally expected to remain housebound in order to keep safe and maintain their reputation. Put another way, a moral woman doesn't wander too far, especially at night. In conjunc-tion, blood, specifically women's menstrual blood, also has an immobilizing effect because it is symbolized as degrading the moral order of sacred space.

Metaphorically speaking, these two beliefs speak volumes about how gen-dered notions of womanhood and place are both symbolized and spatialized. Women's menstrual blood—marked as feminine contamination that is released every month—is considered a polluting force on sacred spaces such as Hindu temples. Women's bodies, keepers of the family's reputation, become contaminated when made mobile in the urban night.[5] These beliefs provide insight into how the interplay between space and time recirculates negative depictions of women. When women enter a space during a time deemed "bad" (such as the urban night), they experience disdain from society. When women enter a space deemed sacred during their "bad" time of the month, they are marked as the polluting force. These forms of censure, of both bodies and the spaces traversed, hinder women's lives.

Contributions to Theoretical Literature

The women who participated in this study move through a variety of spaces that in some cases bring about changes in their social mobility, while in other cases leads to more dramatic shifts in spatial mobility, physical mobility, and temporal mobility. These varying forms of mobility overlap and inform one another. In the end, reaction to women's employment in the call center industry draws from the spatiotemporal narratives that society creates in order to define an individual's place in the larger community.

Figure 1 in Chapter One provides a visual representation of how women have come to embody and experience call center employment. Throughout the course of writing this book, it was apparent that the perceptions and beliefs outlined in this diagram do continue to affect, and in many cases limit, women's mobility and spatial access. At the same time, it was also apparent that experiences of empowerment and exploitation were not distinct experiences that operate in a vacuum, void of their opposites. Instead, there is fluidity and overlap.

Many women, for instance, gained a sense of empowerment and liberation from earning their own money and going out at night. At the same time, they felt exploited and harassed because they believed they were held to higher productivity standards relative to their U.S. counterparts, and in some cases they had to deal with police and nosy neighbors who believed it was their right to know why they were out at night.

To expand on the idea that there is fluidity and overlap in how women experience empowerment and exploitation, at the conclusion of this research I realized that I needed to reconfigure the matrix I presented in Chapter One. Thus I have created a new theoretical matrix (see Figure 6) to expand on the ideas crafted in Chapter One. By reformulating the matrix, I am better able to illustrate and convey some of the findings from this study. The new matrix demonstrates that the ways in which women experience working the night shift—be it backlash for going out at night or liberation through earning their own money—are linked to larger structural forces such as global labor relations and nationalism.[6]

Indeed, there are direct connections—albeit at times subtle and nuanced—between how women who work outside the household are used as a platform for promoting and opposing issues such as globalization, nation-building, and economic development. Class also plays a role in fueling such agendas. For instance, concern related to global forces fueling the growth of India's economy invokes class narratives about who benefits from globalization and who does not. The growth of the middle class is certainly considered a positive result of working in the IT sector.

Yet the ways in which the emergence of the IT sector disrupts the nation's understanding of women's roles and positions in society are made evident in light of reaction to changes in their mobility. When middle-class women who travel at night to service global corporations meet with rape and murder (as in the Bangalore rape case), the idea of the nation and the image of the ideal "Mother India" female figure is disrupted by gendered conceptions of space, mobility, and violence (see Figure 6).

The media frenzy surrounding the Bangalore rape case not only made apparent the disparate attention given to women's safety in relation to their class status, but also demonstrates how women's bodies are used to convey Indian nationalist anxiety related to economic development and globalization.

Literature on body politics was also key to contextualizing how women experience night shift employment. By framing the body as a geographical site that produces and performs gender in a variety of settings, the spatiotemporal narratives that dictate women's lives were given a space to emerge. These narratives are significant because beliefs surrounding night shift work affect women's participation in this rapidly expanding labor force and have implications for how we theorize feminization-of-labor discourse. More aptly, when low-wage day shift employment moves into the realm of high-wage night shift employment and brings with it an increase in men's participation, it suggests that "ladies work" is not only about the actual content of the job. The demand for emotional labor and the supposed preference for women as call center workers were not enough to minimalize men's participation in the industry.

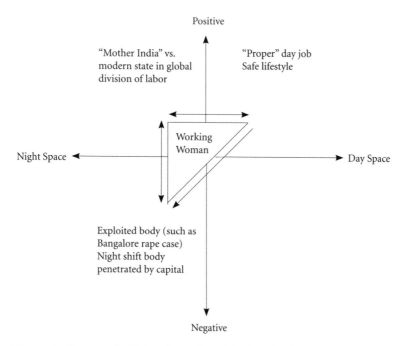

Figure 6. Spaces embodied and experienced by female call center employees

The time-space geography of this industry—a night shift global environment—also has implications for how work is gendered.

Personal Aspects Related to This Book

Although this book is based on a scholarly interest in how gender roles fare in the midst of global technology and development, it also entails the experience of learning about a part of my identity that had remained cloistered. As an American woman returning to the country of her grandparents (my parents hail from East Africa), this research brought up issues of identity, belonging, and gender roles. It also left me deeply troubled, because the contradictory reactions I had to living in Mumbai left me with more questions than answers. I expected that returning to India would put me in touch with my roots in a way that would forge a sense of connection and belonging. It didn't. Instead, I was anxious to leave. When I would travel out of Mumbai, the return would inevitably leave me bereft. At times I didn't want to go back, because of the disappointment of living in an area I viewed as ghetto-like. The sense of not belonging, and not wanting to belong, for that matter, made me want to run away.

The dilapidated building I lived in was certainly not what I had envisioned when people familiar with Mumbai said that I lived in a "posh" area. Going in and out of my flat on a daily basis, I climbed four flights of stairs—uneven stairs for that matter—and could not take my eyes off the stairwell walls, which were covered with decades of red and brown tobacco and betel nut spit. Never once did I even place my bare hand on the stair rail, because I could not bear the dirt and grime that surrounded me. I was disgusted to live in a building where people hired maids to keep their homes spotless, but outside their front door it was absolutely filthy. To give an example of how dirty the neighborhood I resided in was, I was stunned to find that after returning from twenty- to thirty-minute walks, brown grime would come off my hands when I washed them. The air quality was in fact so bad (at least compared to what I was used to) that upon return to the United States after ten months of research, I was prescribed nose and throat inhalers because I was unable to breathe properly.

During preliminary fieldwork in 2005, I wanted to leave by day five of a two-week visit and began counting the days until my return to the United States. I spent the next year wondering how I would fare during the ten months of fieldwork that lay ahead. At the same time, I could not imagine *not* doing the work. Beyond a sense of commitment and follow-through, I was drawn to this research for other reasons. Reasons that to date I am unable to fully comprehend.

Defined as the "City of Dreams," a place where a person can become somebody, Mumbai was my nightmare. I felt like a caged animal, mobility ripped away, unable to speak, unable to drive. Eventually I stopped wanting to go out. The simplest aspects of upper-middle-class life—such as figuring out where and what to eat—were an ordeal merely because I didn't want to take a twenty-minute walk that would leave me grimy from the pollution, agitated from the noise, and hypervigilant from the aggression of drivers, beggars, and street children, as well as from navigating between hawkers and other pedestrians. Although I had the money to get on a plane and leave, within my neighborhood setting I felt suffocated and trapped, and was often looking for a way out.

No one told me I would experience more than one moment of hating my research site. Frustration and anguish were to be expected, hatred was not. I came to view my surroundings as a representation of everything I did not want to become: immobilized, poor, and afraid. In addition to witnessing the abject poverty that is part and parcel of the city, the sense of having to justify my existence as a woman who did not aspire to marriage and children left me empty and uninspired. Through my lens of the world, the posh neighborhood I lived in appeared to me to be a ghetto, the first-class train was the "back of the bus," and the "safe" neighborhood my neighbors emphasized was based on it being considered unbecoming for women to go out alone late at night. Safe for whom? became my question.

And just when I thought I couldn't take it anymore, that I was at the end of my rope both personally and professionally, I would inevitably meet women such as Poonam and Anjali. Their bold willingness to behave in ways deemed risky, combined with their "detractors be damned" attitude, cut through the negative stereotypes I was beginning to form. On a rational level, I was aware that these stereotypes were wrong, but I drew on them in a feeble attempt to bring order and understanding to the chaos.

In writing this, what may appear to some people as a critical, inflexible stance imbued with a sense of American superiority is in reality a sense of despair combined with a profound sense of disappointment about the inequalities that remain embedded in society today. Research in Mumbai, Bangalore, and Ahmedabad left me conflicted, and I was concerned about the level of so-called objectivity I would bring to this study. Instead of hiding behind the detached-observer stance, I decided to reveal my personal experience in order to demonstrate that conducting fieldwork is often about much more than just going out and collecting data.[7]

In fact, the decision to pursue research on the call center industry was a happenstance, because I initially planned to conduct research on women working as engineers in the IT sector. This plan changed during a visit to India in 2003—my first since the age of three—when I participated in the Women in IT Conference held in Chidambaram, located in south India. It was here that I first learned that some call center employees were accused of prostitution when they went out at night. This situation sparked my interest, as a geographer-in-the-making, in uncovering how gendered norms of mobility and spatial access met with the demand for night shift workers. It was only later, however, that I also began to see a parallel between this study and my previous work experience. In 1986, for example, I earned $6.50 an hour as an employee of a major bank's call center. My friend and I were the only high school students working in the department, and we considered this salary quite a step up in pay, especially compared to our friends who earned minimum wage. Fast-forward to the twenty-first century and what was for us a $6.50 per hour job twenty years ago is now done for approximately $1.30 per hour in India.

Even though we were still supported by our parents, my friend and I saw ourselves as well-off and independent, similar to some of the women who participated in this study. Nevertheless, we got to keep our names and work the day shift. Workers in India struggle between opportunity and constriction, and also experience on-the-job training differently. Despite the fact that the content of our work was comparable, because some Indian call center employees took on "American-sounding" names in addition to working the night shift, it became evident that our experiences were really not as similar as I had originally suspected.

In closing, I want to thank the women and men who participated in this study. Their willingness to share their experiences and disclose what was for many sensitive information made for the foundation of this book. By taking on the night and entering a globalized work space, women certainly experienced both constriction and opening in their lives. Between tales of exploitation and tales of empowerment is a gray space that shows us that the answer is "it depends" when asking how night shift employment affects women's mobility. From migrating women and stuck women to bold women and homely women, this industry attracts a variety of workers whose experiences and circumstances outside the industry shape the extent to which night shift employment transforms their lives.

Postscript

After I returned from my fieldwork, the Bangalore Rape Case took an unexpected turn. In addition to arresting Shiv Kumar for the rape and murder of Pratibha Srikanth Murthy, the State of Karnataka also filed charges against Som Mittal, the current president of NASSCOM and former managing director of Hewlett Packard Global Soft Ltd. at the time of Ms. Murthy's murder.[1] The charges: Failure to comply with the state's amended Shops and Commercial Establishments Act of 1961, which requires companies to provide for the safety and security of female night shift employees.

That the head of a global IT firm could face charges in connection with the murder and rape of one of its employees—which it did not directly commit—was a first, and it sent shockwaves throughout the IT industry in India. Mittal challenged the charges on the basis of Section 3(1)(h) of the Shops and Commercial Establishments Act, which exempts individuals in management positions from liability.[2] In February 2008, the case went to the Supreme Court of India, and they rejected Mittal's petition, thus allowing the prosecution to continue with its case. As of June 2009, the case remains in the court system.

In addition to keeping abreast of news in the call center industry, I have remained in contact with several employees. In the course of the past two years, the lives of some of the women who contributed to this study changed drastically. This showed me that it's not possible to predict the outcomes for women who move about in ways deemed against "the rules." Remember Anjali, the twenty-seven-year-old who left home at the age of eighteen, used her call center income to start a nonprofit organization, and broke up with her boyfriend, whom she had secretly lived with for a few years? Four months after I left India, out of the blue I received the following e-mail from her:

> I am coming to NY..first 2 weeks of May [2007].. the reason . . . i am getting engaged..with who? Picture attached. I am happy.

In a subsequent conversation, she shared that she and her fiancé had met while they were attending a wedding in Kolkata. Although she didn't refer to their meeting as an arranged marriage, she stated, "It was all very negotiated." He works as a doctor in a suburb of New York City, and Anjali moved to the United States in March 2008 to be with him. She is currently working in the nonprofit sector and is also exploring graduate school opportunities.

Mona, the twenty-five-year-old employee at Company A, veered off in a surprising yet telling direction considering the liberation and empowerment that is associated with call center employment. She was considered a success story among her friends and colleagues. As discussed in Chapter Five, she purchased her first home at the age of twenty-three and rented it out. She bought a car the following year and, during our interview in February 2006, was deciding whether to trade in her older car for a new one or use her savings to take another overseas vacation. As told in Chapter Five, she was hanging out at pubs and discos during her free time.

When I asked Mona what her parents would think if she married a call center employee, she hedged on the subject, citing that they would not approve and that "caste matters" to them. I did not push further because I sensed it was a contentious topic and not one she wished to pursue with me. Months later I learned that her life had changed drastically. Mona was in love with a man she had met at the call center. She was Hindu, he was Catholic. Upon learning of the relationship, her father beat her, took away her mobile phone, and locked her in their home. As a result, she no longer worked in the call center. From working the night shift to taking overseas vacations, her mobility was ripped away and regimes of surveillance and control quickly took over her life.

After a few months her family began to trust her and she was allowed to go outside. She secretly met with her boyfriend and they married, unbeknownst to her parents. His parents, fully aware of the circumstances, were supportive of the relationship. In addition to religious differences and caste concerns, the disdain from her side of the family stemmed from economic issues. Her family, for instance, has more money than his family. Mona's now-husband and his parents came to her home and asked her parents' permission for them to be together. They refused. As a result, Mona ran away and remains out of touch with both family and friends.

Irene, the thirty-two-year-old training manager, is still trying to get the divorce she has spent approximately seven years trying to obtain. In June 2009 she e-mailed to let me know that her husband had finally returned her jewelry to her parents and was supposed to contact her later that month to finalize a court date for their divorce. Irene also completed an exam needed to graduate from the college she had left a few years ago. Her initial plan—upon graduation and finalizing her divorce—was to find a way to migrate to the United States, either through work or with the help of a family member already in the country. She has now, however, decided instead to pursue an MBA either in India or New Zealand and is currently exploring the options available to her.

During an October 2006 interview, Kriti, the twenty-one-year-old who used her savings from call center employment to start a boutique, said that she would marry in the next few years, by age twenty-four, if she had it her way, or earlier if her parents had it their way. She shared that her parents had also agreed to a longer courtship—eight to nine months—in order to get to know the guy. Although she did once meet a man through her job, she stated, "It didn't go anywhere." Her parents want an arranged marriage and although she was initially agreeable, she now does not want this because "it's too risky." Seven months after this interview, in May 2007, Kriti e-mailed to let me know that she had "finally found the right guy and I'm getting married." She continues to put in long hours working the night shift at a call center while growing her business during the day.

One employee's belief that "the call center becomes our marriage pool!" seemed to have rung true for Jyothi, the twenty-five-year-old call center manager. As discussed in Chapter Seven, Jyothi's life was hypermanaged by her parents. In terms of parental control, she led the most restrictive lifestyle of the participants in this study. Nine months after our initial interview, she told me that she had been secretly seeing someone at the office for years and they planned to marry. Neither had yet told their respective families. Rather than not telling because either of their parents would disapprove of them marrying a call center employee, they have held off because both set of parents, upon finding out about the relationship, would want them to marry sooner rather than later. They preferred to wait, hence the secrecy. After the wedding, Jyothi and her husband will live with his family.

Shilpa, the thirty-eight-year-old who candidly spoke of managing her husband's inferiority complex, e-mailed me in February 2008 to let me know that she was no longer working nights for the Fortune 500 company at which I had initially interviewed her. Her experience with this firm provided her entry into a dayshift management position at a competing firm. She writes, "I got what I wanted now." Poonam, the thirty-two-year-old whose first job out of college was in a cement factory and who in recent years had caused waves by her decision to live away from her husband and child, stated that one of her goals was to work abroad again. In January 2008 she achieved this. The company she works for sponsored her H1–B visa to migrate to the United States and she currently resides in the New England area. Her family joined her later that summer.

Appendix

Research Methodology for This Study

This study used an inductive, mixed-methods approach based on in-depth interviews, focus groups, and participant observation. Mixed methods constitute the "third wave" of academia's research movement, with quantitative being the first wave and qualitative being the second wave. Broadly speaking, mixed methods integrate a variety of data-gathering techniques into the study of a single subject.[1] In this research, mixed methods were incorporated for a key reason: the weakness in one set of data is potentially compensated for by other sets of data. For instance, participant observation gave insight into when employees work but did not provide a deep understanding of how women deal with working at night. Thus in-depth interviews were conducted to elucidate the experiences of women workers. In other words, the mixed-method approach served as a form of triangulation with which to double-check the validity of my findings.

This research also draws from the grounded theory approach.[2] In contrast to hypothesis testing, which compares findings to a predetermined set of outcomes, grounded theory is an inductive approach in which new findings emerge from an ongoing interplay between collecting and analyzing data.[3] Given the relative newness of the call center industry in India, the inductive approach allowed me to remain open to key findings that would have gone unnoticed had I remain attached to a strict either-or hypothesis framework.

Notes

Acknowledgments

1. Any opinions, findings, and conclusions or recommendations expressed in this book are those of the author and do not necessarily reflect the views of the National Science Foundation.

Chapter 1

1. Slater, "Call of the West."

2. Chengappa and Goyal, "Housekeepers to the World."

3. A *salwar kameez* is an outfit that consists of a long, tunic-style top worn over loose-fitting pants and adorned with a scarf.

4. Pradhan and Abraham, "Social and Cultural Impact of Outsourcing.

5. NASSCOM, "NASSCOM's Ranking of Third Party Players," http://www.nasscom.org/artdisplay.asp?Art_id=4400

6. The emergence of transnational call centers is also referred to as *outsourcing*, or sometimes *offshoring*, by the mainstream media. The term *outsourcing*, however, does not fully account for this new phenomenon, because U.S. companies have been outsourcing for decades in terms of hiring local firms to handle processes such as payroll and human resources. The word *transnational* is used to account for the geographic scale of this industry, which is based on cartographies of cultural circulation, identification, and action beyond nation-state borders. See Crang, Dwyer, and Jackson, "Transnationalism and the Spaces of Commodity Culture."

7. Gottdiener, *The Social Production of Urban Space*; Keith and Pile, *Place and the Politics of Identity*; Massey, *Spatial Divisions of Labor;* Massey, *Space, Place, and Gender*; Soja, *Postmodern Geographies;* Soja, *Thirdspace*.

8. Fincher and Jacobs, *Cities of Difference*, 73.

9. Agnew, "Representing Space"; Hanson and Pratt, *Gender, Work, and Space*; Harvey, *Spaces of Hope*; Massey, *For Space*.

10. Ghose, "The Dalit in India."

11. Hancock, *Womanhood in the Making.*

12. Cresswell, *In Place/Out of Place.*

13. Siddiqi, "The Sexual Harassment of Industrial Workers; Siddiqi, "Miracle Worker or Womanmachine?"

14. Siddiqi, "The Sexual Harassment of Industrial Workers," 34.

15. Siddiqi, "Miracle Worker or Womanmachine?" L-16.

16. Ibid.

17. Massey, *Space, Place, and Gender*, 150.

18. Hägerstand, "Space, Time, and Human Conditions," 5. Hagerstrand's work on individual mobility gained attention in the 1970s and he became a leader in the field of behavioral geography. See Flowerdew, "Hägerstand, Torsten."

19. Boyer, "Spaces of Change"; Cresswell, "Embodiment, Power and the Politics of Mobility"; Kantor, "Female Mobility in India"; Law, "Gender and Daily Mobility in a New Zealand City"; Kwan, "Gender and Individual Access to Urban Opportunities"; Cristaldi, "Commuting and Gender in Italy."

20. Hanson and Pratt, *Gender, Work, and Space*; Mandel, "Mobility Matters."

21. Vohra, "Q2P."

22. Bapat and Agarwal, "Our Needs, Our Priorities."

23. Madhusree Dutta, interview.

24. Ranade, "The Way She Moves."

25. Ibid., 1524. A paan shop is a corner shop (some are extremely ramshackle) that sells lighters, cigarettes, beedis (hand-rolled cigarettes popular in India), paan (an after-dinner snack and digestive made with betel leaves and other bits and pieces), sweets, toffees, and so on.

26. In an e-mail discussion, Ranade explained that a "dead wall" is a wall that does not have any openings in it and generally rises above eye level. The high walls of industrial compounds are an example of this. These walls are not porous to the outside world, and in the context of Ranade's study, the critical "eyes on the street" (a term used to describe an area that is easily visible or full of people) are missing because of them.

27. Andersen, *Thinking About Women.*

28. Personal communication, March 6, 2003.

29. Peterson, "Rereading Public and Private."

30. Peterson and Runyan, *Global Gender Issues.*

31. Gray, *Men Are from Mars, Women Are from Venus.* From rating it one of the worst books, in terms of providing advice that reflects the latest findings in behavioral sciences, to discussing Grey's questionable credentials—his doctoral degree is from a correspondence school that was shut down for having a virtually nonexistent staff and questionable coursework—Barnett and Rivers uncover how Grey's prescription for communicating with the opposite sex actually causes more harm than good, particularly for women. See Barnett and Rivers, *Same Difference,* 106–112.

32. For an example of this, see Sengupta, "Careers Give India's Women New Independence."

33. Patel and Parmentier, "The Persistence of Traditional Gender Roles in the Technology Sector."

34. Parikh and Sukhatme, "Women in the Engineering Profession in India," 248.

35. Fountain, "Constructing the Information Society"; Hafkin and Taggart, "Gender, Information Technology, and Developing Countries"; Varma, "Women in Information Technology."

36. Cresswell, *In Place / Out of Place.*

37. See Singh, "Social and Cultural Aspects of Gender Inequality and Discrimination in India."

38. Wright, *Disposable Women and Other Myths of Global Capitalism,* 156.

39. Faludi, *Backlash;* Wilson, *The Sphinx in the City;* Bordo, *Unbearable Weight;* McDowell, *Gender, Identity and Place.*

40. Haraway, "Situated Knowledge.

41. Longhurst, *Bodies;* Longhurst, "The Body and Geography"; Duncan, *Bodyspace;* Silvey, "Borders, Embodiment, and Mobility; Pratt, "Geography and Body."

42. Geographers from a variety of subspecialties have demonstrated that the body is a key site for understanding how difference is maintained and spatialized. On medical geography, see Laws and Radford, "Women with Disabilities and Everyday Geographies." See also Agot, "HIV/Aids Interventions and the Politics of the African Woman's Body." On sports geography, see Johnston, "Crossing Boundaries." On political geography, see Hyndman, "Towards a Feminist Geopolitics." On social geography, see Longhurst, "Fat Bodies." See also McKittrick, "Who Do You Talk to, When a Body's in Trouble?"

43. Brownmiller, *Femininity.*

44. Wadley, "Women and the Hindu Tradition," 121.

45. Ranjit, "Sabarimalai."

46. Butler, *Gender Trouble.*

47. Ibid.

48. Secor, *The Veil and Urban Space in Istanbul,* 5.

49. Phadke, "'You Can Be Lonely in a Crowd,'" 52.

50. Nagar, Lawson, McDowell, and Hanson, "Locating Globalization," 267.

51. Cox, "Mumbai Wards & Districts." In an e-mail discussion, Cox confirmed that his numbers are derived from the Census of India data on the Municipality of Greater Mumbai. He further explained that access to these data is now limited to employees, but they can be validated on the United Way's Mumbai Helpline Web site: http://www.mumbaihelpline.org/YourWardList.asp.

52. Shaw, *The Making of Navi Mumbai*.

53. Ibid., 4.

54. Ibid., 4.

55. Sahu, "Present Scenario of Municipal Solid Waste (MSW) Dumping Grounds in India."

56. Poster, "Saying 'Good Morning' in the Middle of the Night," 102.

57. Patel, *The Economic Times IT Enabled Services 2002*.

58. Phadke, "'You Can Be Lonely in a Crowd.'"

59. Bangalore changed to Bengaluru during the course of this study. Throughout the book, however, I continue to use the name Bangalore because it reflects how interviewees referred to the city even after the official name change.

60. Skop, "The Methodological Potential of Focus Groups in Population Geography."

61. NASSCOM, "Nasscom's Ranking of Third Party Players."

62. Based on the April 16, 2005, currency exchange of US$1 = Rs 43.775.

63. All amounts going forward are based on an exchange rate of Rs 45.10474 to US$1. This rate was calculated on the basis of a twelve–month average of the 2006 rupee to U.S. dollar exchange, derived from Federal Reserve Bank of New York data. Amounts in U.S. dollars are rounded to the nearest dollar.

64. Bhagat, *One Night @ the Call Center*.

65. Vohra, "Q2P"; Girls Media Group, *Do You Know How We Feel? Aaaaaaargh!*

66. Strauss and Corbin, *Basics of Qualitative Research;* Rubin and Rubin, *Qualitative Interviewing.*

67. Peppered throughout the book are names such as Sandra, Valerie, and Irene. These pseudonyms reflect the English names of the Catholic Indians who participated in this study and are not the American identities that some employees are required to take on as part of their job. Although accurate data on the actual number of Catholic Indians working in the industry are unavailable, interviewees noted that they are in demand because of their English skills and anglicized accent derived from speaking English in the house and attending Catholic schools.

68. Haraway, "Situated Knowledge."

69. Haraway, *Simians, Cyborgs, and Women*.

70. Holloway, "Donna Haraway."

71. Harding, *Whose Science? Whose Knowledge?* Hickey and Lawson, "Beyond Science?"

72. On ethnography, see Kirschner, "'Then What Have I to Do with Thee?'"; Behar, "The Vulnerable Observer"; Foley, "Critical Ethnography"; Parameswaran, "Feminist Media Ethnography in India." On feminist geography, see England, "Getting Personal"; Kobayashi, "GPC Ten Years On"; Chacko, "Positionality and Praxis"; Rose, "Situating Knowledges"; Raju, "We Are Different, but Can We Talk?"

73. Skop, *Saffron Suburbs.*

74. Tuan, "Cultural Geography."

Chapter 2

1. Although India has the highest concentration of transnational call centers thus far, the centers also have a presence in Kenya, the Philippines, China, Pakistan, Ireland, Lithuania, Panama, and the Caribbean.

2. For an insightful reading on the training and communications aspect of transnational call center employment, see Aneesh, "Specters of Global Communication."

3. A maquiladora is a duty-free manufacturing plant located in Mexico, often near the U.S. border.

4. For further reading on the identity aspects of this industry see Krishnamurthy, "Outsourced Identities"; Poster, "Who's on the Line?"; Mirchandani, "Practices of Global Capital." The identity aspect of this industry is also the subject of a documentary filmed in Mumbai. See Ahluwalia, *John and Jane.*

5. Labeling Indian employees as cheap labor is a source of contention. As Parul Baxi points out, some scholars believe this characterization perpetuates a Eurocentric view of Indians. See Baxi, "Globalizing Identity?"

6. Adam, "The Gendered Time Politics of Globalization," 21.

7. Ibid.; Patel, "Working the Night Shift"; Fitzpatrick, "Social Policy and Time."

8. The push for protectionist policies during times of economic insecurity is not new. The U.K. 1883 Factory Act, enacted during British Colonial rule in India, was introduced under the rubric of implementing fairer work practices. Yet Babu Mathew argues that it was a protectionist measure brought about by textile conglomerate groups in Britain who were threatened by competition from India's textile industry. See Mathew, "A Brief Note on Labour Legislation in India."

Although considerable media attention is given to the loss of U.S. jobs due to outsourcing in India, this trend should not be exaggerated. Kavita Pandit, for example, finds that the actual number of U.S. jobs that have moved overseas thus far is not significant. In fact, "reverse outsourcing" is also emerging slowly as Indian companies such as Wipro Technologies hire hundreds of U.S. graduates to work at their offices in India. See Pandit, "Elite Migration from 'Body Shopping' to 'Reverse Migration.'"; "U.S. Business Grads Take Jobs in India." Furthermore, the actual number of U.S.

jobs lost, both long-term and short-term, is a highly debated subject. Critics view the BPO industry as taking jobs away from U.S. workers. Proponents view it as a means to export monotonous work, thus providing U.S. workers with the means to focus on higher levels of "knowledge work." See Nichols, "Global Fights Go Local"; Delaney, "Outsourcing Jobs—and Workers—to India"; Harrison and McMillan, "Dispelling Some Myths About Offshoring"; Reich, "Plenty of Knowledge Work to Go Around"; "The New Jobs Migration"; Thibodeau, "Inaction on Offshoring Will Hurt U.S. IT, Author Says"; Miller, "Hello, India? Er, Des Moines?"

9. Greenspan, *India and the IT Revolution.*

10. NASSCOM, "Indian Software and Services Exports"; NASSCOM, "Nasscom's Ranking of Third Party Players."

11. Although the BPO industry provided much-needed jobs, it inadvertently created employment competition for local industries. Jagdish, owner of a graphic design firm in Mumbai, declared that "the call center industry is hurting my business!" He attributed this to being unable to compete with the salaries of the call center industry. Indeed, entry-level wages in the call centers range between Rs 9,000 per month to Rs 15,000 per month (US$200 to US$333), depending on the company. Jagdish noted that even when he offered a salary that was on par with the starting salary of a call center, his workers still quit to work at the call center. Given that the salaries of the call center industry are far higher than the average wages paid to individuals qualified to work in this industry, call center employment is clearly an attractive choice on the basis of salary alone.

12. Belt, Richardson, and Webster, "Women's Work in the Information Economy"; Hunt, "Call Centre Work for Women"; Breathnach, "Information Technology, Gender Segmentation and the Relocation of Back Office Employment"; Bonds, "Calling on Femininity?"

13. *Pink collar* is used to denote a field that is made up mostly of women workers. For background on how some women have experienced pink-collar employment, see Howe, *Pink Collar Workers.*

14. Bonds, "Calling on Femininity?"

15. Hochschild and Machung, *The Second Shift.*

16. Breathnach, "Information Technology, Gender Segmentation and the Relocation of Back Office Employment," 320.

17. Wright, *Disposable Women;* Ong, *Spirits of Resistance and Capitalist Discipline;* Elson and Pearson, "'Nimble Fingers Make Cheap Workers'"; Elson, "Nimble Fingers and Other Fables"; Domosh and Seager, *Putting Women in Place;* Poster, "Dangerous Places and Nimble Fingers."

18. Freeman, *High Tech and High Heels in the Global Economy,* 5.

19. A dowry, similar to a trousseau, involves money and material items that a woman's family provides to their daughter upon marriage, to bring to her future hus-

band's household. This practice is rife with negative social implications. The demand for large dowries on the part of the groom's family, for instance, perpetuates the preference for boys because girls are viewed as an expense. It is also the cause of dowry murder, in which families kill their daughters-in-law because they did not bring enough money or goods to the union. See Saxena, "The Menace of Dowry."

20. Kelkar and Nathan, "Gender Relations and Technological Change in Asia."

21. Pradhan and Abraham, "Social and Cultural Impact of Outsourcing," 24.

22. Hochschild, *The Managed Heart.* For a discussion on how "emotional labor" fares in customer service jobs that move abroad, see Bryson, "The 'Second' Global Shift."

23. The conception of the industry as middle-class also stems from the fact that it initially recruited college graduates to be employees. During a 2004 interview with Nilesh, the industry consultant for one of India's first call centers, he argued that by transferring call center operations to India, companies got more value for their money because the Indian counterparts of workers in the United States—where he believed most workers have only a high school education—came with a college degree and could be hired at a much lower cost.

24. Raju and Bagchi, *Women and Work in South Asia.*

25. In addition, companies provide transportation because the Indian government does not have an adequate public transportation infrastructure in place for its citizens. Transportation during the day shift in an urban area, for instance, is rife with pollution, overcrowding, and traffic that can take some employees upwards of two hours to traverse 24 kilometers (14.9 miles). The traffic is the same or worse in Bangalore. In contrast, traffic at night is relatively sparse, and for women in particular it is not deemed safe. Despite concerns for safety voiced by family members, some women said they preferred night shift employment because they did not have to deal with the dilemmas of day shift traffic, congestion, and harassment on public transportation.

26. Poster, "Saying 'Good Morning' in the Middle of the Night," 104.

27. Weinberg, "Computer Use and the Demand for Female Workers."

28. This is not to infer that all customer service positions in the United States are day shift, because 24/7 customer service centers also have night shift employees. Relatively speaking, however, they are far fewer in number.

29. Poster, "Who's on the Line?"; Mirchandani, "Gender Eclipsed?"

30. Chengappa and Goyal, "Housekeepers to the World."

31. Although neither WebCorp nor MedCorp are voice-based call centers, both companies do fall under the umbrella of the BPO industry, in which working the night shift and proficiency in English is the primary requirement. WebCorp is a Web-based processing facility that addresses customer queries, and MedCorp is a medical transcription firm that services U.S. clients.

32. Parvati, a collections agent, had ten days to decide if she wanted to take a day

shift position. Although it might be expected that going from a night shift position to a day shift position would be a promotion, she was undecided because of two key drawbacks: (1) a Rs 2,500 (US$55) reduction in her current monthly salary, and (2) no more shuttle transportation. She would only be able to access a central pickup, which would increase her commuting time considerably or increase her transportation expense in that she would have to travel by rickshaw.

33. Singh and Pandey, "Women in Call Centres."

34. Chengappa and Goyal, "Housekeepers to the World."

35. Ramesh, "Cyber Coolies' in BPO."

36. "Out of India."

37. Dhillon, "Call Centres Are Blamed for a Rise in Loose Living"; Ramesh, "'Cyber Coolies' in BPO."

38. Dina Siddiqi found that, similar to the way transnational call centers are viewed as safer compared to local industry, factories located within export processing zones (EPZs) in Dhaka, Bangladesh, are safer for women in comparison to factories that operate outside the EPZs. This was ironic given that EPZs are immune from legal provisions that require them to adhere to national labor laws. Siddiqi found that workers experience higher levels of safety because of the lack of men in the work space and, as stated by one of her interviewees, "Men in the EPZ are like sheep. . . . They've been silenced, the ones who remain are terrified of losing their jobs." See Siddiqi, "The Sexual Harassment of Industrial Workers," 37.

39. Captive call centers are directly owned and operated by the off-shore corporation whereas a call center that is operated by an Indian-owned company or that is a joint venture with an Indian firm is labeled a third-party process.

40. An experiential, how-to book that focuses on gaining entry into the call center industry and offers advice on navigating the industry is now available. See Yadav, *Winning @ Call Centre.*

41. Sharma, "Headcount Crisis at Call Centres"; Thanawala, "India's Call-Center Jobs Go Begging."

42. Wright, *Disposable Women and Other Myths of Global Capitalism*; Sandburg, "'It Says Press Any Key. Where's the Any Key?'"

43. Eighth standard is similar to middle school in the United States.

44. To illustrate Parag's point, Shivani, a twenty-three-year-old employee at WebCorp, has an engineering degree but joined WebCorp in Ahmedabad because she could not get a job in her field. As is reflected in the findings of Pravina Parikh and Suhas Sukhatme's twenty-year study, during college, Shivani recalled, women were excluded from participating in the on-campus job interviews that were vital to gaining employment.

45. For an account of the move from an American accent to a neutral accent, see Cowie, "The Accents of Outsourcing."

46. Johnson, "Bangalore Hit by English Ban in Schools"; "Students Upset over Ban on Alternate English." As of April 2007, the government has held back on closing schools that continue to teach in English and has planned to fine schools instead. See "Bangalore Schools Face English Fines."

47. Boyer, "Place and the Politics of Virtue"; Tanner and Cockerill, "Gender, Social Change, and the Professions"; Ehrenreich and Hochschild, *Global Woman.*

Chapter 3

1. Cresswell, *In Place / Out of Place.*

2. This act was an extension of the 1883 Factory Act, which stipulated eight-hour work shifts and provision for overtime wages, and made child labor illegal. See Barker, "Factory Legislation in India," 644.

3. Kumar, *The History of Doing.*

4. Dutta, "7 Islands and a Metro."

5. "Factories Act, 1948."

6. Rao, "The Factories (Amendment) Bill, 2005." Emphasis added.

7. The term *mobility-morality narrative* was inspired by previous research on women's mobility and spatial access. See Liddle and Joshi, *Daughters of Independence;* Bondi and Domosh, "On the Contours of Public Space"; Bondi and Rose, "Constructing Gender, Constructing the Urban"; Nagar, "Communal Discourses, Marriage, and Politics of Gendered Social Boundaries"; Nast, "Unsexy Geographies."

8. Wright, "From Protests to Politics"; Castillo, Gomez, and Delgado, "Border Lives."

9. For an insightful account of life under the purdah regimes, see Lalithambika and Krishnakutty, *Cast Me Out If You Will;* Minturn and Kapoor, *Sita's Daughters.* See also Deshmukh-Ranadive, *Space for Power;* Raju and Bagchi, *Women and Work in South Asia;* Kantor, "Female Mobility in India." In addition, Dagmar Engels uncovers how purdah affected women's political activism, particularly as it related to their involvement in the nationalist movements. See Engels, *Beyond Purdah?*

10. Deshmukh-Ranadive, *Space for Power;* Raju and Bagchi, *Women and Work in South Asia;* Kantor, "Female Mobility in India."

11. Some scholars contend that viewing the mobility of urban, middle-class women in the twenty-first century as a continued reflection of purdah regimes is problematic, for two reasons. First, it is believed that purdah no longer applies to the lives of women because it is ahistorical. The stringent confinement rules that define purdah are viewed as a thing of the past. Second, to draw on purdah to gain a comparative context for the women in twenty-first-century India could be a form of *Orientalism,* a term used to describe how Westerners create discourses about Asia from an us-versus-them perspective that positions Westerners as superior to their studied subject. See Said, *Orientalism.*

12. The *women's question* is a commonly used term in literature that focuses on women in India.

13. Research on sati, the practice of widow burning, generally focuses on India. Joerg Fisch, however, found that both the ritualized and the nonritualized practice of widow sacrifice occurred in many parts of the world, from Japan to the United States. See Fisch, *Burning Women*.

14. Burton, *Burdens of History*. In addition, Barbara Ramusack coined the term *maternal imperialists* to describe the deferential treatment that some British women demanded from Indian women during the colonizing mission. See Ramusack, "Cultural Missionaries, Maternal Imperialists, Feminist Allies."

15. Pradhan and Abraham, "Social and Cultural Impact of Outsourcing," 25.

16. Agnew, *Hegemony*, 4–5.

17. The sense of modernity that Valerie associated with India's Catholic population in relation to other groups such as Hindus and Muslims was not an isolated incident. This belief was also voiced by other women and men I interviewed during the course of fieldwork.

18. Phadke, "Dangerous Liaisons," 1512.

19. Going to a woman's home to convince her family to allow her to work in a call center is not a common practice throughout the industry. Girija, a human resources manager for a firm located in Mindspace, stated, "It's already known the hours of the job, so it's up to the girl to sort it out."

20. Joseph, "God, Sex, and Call Centres"; Arora, "Bad BPOs: A Case of Wrong Image?" Tejaswi, "India Calling."

21. "Delhi: The Rape Capital of India."

22. Puri, "Stakes and States."

23. Some scholars argue that marking women as a site to protect (that is, keep safe) is a means to reinforce patriarchal regimes of control over their bodies. See Bordo, *Unbearable Weight*.

24. Ranade, "The Way She Moves."

25. Girls Media Group, "Do You Know How We Feel? *Aaaaaaargh!*"

26. Haraway, *Simians, Cyborgs, and Women*, 165.

27. Suvarna, "Ways of the Indian Pervert."

Chapter 4

1. Borkar, "Midnight Melange."

2. Hanson and Pratt, *Gender, Work, and Space*; Burns, "Women's Travel to Inner City Employment"; Burns and Gober, "Job Linkages in Inner City Phoenix."

3. NASSCOM, "Third Party ITES-BPO Companies Rankings for FY 05–06."

4. Wright, *Disposable Women and Other Myths of Global Capitalism*.

5. According to Edward S. Herman and Noam Chomsky, unequal media atten-

tion given to similar crimes is linked to a political economy that deems some victims as "worthy" and others as "unworthy." See Herman and Chomsky, *Manufacturing Consent.*

6. Wright, *Disposable Women and Other Myths of Global Capitalism.*

7. Livingston, "Murder in Juarez"; Garwood, "Working to Death."

8. Thompson, "Chasing Mexico's Dream into Squalor," 2.

9. Wright, *Disposable Women and Other Myths of Global Capitalism.*

10. Elliot, "India, Inc."; "India's Shining Hopes."

11. Sharma, "Headcount Crisis at Call Centres"; Thanawala, "India's Call-Center Jobs Go Begging."

12. Hyndman, "Mind the Gap."

13. Ibid., 318.

14. Kirshenbaum, "Jadranka, Cigelj, and Nusreta Sivac," 64.

15. Oza, "Showcasing India"; Chatterjee, *The Nation and Its Fragments.* For further reading on the gendering of nations and nationalism, see Mohammed, "British Pakistani Muslim Women"; West, "Nation"; Yuval-Davis, *Gender and Nation*; Burton, "House/Daughter/Nation"; Sharp, "Gendering Nationhood."

16. Oza, "Showcasing India."

17. This dynamic is not confined to "the women's question" within India. Sheba Mariam George's work on the transnational marriage market between Kerala and the United States uncovers how "the control of women's sexuality becomes linked to notions of nationalism and the upholding of religion, tradition, and Indian culture." See George, *When Women Come First,* 173.

18. Oza, "Showcasing India," 1068–1069.

19. Certainly the home itself is also a site of tyranny and violence for some women, and in such instances getting out of the house is a means of escape. See Rose, *Feminism and Geography;* Phadke, "Dangerous Liaisons"; Bhattacharya, *Behind Closed Doors.*

20. Gibson-Graham, *The End of Capitalism (As We Knew It),* 146.

21. Chatterjee, *The Nation and Its Fragments,* 117.

22. Phadke, "Dangerous Liaisons," 1510.

23. Chatterjee, *The Nation and Its Fragments.*

24. Raju, "Contextualizing Critical Geography in India."

25. Hancock, "Gendering the Modern."

26. The term *colonization of time* is from Barbara Adam's work on gender and global labor processes. See Adam, "The Gendered Time Politics of Globalization."

Chapter 5

1. Singh and Pandey, "Women in Call Centres"; Upadhya and Vasavi, "Work, Culture, and Sociality in the Indian IT Industry."

2. Sandburg, "'It Says Press Any Key.'"

3. Sassen, "Women's Burden."

4. That a single woman such as Manisha, who also is a college dropout, had the ability to buy her own home was significant given the discrimination that both urban and rural women experience in terms of land and property rights. See Kumar and Menon-Sen, "Women in India"; Panda and Agarwal, "Marital Violence, Human Development and Women's Property Status in India"; Agarwal, *A Field of One's Own;* Patel, *Hindu Women's Property Rights in Rural India.*

5. As illustrated in Veena Grover's story in the documentary film "A Woman's Place," the refusal of men to support a girl-child due to the entrenched preference for boys is not uncommon. See Vohra, "A Woman's Place."

6. The term *backlash* draws from Susan Faludi's research on the ways in which U.S. women face hostility in the midst of their progress. See Faludi, *Backlash.*

7. The term *leapfrog* is drawn from IT and development discourse. It is based on the idea that by leapfrogging into new technologies (such as going straight to mobile phones rather than working on landline infrastructure), developing countries have the potential to modernize at a much faster rate. See Mansell and de Montalvo, *Knowledge Societies;* Castells, *End of Millennium.*

8. Singh, "Social and Cultural Aspects of Gender Inequality and Discrimination in India"; Varma, "Technological Fix."

9. Kumar and Menon-Sen, "Women in India."

10. The term *capital accumulation* draws from David Harvey, who, inspired by Donna Haraway's theorizing of the body, conceptualizes the body as a site of "capitalist accumulation" vis-à-vis the political economy. Building on this conception, feminist geographers such as Melissa Wright uncover how the feminization of labor on a global scale intersects with women workers being scripted as the bodily site of capital accumulation that is deemed disposable and easily replaced. See Harvey, *Justice, Nature, and the Geography of Difference;* Wright, *Disposable Women and Other Myths of Global Capitalism.*

11. A bachelor of commerce degree is similar to an economics degree in the United States.

12. For further reading on consumerism in India, see Jackson, "Local Consumption Cultures in a Globalizing World." See also Bellman, "A Dollar Store's Rich Allure in India."

13. Patel, "Working the Night Shift."

14. The health ramifications of night shift employment and its effects on women's mobility were not fully taken into account during the design phase of this research. This was a mistake. During in-depth interviews it became clear that the constriction some women faced in their lives was not only about having no time to hang out. It was also related to health problems that employees linked to working at night, such as digestive problems and depression. These issues impeded their ability and desire to

go out during their days off. Furthermore, the night shift requirement not only meant sleeping all day, thus losing access to daytime activities, but employees also spoke of needing more sleep than before because they were exhausted. "I'm too tired to go out!" was a theme that emerged.

15. Rekha Pande's research on the call center industry in Hyderabad also reflects this finding. See Pande, "Looking at Information Technology from a Gender Perspective."

16. Poster, "Saying 'Good Morning' in the Middle of the Night."

17. Ong, *Spirits of Resistance and Capitalist Discipline*; Wright, *Disposable Women and Other Myths of Global Capitalism*; Freeman, *High Tech and High Heels in the Global Economy.*

18. Gulati, "Nalini by Day, Nancy by Night."

19. Menon and Lobo, "Freedom Before 11. "

20. Manju, "A Supersonic Boom" ; "Ready for Take-Off."

21. Poster, "Who's on the Line?"

22. Ibid., 273.

Chapter 6

1. Domosh, "Geography and Gender: Home, Again?" 276.

2. Marston and Smith, "States, Scales and Households," 618.

3. Marston, "The Social Construction of Scale."

4. Chant, "Households, Gender and Rural-Urban Migration," 5.

5. Kelkar, Shrestha, and Nagarjan, "IT Industry and Women's Agency."

6. George, *When Women Come First.*

7. This finding reflects Govind Kelkar, Girija Shrestha, and Veena Nagarjan's argument that call center employment does not lead to a drastic shift in gender relations in the household. See Kelkar, Shrestha, and Nagarjan, "IT Industry and Women's Agency."

8. Two focus groups I conducted also provided another glimpse into gender relations in the household. One Sunday afternoon at a Catholic church in Mumbai, I interviewed a focus group consisting of five female employees, one of whom was married. Her husband participated in the group. Interestingly, the husband tried to speak on behalf of his wife and at times expressed what it is like to be a call center employee even though he is not one himself. In another focus group of three women and three men the same dynamic emerged. The boyfriend of a call center employee insisted on answering on behalf of his girlfriend.

9. Control of the dowry and even the murder of young women because they lack the expected dowry is an ongoing issue. See Kumar and Menon-Sen, "Women in India"; Vohra, "A Woman's Place."

10. Poonam pointed out that very few women are in the field of civil engineer-

ing. This finding is reflected in a twenty-year study conducted by Pravina Parekh and Suhas Sukhatme. See Parikh and Sukhatme, "Women Engineers in India"; Parikh and Sukhatme, "Women in the Engineering Profession in India."

11. McCann and Kim, *Feminist Theory Reader;* Talpade Mohanty, Ann Russo, and Lourdes Torres, *Third World Women and the Politics of Feminism.*

12. García, *Chicana Feminist Thought;* Moraga and Anzaldúa, *This Bridge Called My Back;* Hooks, *Feminist Theory;* Mohanty, *Feminism Without Borders.*

13. On how some migrant Indian women experience being part of a global network of skilled workers via the IT sector, see Raghuram, "Migration, Gender, and the IT Sector."

14. Sassen, "Women's Burden"; Pratt, *Working Feminism*; Ehrenreich and Hochschild, *Global Woman;* Yeoh and Huang, "Negotiating Public Space"; Wright, "Crossing the Factory Frontier."

Chapter 7

1. Ramesh, "'Cyber Coolies' in BPO"; Gulati, "Nalini by Day, Nancy by Night"; Kelkar and Nathan, "Gender Relations and Technological Change in Asia."

2. Patel, "Working the Night Shift," 20.

3. In Indian society it is easier for a divorced man than for a divorced woman to remarry. This fact is linked to the expectation that a woman must be sexually chaste prior to marriage. To counteract this imperative, some female divorcees label their previous marriages as "unconsummated."

4. Concern about causing problems for the very individuals from whom I sought to learn stemmed from an experience in my neighborhood. The flat in which I resided was in Juhu-Vile Parle Scheme, which was demarcated a conservative, Gujarati neighborhood. About six months into my fieldwork, neighbors in the building told me to "talk to the girl on the second floor; she works in a call center." After three families suggested this, I did as advised, but the young woman who answered the door responded defensively that no one in her home works at a call center. In contrast to other residents, who made it a habit to chat in a social, neighborly fashion, she did not, it was clear, want anything to do with me. She promptly ended our conversation and shut the door. When I told the neighbors that she did not work in a call center, they claimed she was lying. "We see her coming and going," one elderly woman stated. I never learned who was telling the truth and who wasn't, but the gossip and sense of secrecy connected with the matter reminded me of the importance of respecting boundaries, particularly those of people who are the subject of "nosy neighbors."

5. Phadke, "Dangerous Liaisons"; Phadke, "'You Can Be Lonely in a Crowd.'"

6. Phadke, "Dangerous Liaisons," 1510.

7. George, *When Women Come First.*

8. Ibid., 180.

9. Kibria, "Culture, Social Class, and Income Control in the Lives of Women Garment Workers in Bangladesh."

10. ibid., 304

11. George, *When Women Come First,* 176.

12. Ibid.

Chapter 8

1. Baker, "In Search of the Next Bangalore," 43.

2. "Out of India."

3. Pradhan and Abraham, "Social and Cultural Impact of Outsourcing," 24.

4. For instance, Anjali spoke of how on public buses she finds it necessary to contain herself due to *Eve-teasing.* This need stems from an incident in which a male passenger on the bus tried to fondle her breast. For this reason, Anjali believes, women need to be hyperaware of who surrounds them and situate themselves accordingly. For example, when seated next to a man, Anjali makes sure to place her purse between her underarm and breast as a buffer. When walking down the street or through the train station, she is required to maintain vigilance on the men who pass her, because of harassment and stares. "It's exhausting" is how she describes the energy she has to put into protecting herself from men when she goes out. "It's like we don't even have a right to exist," she stated.

5. For further readings on women as the bodily site of maintaining their family's reputation, see Nagar, "Communal Discourses, Marriage, and Politics of Gendered Social Boundaries Among South Asian Immigrants in Tanzania"; Mathur, "Body as Site, Body as Space."

6. According to Margaret Abraham, the globalization of customer service not only brings forth much-needed employment opportunities to India, but also the nation-state uses the influx of such foreign investment to shift its role from being a provider of public benefits such as electricity and education to privatizing such public essentials. She also contends that when a nation-state moves in the direction of reducing the social protections provided to citizens—under the rubric of private companies providing such protections—we should proceed with caution when analyzing women's participation in the service sector and its subsequent benefits and drawbacks. See Abraham, "Globalization, Work and Citizenship"; Abraham and Manning, "Business Process Outsourcing."

7. Haraway, "Situated Knowledge."

Postscript

1. "Boss Faces Call-Centre Death Case."

2. "SC dismisses Som Mittal's plea."

Appendix

1. Onwuegbuzie and Johnson, "Mixed Method and Mixed Model Research"; Onwuegbuzie and Leech, "On Becoming a Pragmatic Researcher: The Importance of Combining Quantitative and Qualitative Research Methodologies."

2. Strauss and Corbin, *Basics of Qualitative Research;* Strauss and Corbin, *Grounded Theory in Practice.*

3. Cresswell, *Qualitative Inquiry and Research Design;* Russell, *Research Methods in Anthropology.*

References

Abraham, Margaret. "Globalization, Work and Citizenship: The Call Centre Industry in India." In *Contours of Citizenship: Women in a Local-Global World*, ed. Margaret Abraham, Esther Ngan-ling Chow, Laura Maratou-Alipranti, and Evangelia Tastsoglou. Aldershot, England: Ashgate, forthcoming.

Abraham, Margaret, and Susan Manning. Business Process Outsourcing: The U.S. and India in the New Global Market. Paper presented at the Annual Meeting of the American Sociological Association, San Francisco, CA, August 14–17, 2004.

Adam, Barbara. "The Gendered Time Politics of Globalization: Of Shadowlands and Elusive Justice." *Feminist Review* 3, no. 70 (2002): 3–30.

Agarwal, Bina. *A Field of One's Own: Gender and Land Rights in South Asia*. Cambridge, UK: Cambridge University Press, 1994.

Agnew, John. *Hegemony: The New Shape of Global Power*. Philadelphia: Temple University Press, 2005.

———. "Representing Space: Space, Scale, and Culture in Social Science." In *Place/Culture/Representation*, ed. James Duncan and David Ley. New York: Routledge, 1993.

Agot, Kawango. "HIV/Aids Interventions and the Politics of the African Woman's Body." In *A Companion to Feminist Geography*, ed. Lise Nelson and Joni Seager, 363–378. Malden, MA: Blackwell, 2005.

Ahluwalia, Ashim, dir. *John and Jane*. Mumbai, India: Future East Film, 2005.

Andersen, Margaret L. *Thinking About Women: Sociological Perspectives on Sex and Gender*, 7th ed. Boston: Pearson/Allyn & Bacon, 2006.

Aneesh, Aneesh. "Specters of Global Communication." *Frakcija* 43/44 (2007), 26–33.

Arora, Chandna. "Bad BPOs: A Case of Wrong Image?" *Times of India, Mumbai*, November 11, 2006.

Baker, Aryn. "In Search of the Next Bangalore." *Time*, June 26, 2006, 42–43.

"Bangalore Schools Face English Fines." *Guardian Weekly,* April 13, 2007, http://education.guardian.co.uk/tefl/story/0,,2055731,00.html (accessed November 28, 2007).

Bapat, M., and I. Agarwal. "Our Needs, Our Priorities: Women and Men from the Slums in Mumbai and Pune Talk About Their Needs for Water and Sanitation." *Environment and Urbanization* 15, no. 2 (2003): 71–86.

Barker, D. A. "Factory Legislation in India." *The Economic Journal* 21, no. 84 (1911): 643–648.

Barnett, Rosalind, and Caryl Rivers. *Same Difference: How Gender Myths Are Hurting Our Relationships, Our Children, and Our Jobs.* New York: Basic Books, 2004.

Bhattacharya, Rinki, ed. *Behind Closed Doors: Domestic Violence in India.* New Thousand Oaks, CA: Sage, 2004.

Baxi, Parul. "Globalizing Identity? Voices of Call Center Workers from Gurgaon, India." Hayward: California State University, East Bay, 2006.

Behar, Ruth. "The Vulnerable Observer." In *The Vulnerable Observer: Anthropology That Breaks the Heart,* ed. Ruth Behar, 1–33. Boston: Beacon Press, 1996.

Bellman, Eric. "A Dollar Store's Rich Allure in India---A U.S. Franchise's Success Shows 'Made in America' Sells: Lessons for Wal-Mart's Entry?" *Wall Street Journal,* January 23, 2007, B1.

Belt, Vicki, Ranald Richardson, and Juliet Webster. "Women's Work in the Information Economy: The Case of Telephone Call Centres." *Information Communication & Society* 3, no. 3 (2000): 366–386.

Bhagat, Chetan. *One Night @ the Call Center.* New Delhi: Rupa & Co., 2005.

Bondi, Liz, and Mona Domosh. "On the Contours of Public Space: A Tale of Three Women." *Antipode* 30, no. 3 (1998): 270–289.

Bondi, Liz, and Damaris Rose. "Constructing Gender, Constructing the Urban: A Review of Anglo-American Feminist Urban Geography." *Gender, Place & Culture: A Journal of Feminist Geography* 10, no. 3 (2003): 229–246.

Bonds, Anne. "Calling on Femininity? Gender, Call Centers, and Restructuring in the Rural American West." *ACME: An International E-Journal for Critical Geographies* 5, no. 1 (2006): 28–49.

Bordo, Susan. *Unbearable Weight: Feminism, Western Culture, and the Body.* Berkeley: University of California Press, 1993.

Borkar, Pallavi. "Midnight Melange." *Mid Day, Mumbai,* May 26, 2006, CV11.

"Boss Faces Call-Centre Death Case." *BBC News,* February 22, 2008, http://news.bbc.co.uk/2/hi/business/7258837.stm (accessed May 27, 2009).

Boyer, Kate. "Place and the Politics of Virtue: Clerical Work, Corporate Anxiety, and Changing Meanings of Public Womanhood in Early Twentieth-Century Montreal." *Gender Place & Culture: A Journal of Feminist Geography* 5, no. 3 (1998): 261–276.

———. "Spaces of Change: Gender, Information Technology, and New Geographies of Mobility and Fixity in the Early Twentieth Century Information Economy." In *A*

Companion to Feminist Geography, ed. Lise Nelson and Joni Seager, 228–256. Malden, MA: Blackwell, 2005.

Breathnach, Proinnsias. "Information Technology, Gender Segmentation and the Relocation of Back Office Employment." *Information, Communication & Society* 5, no. 3 (2002): 320–335.

Brownmiller, Susan. *Femininity.* New York: Fawcett Books, 1985.

Bryson, John R. "The 'Second' Global Shift: The Offshoring or Global Sourcing of Corporate Services and the Rise of Distanciated Emotional Labour." *Geografiska Annaler Series B: Human Geography* 89 (2007): 31–43.

Burns, Elizabeth. "Women's Travel to Inner City Employment." Women's Travel Issues: Proceedings from the Second National Conference, Federal Highway Administration, U.S. Department of Transportation, 1996. http://www.fhwa.dot.gov/ohim/womens/chap10.pdf (accessed October 22, 2009).

Burns, Elizabeth, and Patricia Gober. "Job Linkages in Inner City Phoenix." *Urban Geography* 19, no. 1 (1998): 12–23.

Burton, A. "House/Daughter/Nation: Interiority, Architecture, and Historical Imagination in Janaki Majumdar's 'Family History.'" *Journal of Asian Studies* 56, no. 4 (1997): 921–946.

Burton, Antoinette M. *Burdens of History: British Feminists, Indian Women, and Imperial Culture, 1865–1915.* Chapel Hill: University of North Carolina Press, 1994.

Butler, Judith. *Gender Trouble: Feminism and the Subversion of Identity.* New York: Routledge, 1990.

Castells, Manuel. *End of Millennium.* Malden, MA: Blackwell, 1998.

Castillo, Debra A., Maria Gudelia Rangel Gomez, and Bonnie Delgado. "Border Lives: Prostitute Women in Tijuana." *Signs* 24, no. 2 (1999): 387–422.

Chacko, Elizabeth. "Positionality and Praxis: Fieldwork Experiences in Rural India." *Singapore Journal of Tropical Geography* 25, no. 1 (2004): 51–63.

Chant, Sylvia. "Households, Gender and Rural-Urban Migration: Reflections on Linkages and Considerations for Policy." *Environment and Urbanization* 10, no. 1 (1998): 5–21.

Chatterjee, Partha. *The Nation and Its Fragments: Colonial and Postcolonial Histories.* Princeton, NJ: Princeton University Press, 1993.

Chengappa, Raj, and Malini Goyal. "Housekeepers to the World." *India Today,* November 18, 2002, 36–49.

Cowie, Claire. "The Accents of Outsourcing: The Meanings Of 'Neutral' in the Indian Call Centre Industry." *World Englishes* 26, no. 3 (2007): 316–330.

Cox, Wendell, "Mumbai Wards & Districts: Population & Density by Sector 2001," http://www.demographia.com/db-mumbaidistr91.htm (accessed October 1, 2007).

Crang, Philip, Claire Dwyer, and Peter Jackson. "Transnationalism and the Spaces of Commodity Culture." *Progress in Human Geography* 27, no. 4 (2003): 438–457.

Cresswell, Tim. "Embodiment, Power and the Politics of Mobility: The Case of Female Tramps and Hobos." *Transactions of the Institute of British Geographers* 24, no. 2 (1999): 175–192.

———. *In Place / Out of Place: Geography, Ideology, and Transgression.* Minneapolis: University of Minnesota Press, 1996.

———. *Qualitative Inquiry and Research Design: Choosing Among Five Traditions.* Thousand Oaks, CA: Sage, 1998.

Cristaldi, Flavia. "Commuting and Gender in Italy: A Methodological Issue." *Professional Geographer* 57, no. 2 (2005): 268–285.

Delaney, Kevin J. "Outsourcing Jobs--and Workers--to India." *Wall Street Journal,* October 13, 2003, B1.

"Delhi: The Rape Capital of India." *Times of India,* July 2, 2004, http://timesofindia. indiatimes.com/India/Delhi_The_Rape_Capital_of_India/articleshow/msid-762338,curpg-1.cms (accessed September 27, 2007).

Deshmukh-Ranadive, Joy. *Space for Power: Social and Cultural Aspects of Gender Inequality and Discrimination in India.* Noida, India: Rainbow Publishers, in collaboration with Centre for Women's Development Studies, 2002.

Dhillon, Amrit. "Call Centres Are Blamed for a Rise in Loose Living Among India's Affluent New Elite," *Telegraph.co.uk,* August 10, 2006, http://www.telegraph.co.uk/news/ main.jhtml?xml=/news/2006/10/08/windia08.xml (accessed October 22, 2007).

Domosh, Mona. "Geography and Gender: Home, Again?" *Progress in Human Geography* 22, no. 2 (1998): 276–282.

Domosh, Mona, and Joni Seager. *Putting Women in Place: Feminist Geographers Make Sense of the World.* London: Guilford Press, 2001.

Duncan, Nancy. *Bodyspace: Destabilizing Geographies of Gender and Sexuality.* London: Routledge, 1996.

Dutta, Madhusree, dir. "7 Islands and a Metro." Mumbai, India: Majlis, 2006.

Ehrenreich, Barbara, and Arlie Russell Hochschild. *Global Woman: Nannies, Maids, and Sex Workers in the New Economy.* New York: Metropolitan Books, 2003.

Elliot, Michael. "India, Inc.: Why the World's Biggest Democracy Is the Next Great Economic Superpower--and What It Means for America." *Time,* June 26, 2006, 36–46.

Elson, Diane. "Nimble Fingers and Other Fables." In *Of Common Cloth: Women in the Global Textile Industry,* ed. Wendy Chapkis and Cynthia Enloe, 5–15. Amsterdam: Transnational Institute, 1983.

Elson, Diane, and Ruth Pearson. "'Nimble Fingers Make Cheap Workers': An Analysis of Women's Employment in Third World Export Manufacturing." *Feminist Review,* no. 7 (1981): 87–107.

Engels, Dagmar. *Beyond Purdah? Women in Bengal 1890–1939.* Delhi, India: Oxford University Press, 1996.

England, Kim. "Getting Personal: Reflexivity, Positionality, and Feminist Research." *The Professional Geographer* 46, no. 1 (1994): 80–89.

"Factories Act, 1948." Delhi, India: Office of the Labour Commissioner. http://labour.delhigovt.nic.in/act/html_ifa/fa1948_index.html (accessed April 13, 2006).

Faludi, Susan. *Backlash: The Undeclared War Against American Women*. New York: Crown, 1991.

Fincher, Ruth, and Jane M. Jacobs. *Cities of Difference*. New York: Guilford Press, 1998.

Fisch, Joerg. *Burning Women: A Global History of Widow-Sacrifice from Ancient Times to the Present*. London: Seagull Books, 2005.

Fitzpatrick, Tony. "Social Policy and Time." *Time & Society* 13, no. 2–3 (2004): 197–219.

Flowerdew, Robin. "Hägerstand, Torsten." In *Key Thinkers on Space and Place*, ed. Phil Hubbard, Rob Kitchin, and Gill Valentine, 149–153. London: Sage, 2004.

Foley, Douglas E. "Critical Ethnography: The Reflexive Turn." *Qualitative Studies in Education* 15, no. 5 (2002): 469–490.

Fountain, Jane. "Constructing the Information Society: Women, Information Technology, and Design." *Technology in Society* 22 (2000): 45–62.

Freeman, Carla. *High Tech and High Heels in the Global Economy: Women, Work, and Pink-Collar Identities in the Caribbean*. Durham, NC: Duke University Press, 2000.

García, Alma M. *Chicana Feminist Thought: The Basic Historical Writings*. New York: Routledge, 1997.

Garwood, S. "Working to Death: Gender, Labour, and Violence in Ciudad Juárez, México." *Peace, Conflict and Development*, no. 2 (2002), http://www.peacestudiesjournal.org.uk/dl/working2.pdf (accessed October 19, 2009).

George, Sheba Mariam. *When Women Come First: Gender and Class in Transnational Migration*. Berkeley: University of California Press, 2005.

Ghose, Sagarika. "The Dalit in India." *Social Research* 70, no. 1 (2003): 83–109.

Gibson-Graham, J. K. *The End of Capitalism (as We Knew It): A Feminist Critique of Political Economy*. Malden, MA: Blackwell, 1996.

Girls Media Group. "Do You Know How We Feel?" Mumbai, India: PUKAR: A Woman's Place Project, 2003.

Gottdiener, Mark. *The Social Production of Urban Space*. Austin: University of Texas Press, 1985.

Greenspan, Anna. *India and the IT Revolution: Networks of Global Culture*. New York: Palgrave Macmillan, 2004.

Gray, John. *Men Are from Mars, Women Are from Venus: A Practical Guide for Improving Communication and Getting What You Want in Your Relationships*. New York: HarperCollins, 1992.

Gulati, Sonali. "Nalini by Day, Nancy by Night." New York: Women Make Movies, 2005.

Hafkin, Nancy, and Nancy Taggart. "Gender, Information Technology, and Developing Countries: An Analytic Study." Washington DC: United States Agency for International Development, 2001.

Hägerstand, Torsten. "Space, Time, and Human Conditions." In *Dynamic Allocation of*

Urban Space, ed. Anders Karlqvist, L. Lundqvist, and F. Snickars, 3–14. Lexington, MA: Saxon House, Lexington Books, 1975.

Hancock, Mary Elizabeth. "Gendering the Modern: Women and Home Science in British India." In *Gender, Sexuality and Colonial Modernities*, ed. Antoinette Burton 148-160. New York: Routledge, 1999.

———. *Womanhood in the Making: Domestic Ritual and Public Culture in Urban South India*. Boulder, CO: Westview Press, 1999.

Hanson, Susan, and Geraldine Pratt. *Gender, Work, and Space*. New York: Routledge, 1995.

Haraway, Donna. *Simians, Cyborgs, and Women: The Reinvention of Nature*. New York: Routledge, 1991.

———. "Situated Knowledge: The Science Question in Feminism and the Privilege of Partial Perspective." *Feminist Studies* 14 (1988): 575–599.

Harding, Sandra G. *Whose Science? Whose Knowledge? Thinking from Women's Lives*. Ithaca, NY: Cornell University Press, 1991.

Harrison, Ann E., and Margaret S. McMillan. "Dispelling Some Myths About Offshoring." *Academy of Management Perspectives (formerly Academy of Management Executive)* 20, no. 4 (2006): 6–22.

Harvey, David. *Justice, Nature, and the Geography of Difference*. Malden, MA: Blackwell, 1996.

———. *Spaces of Hope*. Berkeley: University of California Press, 2000.

Herman, Edward S., and Noam Chomsky. *Manufacturing Consent: The Political Economy of the Mass Media*. New York: Pantheon Books, 1988.

Hickey, M., and V. Lawson. "Beyond Science? Human Geography, Interpretation, and Critique." In *Questioning Geography: Fundamental Debates*, ed. Noel Castree and Alisdair Rogers, 96–114. Malden, MA: Blackwell, 2005.

Hochschild, Arlie. *The Managed Heart*. University of California Press, 1983.

Hochschild, Arlie Russell, and Anne Machung. *The Second Shift: Working Parents and the Revolution at Home*. New York: Viking, 1989.

Holloway, Lewis. "Donna Haraway." In *Key Thinkers on Space and Place*, ed. Phil Hubbard, Rob Kitchin, and Gill Valentine, 167–173. Thousand Oaks, CA: Sage, 2004.

Hooks, Bell. *Feminist Theory: From Margin to Center*. Boston: South End Press, 1984.

Howe, Louise. *Pink Collar Workers: Inside the World of Women's Work*. New York: Putnam, 1977.

Hunt, V. "Call Centre Work for Women: Career or Stopgap?" *Labour & Industry* 14, no. 3 (2004): 139–155.

Hyndman, Jennifer. "Mind the Gap: Bridging Feminist and Political Geography Through Geopolitics." *Political Geography* 23, no. 3 (2004): 307–323.

———. "Towards a Feminist Geopolitics." *Canadian Geographer* 45, no. 2 (2001): 210–223.

"India's Shining Hopes: A Survey of India." *Economist* 53 (February 19, 2004), 20-page insert.

Jackson, Peter. "Local Consumption Cultures in a Globalizing World." *Transactions of the Institute of British Geographers* 29, no. 2 (2004): 165–179.

Johnson, Jo. "Bangalore Hit by English Ban in Schools." *Financial Times*, September 26, 2006, http://www.ft.com/cms/s/0/5f5bfade-4cec-11db-b03c-0000779e2340.html?nclick_check=1 (accessed November 28, 2007).

Johnston, Lynda. "Crossing Boundaries : Gendered Spaces and Bodies in Golf." In *Subjectivities, Knowledges, and Feminist Geographies: The Subjects and Ethics of Social Research*, ed. Liz Bondi, 90–105. Lanham, MD: Rowman & Littlefield, 2002.

Joseph, Manu. "God, Sex, and Call Centres." *Times of India, Mumbai*, October 22, 2006, 15.

Kantor, Paula. "Female Mobility in India--The Influence of Seclusion Norms on Economic Outcomes." *International Development Planning Review* 24, no. 2 (2002): 145–159.

Katz, Cindi. *Growing Up Global: Economic Restructuring and Children's Everyday Lives*. Minneapolis: University of Minnesota Press, 2004.

Keith, Michael, and Steve Pile. *Place and the Politics of Identity*. New York: Routledge, 1993.

Kelkar, Govind, and D. Nathan. "Gender Relations and Technological Change in Asia." *Current Sociology* 50, no. 3 (2002): 427–441.

Kelkar, Govind, Girija Shrestha, and Veena Nagarjan. "IT Industry and Women's Agency: Explorations in Bangalore and Delhi, India." *Gender, Technology and Development* 6, no. 1 (2002): 63–82.

Kibria, Nazli. "Culture, Social Class, and Income Control in the Lives of Women Garment Workers in Bangladesh." *Gender and Society* 9, no. 3 (1995): 289–309.

Kirschner, Suzanne R. "'Then What Have I to Do with Thee?': On Identity, Fieldwork, and Ethnographic Knowledge." *Cultural Anthropology* 2, no. 2 (1987): 211–234.

Kirshenbaum, G. "Jadranka, Cigelj, and Nusreta Sivac: Efforts to Bring the Rapists of Bosnian Women to Justice." *Ms.* 7, no. 4 (1997): 64–68.

Kobayashi, Audrey. "GPC Ten Years On: Is Self-Reflexivity Enough?" *Gender Place & Culture* 10, no. 4 (2003): 345–350.

Krishnamurthy, Mathangi. "Outsourced Identities: The Fragmentations of the Cross-Border Economy." *Anthropology News* 46, no. 3 (2005): 22–23.

Kumar, A. K. Shiva, and Kalyani Menon-Sen. "Women in India: How Free? How Equal?" New Delhi: United Nations Development Assistance Framework, Office of the Resident Coordinator in India, 2001.

Kumar, Radha. *The History of Doing: An Illustrated Account of Movements for Women's Rights and Feminism in India, 1800–1990*. New York: Verso, 1993.

Kwan, Mei Po. "Gender and Individual Access to Urban Opportunities: A Study Using

Space-Time Measures." *Professional Geographer* 51, no. 2 (1999): 210–227.

Lalithambika, Antharjanam, and Gita Krishnakutty. *Cast Me Out If You Will: Stories and Memoir.* New York: Feminist Press, 1998.

Law, Robin. "Gender and Daily Mobility in a New Zealand City, 1920–1960." *Social & Cultural Geography* 3, no. 4 (2002): 425–446.

Laws, Glenda, and John Radford. "Women with Disabilities and Everyday Geographies: Home Space and the Contested Body." In *Putting Health into Place: Landscape, Identity, and Well-Being,* ed. Robin A. Kearns and Wilbert M. Gesler. Syracuse, NY: Syracuse University Press, 1998.

Liddle, Joanna, and Rama Joshi. *Daughters of Independence: Gender, Caste, and Class in India.* New Delhi, India: Kali for Women, 1986.

Livingston, Jessica. "Murder in Juarez: Gender, Sexual Violence, and the Global Assembly Line." *Frontiers: A Journal of Women's Studies* 25, no. 1 (2004): 59–77.

Longhurst, Robyn. *Bodies: Exploring Fluid Boundaries.* New York: Routledge, 2000.

———. "The Body and Geography." *Gender, Place & Culture: A Journal of Feminist Geography* 2, no. 1 (1995): 97–106.

———. "Fat Bodies: Developing Geographical Research Agendas." *Progress in Human Geography* 29, no. 3 (2005): 247–259.

Mandel, Jennifer. "Mobility Matters: Women's Livelihood Strategies in Porto Novo, Benin." *Gender, Place, and Culture* 11, no. 2 (2004): 257–388.

Manju, V. "A Supersonic Boom." *Times of India, Mumbai,* September 20, 2006, 4.

Mansell, Robin, and Uta Wehn de Montalvo. *Knowledge Societies: Information Technology for Sustainable Development.* Oxford, UK: Oxford University Press, for and on behalf of the United Nations, 1998.

Marston, Sallie. "The Social Construction of Scale." *Progress in Human Geography* 24, no. 2 (2000): 219–243.

Marston, Sallie, and Neil Smith. "States, Scales and Households: Limits to Scale Thinking? A Response to Brenner." *Progress in Human Geography* 25, no. 4 (2001): 615–620.

Massey, Doreen. *For Space.* Thousand Oaks, CA: Sage, 2005.

———. *Space, Place, and Gender.* Minneapolis: University of Minnesota Press, 1994.

———. *Spatial Divisions of Labor: Social Structures and the Geography of Production.* New York: Methuen, 1984.

Mathew, Babu. "A Brief Note on Labour Legislation in India." *Asia Labour Update,* no. 46 (2003), http://www.amrc.org.hk/alu_article/labour_law/a_brief_note_on_labour_legislation_in_india (accessed October 17, 2009).

Mathur, Kanchan. "Body as Site, Body as Space: Bodily Integrity and Women's Empowerment in India." *Economic and Political Weekly* 43, no. 17 (2008): 54–63. http://save-intl.org/women_epw.pdf (accessed October 31, 2009).

McCann, Carole R., and Seung-Kyung Kim. *Feminist Theory Reader: Local and Global Perspectives.* New York: Routledge, 2003.

McDowell, Linda. *Gender, Identity and Place: A Feminist Perspective.* Cambridge, UK: Polity Press, 1999.

McKittrick, Katherine. "Who Do You Talk to, When a Body's in Trouble? M. Nourbese Philip's (Un)Silencing of Black Bodies in the Diaspora." *Social & Cultural Geography* 1, no. 2 (2000): 223.

Menon, Radhika, and Roseanne Lobo, dirs. "Freedom Before 11." 25 minutes. Mumbai, India: PUKAR: Gender and Space Project, 2005.

Miller, Kerry. "Hello, India? Er, Des Moines?" *Business Week*, June 25, 2007, 14.

Minturn, Leigh, and Swaran Kapoor. *Sita's Daughters: Coming Out of Purdah: The Rajput Women of Khalapur Revisited.* New York: Oxford University Press, 1993.

Mirchandani, Kiran. "Gender Eclipsed? Racial Hierarchies in Transnational Call Center Work." *Social Justice* 32, no. 4 (2005): 105–119.

———. "Practices of Global Capital: Gaps, Cracks, and Ironies in Transnational Call Centres in India." *Global Networks* 4, no. 4 (2004): 255–373.

Mohammed, Robin. "British Pakistani Muslim Women: Marking the Body, Marking the Nation." In *A Companion to Feminist Geography*, ed. Lise Nelson and Joni Seager, 379–397. Malden, MA: Blackwell, 2005.

Mohanty, Chandra Talpade. *Feminism Without Borders: Decolonizing Theory, Practicing Solidarity.* Durham, NC: Duke University Press, 2003.

Mohanty, Chandra Talpade, Ann Russo, and Lourdes Torres. *Third World Women and the Politics of Feminism.* Bloomington: Indiana University Press, 1991.

Moraga, Cherríe, and Gloria Anzaldúa. *This Bridge Called My Back: Writings by Radical Women of Color.* Watertown, MA: Persephone Press, 1981.

Nagar, Richa. "Communal Discourses, Marriage, and Politics of Gendered Social Boundaries Among South Asian Immigrants in Tanzania." *Gender, Place and Culture* 5, no. 2 (1998): 117–139.

Nagar, Richa, Victoria Lawson, Linda McDowell, and Susan Hanson. "Locating Globalization: Feminist (Re)Readings of the Subjects and Spaces of Globalization." *Economic Geography* 78, no. 3 (2002): 257–285.

NASSCOM, "Indian Software and Services Exports," http://www.nasscom.in/Nasscom/templates/NormalPage.aspx?id=2635 (accessed June 20, 2009).

———. "Nasscom's Ranking of Third Party Players," http://www.nasscom.org/artdisplay.asp?Art_id=4400 (accessed March 3, 2009).

———. "Third Party ITES-BPO Companies Rankings for FY 05–06," http://www.nasscom.in/Nasscom/templates/NormalPage.aspx?id=43383 (accessed February 14, 2009).

Nast, Heidi. "Unsexy Geographies." *Gender, Place, and Culture* 5 (1998): 191–206.

"The New Jobs Migration." *Economist*, February 21, 2004, 27–29.

Nichols, John. "Global Fights Go Local." *Nation*, August 30, 2004, 22.

Oberhauser, Ann, Donna Rubinoff, Karen De Bres, Susan Mains, and Cindy Pope. "Geographic Perspectives on Women." In *Geography in America at the Dawn of the 21st Century*, ed. Gary L. Gaile and Cort J. Willmott, 736–758. Oxford, UK: Oxford University Press, 2003.

Ong, Aihwa. *Spirits of Resistance and Capitalist Discipline*. Albany: State University of New York Press, 1987.

Onwuegbuzie, A. J., and R. B. Johnson. "Mixed Method and Mixed Model Research." In *Educational Research: Quantitative, Qualitative, and Mixed Approaches*, ed. R. B. Johnson and L. B. Christensen, 408–431. Needham Heights, MA: Allyn & Bacon, 2004.

Onwuegbuzie, A. J., and N. L. Leech. "On Becoming a Pragmatic Researcher: The Importance of Combining Quantitative and Qualitative Research Methodologies." *International Journal of Social Research Methodology* 8, no. 5 (2005): 375–387.

"Out of India." *60 Minutes*. CBS News, January 11, 2004, http://www.cbsnews.com/stories/2003/12/23/60minutes/main590004.shtml (accessed October 17, 2009).

Oza, Rupal. "Showcasing India: Gender, Geography, and Globalization." *Signs: Journal of Women in Culture & Society* 26, no. 4 (2001): 1067–1095.

Panda, Pradeep, and Bina Agarwal. "Marital Violence, Human Development and Women's Property Status in India." *World Development* 33, no. 5 (2005): 823–850.

Pande, Rekha. "Looking at Information Technology from a Gender Perspective: A Look at Call Centers in India." *Asian Journal of Women's Studies* 11, no. 1 (2005): 58–82.

Pandit, Kavita. "Elite Migration from 'Body Shopping' to 'Reverse Migration': The Restructuring of the Flows of Indian Technology Workers to the United States. Paper presented at Geography and the Environment Colloquium, University of Texas at Austin. February 4, 2005.

Parameswaran, Radhika "Feminist Media Ethnography in India: Exploring Power, Gender, and Culture in the Field." *Qualitative Inquiry* 7, no. 1 (2001): 69–103.

Parikh, Pravina, and Suhas Sukhatme. "Women Engineers in India." Bombay: Indian Institute of Technology, Department of Mechanical Engineering, 1992.

———. "Women in the Engineering Profession in India: The Millennium Scenario." Mumbai: Indian Institute of Technology, Department of Mechanical Engineering, 2002.

Patel, Meenakshi Dhar. *The Economic Times IT Enabled Services 2002*. Mumbai, India: Bennett Coleman, 2002.

Patel, Reena. *Hindu Women's Property Rights in Rural India: Law, Labour and Culture in Action*. Aldershot, UK: Ashgate, 2007.

———. "Working the Night Shift: Gender and the Global Economy." *ACME: An International E-Journal for Critical Geographies* 5, no. 1 (2006): 9–27.

Patel, Reena, and Mary Jane Parmentier. "The Persistence of Traditional Gender Roles in the Technology Sector: A Study of Female Engineers in India." *Information Technologies and International Development* 2, no. 3 (2005): 29–46.

Peterson, V. Spike. "Rereading Public and Private: The Dichotomy That Is Not One." *SAIS Review* 20, no. 11–29 (2000): 11–29.

Peterson, V. Spike, and Anne Sisson Runyan. *Global Gender Issues.* Boulder, CO: Westview Press, 1999.

Phadke, Shilpa. "Dangerous Liaisons: Men and Women: Risk and Reputation in Mumbai." *Economic and Political Weekly* 42, no. 17 (2007): 1510–1518.

———. "'You Can Be Lonely in a Crowd': The Production of Safety in Mumbai." *Indian Journal of Gender Studies* 12, no. 1 (2005): 41–62.

Poster, Winifred. "Dangerous Places and Nimble Fingers: Discourses of Gender Discrimination and Rights in Global Corporations." *International Journal of Politics, Culture, and Society* 15, no. 1 (2001): 77–105.

———. "Saying 'Good Morning' in the Middle of the Night: The Reversal of Work Time in Globalized ICT Service Work." *Research in the Sociology of Work* 17 (2007): 55–112.

———. "Who's on the Line? Indian Call Center Agents Pose as Americans for US-Outsourced Firms." *Industrial Relations* 46, no. 2 (2007): 271–304.

Pradhan, J. P., and V. Abraham. "Social and Cultural Impact of Outsourcing: Emerging Issues from Indian Call Centers." *Harvard Asia Quarterly* 9, no. 3 (2005): 22–30.

Pratt, Geraldine. "Geography and Body." In *The Dictionary of Human Geography,* ed. Ronald John Johnston, Derek Gregory, Geraldine Pratt, and Michael Watts, 48–49. Malden, MA: Blackwell, 2000.

———. *Working Feminism.* Philadelphia: Temple University Press, 2004.

Puri, Jyoti. "Stakes and States: Sexual Discourses from New Delhi." *Feminist Review* 83, no. 1 (2006): 139–148.

Raghuram, Parvati. "Migration, Gender, and the IT Sector: Intersecting Debates." *Women's Studies International Forum* 27, no. 2 (2004): 163–176.

Raju, Saraswati. "Contextualizing Critical Geography in India: Emerging Research and Praxis." *Geoforum* 35 (2004): 539–544.

———. "We Are Different, but Can We Talk?" *Gender, Place & Culture: A Journal of Feminist Geography* 9, no. 2 (2002): 173–177.

Raju, Saraswati, and Deipica Bagchi. *Women and Work in South Asia: Regional Patterns and Perspectives.* London: Routledge, 1993.

Ramesh, Babu P. "Cyber Coolies in BPO: Insecurities and Vulnerabilities of Non-Standard Work." *Economic and Political Weekly* 39, no. 5 (2004): 492–497.

Ramusack, Barbara N. "Cultural Missionaries, Maternal Imperialists, Feminist Allies: British Women Activists in India, 1865–1945." *Women's Studies International Forum* 13, no. 4 (1990): 295–308.

Ranade, Shilpa. "The Way She Moves: Mapping the Everyday Production of Gender-Space." *Economic and Political Weekly* 42, no. 17 (2007): 1519–1526.

Ranjit, Shan, "Sabarimalai: The Banning of Menstruating Women," http://www.tamil-nation.org/forum/shanranjit/sabarimalai.htm (accessed September 29, 2007).

Rao, K. Chandra Sekhar, "The Factories (Amendment) Bill, 2005 " www.prsindia.org/docs/bills/1171264974/1171264974_The_Factories__Amendment__Bill_2005.pdf (accessed August 18, 2007).

"Ready for Take-Off." *Economist*, June 16, 2007, 8–10.

Reich, Robert. "Plenty of Knowledge Work to Go Around." *Harvard Business Review* 83, no. 4 (2005): 17.

Rose, Gillian. *Feminism and Geography: The Limits of Geographical Knowledge.* Cambridge, UK: Polity Press, 1993.

———. "Situating Knowledges: Positionality, Reflexivities and Other Tactics." *Progress in Human Geography* 21, no. 3 (1997): 305–320.

Rubin, Herbert, and Irene S. Rubin. *Qualitative Interviewing: The Art of Hearing Data.* Thousand Oaks, CA: Sage, 1995.

Russell, Bernard. *Research Methods in Anthropology: Qualitative and Quantitative Methods.* Walnut Creek, CA: AltaMira Press, 2002.

Sahu, Amiya Kumar. "Present Scenario of Municipal Solid Waste (MSW) Dumping Grounds in India." Paper presented at the International Conference on Sustainable Solid Waste Management, Chennai, India, September 5–7, 2007.

Said, Edward W. *Orientalism.* New York: Pantheon Books, 1978.

Sandburg, Jared. "'It Says Press Any Key. Where's the Any Key?' India's Call-Center Workers Get Pounded, Pampered." *Wall Street Journal,* February 20, 2007, B1.

———. "Women's Burden: Counter-Geographies of Globalization and the Feminization of Survival." *Journal of International Affairs* 53, no. 2 (2000): 503–524.

Saxena, Poonam. "The Menace of Dowry." In *From Patriarchy to Empowerment: Women's Participation, Movements, and Rights in the Middle East, North Africa, and South Asia,* ed. V. M. Moghadam, 258–276. Syracuse, NY: Syracuse University Press, 2007.

"SC dismisses Som Mittal's plea." *Business Standard,* February 21, 2008, http://www.business-standard.com/india/storypage.php?tp=on&autono=33957 (accessed May 27, 2009).

Seager, Joni K., and Mona Domosh. *Putting Women in Place: Feminist Geographers Make Sense of the World.* New York: Guilford Press, 2001.

Secor, Anna. "The Veil and Urban Space in Istanbul: Women's Dress, Mobility and Islamic Knowledge." *Gender, Place and Culture* 9, no. 1 (2002): 5–22.

Sengupta, Somini. "Careers Give India's Women New Independence." *New York Times,* November 23, 2007, http://www.nytimes.com/2007/11/23/world/asia/23india.html?_r=1&oref=slogin (accessed November 27, 2007).

Sharma, Arti. "Headcount Crisis at Call Centres." *Times of India,* July 15, 2005, http://timesofindia.indiatimes.com/articleshow/1173472.cms (accessed June 28, 2007).

Sharp, Joanne. "Gendering Nationhood: A Feminist Engagement with National Identity." In *Bodyspace: Destabilizing Geographies of Gender and Sexuality,* ed. Nancy Duncan, 97–108. London: Routledge, 1996.

Shaw, Annapurna. *The Making of Navi Mumbai.* New Delhi, India: Orient Longman, 2004.

Siddiqi, Dina. "Miracle Worker or Womanmachine? Tracking (Trans) National Realities in Bangladeshi Factories." *Economic and Political Weekly* 35, no. 21–22 (2000): 11–17.

———. "The Sexual Harassment of Industrial Workers: Strategies for Intervention in the Workplace and Beyond." Dhaka, India: Center for Policy Dialogue, 2003.

Silvey, Rachel. "Borders, Embodiment, and Mobility: Feminist Migration Studies in Geography." In *A Companion to Feminist Geography,* ed. Lise Nelson and Joni Seager, 138–149. Malden, MA: Blackwell, 2005.

Singh, J. P. "Social and Cultural Aspects of Gender Inequality and Discrimination in India." *Asian Profile* 30, no. 2 (2002): 163–176.

Singh, Preeti, and Anu Pandey. "Women in Call Centres." *Economic and Political Weekly* 40, no. 7 (2005): 684–688.

Skop, Emily. *Saffron Suburbs: Lessons Learned from an Indian American Community.* Chicago: Center for American Places, forthcoming.

———. "The Methodological Potential of Focus Groups in Population Geography." *Population, Space and Place* 12, no. 2 (2006): 113–124.

Slater, Joanna. "Call of the West: For India's Youth, New Money Fuels a Revolution." *Wall Street Journal,* January 27, 2004, A1.

Soja, Edward W. *Postmodern Geographies: The Reassertion of Space in Critical Social Theory.* London: Verso, 1989.

———. *Thirdspace: Journeys to Los Angeles and Other Real-and-Imagined Places.* Malden, MA: Blackwell, 1996.

Strauss, Anselm L., and Juliet M. Corbin. *Basics of Qualitative Research: Ground Theory Procedures and Techniques.* Newbury Park, CA: Sage, 1990.

———. *Grounded Theory in Practice.* Thousand Oaks, CA: Sage, 1997.

"Students Upset over Ban on Alternate English." *Times of India,* August 5, 2006, http://timesofindia.indiatimes.com/articleshow/1859817.cms (accessed December 5, 2007).

Suvarna, Yatish. "Ways of the Indian Pervert." *Times of India, Mumbai,* December 3, 2006.

Tanner, Julian, and Rhonda Cockerill. "Gender, Social Change, and the Professions: The Case of Pharmacy." *Sociological Forum* 11, no. 4 (1996): 643–660.

Tejaswi, Mina Joseph. "India Calling." *Times of India,* August 4, 2006, 25.

Thanawala, Sudhin, "India's Call-Center Jobs Go Begging," *Time,* October 16, 2007, http://www.time.com/time/business/article/0,8599,1671982,00.html?cnn=yes (accessed October 16, 2007).

Thibodeau, Patrick. "Inaction on Offshoring Will Hurt U.S. IT, Author Says." *Computerworld* 39, no. 27 (2005): 13.

Thompson, Ginger. "Chasing Mexico's Dream into Squalor." *New York Times*, February 11, 2001.

Tuan, Yi Fu. "Cultural Geography: Glances Backward and Forward." *Annals of the Association of American Geographers* 94, no. 4 (2004): 729–734.

"U.S. Business Grads Take Jobs in India." *NPR News*, September 6, 2007, http://www.npr.org/templates/story/story.php?storyId=14204623 (accessed November 15, 2007).

Upadhya, Carol, and A. R. Vasavi. "Work, Culture, and Sociality in the Indian IT Industry: A Sociological Study." Bangalore, India: School of Social Sciences, National Institute of Advanced Studies, 2006.

Varma, Roli. "Technological Fix: Sex Determination in India." *Bulletin of Science, Technology, and Society* 22, no. 1 (2002): 21–30.

———. "Women in Information Technology: A Case Study of Undergraduate Students in a Minority-Serving Institution." *Bulletin of Science, Technology, and Society* 22, no. 4 (2002): 274–283.

Vohra, Paromita. "Q2P." 55 minutes. Mumbai, India: Paromita Vohra/Devi Pictures, 2006.

———. "A Woman's Place." 30 minutes. Mumbai, India: Paromita Vohra/Devi Pictures, 1999.

Wadley, Susan S. "Women and the Hindu Tradition." *Signs* 3, no. 1 (1977): 113–125.

Weinberg, B. A. "Computer Use and the Demand for Female Workers." *Industrial and Labor Relations Review* 53, no. 2 (2000): 290–308.

West, Lois A. "Nation." In *A Companion to Gender Studies*, ed. Philomena Essed, David Theo Goldberg, and Audrey Kobayashi, 145–159. Malden, MA: Blackwell, 2005.

Wilson, Elizabeth. *The Sphinx in the City: Urban Life, the Control of Disorder, and Women.* Berkeley: University of California Press, 1992.

Wright, Melissa W. "Crossing the Factory Frontier: Gender, Place and Power in the Mexican Maquiladora." *Antipode* 29, no. 3 (1997): 278–302.

———. *Disposable Women and Other Myths of Global Capitalism.* New York: Routledge, 2006.

———. "From Protests to Politics: Sex Work, Women's Worth, and Ciudad Juarez Modernity." *Annals of the Association of American Geographers* 94, no. 2 (2004): 369–386.

Yadav, Madhukar. *Winning @ Call Centre: Confessions of a Calling Agent.* New Delhi, India: Wisdom Tree, 2007.

Yeoh, Brenda, and Shirlena Huang. "Negotiating Public Space: Strategies and Styles of Migrant Female Domestic Workers in Singapore." *Urban Studies* 35, no. 3 (1998): 583–602.

Yuval-Davis, Nira. *Gender and Nation.* London: Sage, 1997.

Index

accent acquisition and training, 43, 46, 103, 104, 162n67, 166n45
American-Born Confused Desi (ABCD), 22

Bangalore rape case, 74–79, 153
blood, 146–47
Bombay Calling (documentary), 16
Bombay Maternity Benefit Act, 49
business process outsourcing (BPO) industry, 2, 164nn8, 11; emergence of industry, 28–29; and "English imperialism," 46; and feminization of labor, 30–33; job fair photo, 17; *see also* call center industry
Butler, Judith, 13

call center industry; distinction from other transnational industries, 27–28; educational background of workers, 33–34; employee reasons for becoming part of, 84; "Because I want to!," 91–93; as an escape, 98–99; family survival, 84–91; independence as a single woman, 99–102; joining the airline industry, 103–4; money for spending, saving, and venture capital, 93–97; emotional labor, 32; English fluency, 46, 88, 104; feminization of labor, 30–33; and technological development, 36; gender dynamics changes in households, 108–10; gender makeup of the industry, 37, 40; household effects when women become employed in, 107–22; "housekeepers to the world," 1, 36, 38; and husband–wife relationships, 110–16; and immoral behavior, 58–59; Indian industry background, 2, 28–29, 164n11; and marriage, 130–36, 172n3; men employed in growing numbers in, 40; as middle-class employment, 33, 165n23; off-hour activities of workers, 127–30; and parent–child relationships, 116–21; as part of larger BPO industry, 29; popular opinions and concerns regarding, 41–46; rape and capital penetration, 74–79; safety concerns, 3–4, 43, 60–62, 166n38; and employer-provided transportation, 71–74; spending habits of employees, 93–97; wages, 87–89, 92, 99, 100, 112, 113–14, 129, 164n11; transportation options, 69–74; variety of educational, social, and economic backgrounds of workers, 124–27; "What will people think?," 145. *See also* night shift employment
capital accumulation, 91, 170n10
Chatterjee, Partha, 79–80
colonization of time, 28
consumerism, 93–94
"Company A," 19, 20, 53–57, 60, 84, 87, 95, 101, 125, 134, 135, 154; anniversary party and mobility-morality narratives, 56; percentage of men employed at, 37; transportation for employees, 69, 70, 71, 73, 76
coolies, 41
credit cards, 97
"Culture, Social Class, and Income Control in the Lives of Women Garment Workers in Bangladesh" (Kibria), 138–39
cyber-coolies, 41, 46, 76

189